ARCHITECTS IN COMPETITION

ARCHITECTS IN COMPETITION

International Architectural Competions
of the last 200 years

HILDE DE HAAN AND IDS HAAGSMA

With essays by
DENNIS SHARP AND KENNETH FRAMPTON

THAMES AND HUDSON

ISBN 90 290 8134 1

First published in Great Britain in 1988 bij Thames and Hudson Ltd.London

First published in the USA in 1988 by Thames and Hudson Inc., 500 fifth Avenue, New York. New York 10110

© 1988
Vorm + Kleur grafische ontwerpers. Naarden, The Netherlands

Library of Congress Catalog card Number 87-50250

Printed and bound in Spain
DLB - 1557 - 88

On the jacket:
Competition design by George Gilbert Scott and John Oldrid Scott for the Berlin parliament buildings, 1872.

Facing p.3: sealed envelope with motto and name of entrant in competition for the Vienna Savings Bank, 1903.

CONTENTS

7 Prologue

9 Competitions, the treasure houses of architecture

22 The White House in Washington
1792

30 Houses of Parliament, London
1835

41 The Paris Opera
1860

54 The Reichstag in Berlin
1882

64 The Eiffel Tower
1886

72 The Austrian Savings Bank in Vienna
1903

82 Stockholm Town Hall
1903

94 Helsinki Station
1903

105 The Peace Palace, The Hague
1905

115 Chicago Tribune Tower
1922

127 Termini Station, Rome
1947

136 Sydney Opera House
1956

147 Congress Building, Kyoto, Japan
1962

156 Amsterdam Town Hall
1967

168 Centre Pompidou in Paris
1970

181 Architectural competitions: a watershed between old and new, by *Dennis Sharp*

193 Le Corbusier at Geneva: the debacle of the Société des Nations, by *Kenneth Frampton*

204 The Standard Regulations of UIA

208 Bibliography

213 Sources of illustrations

214 Index

PROLOGUE

FROM TIME IMMEMORIAL IT HAS been the custom in the building
world - and not only there - to commission work from whoever
is the cheapest. Different builders are asked to give estimates,
and then the commission is usually given to the lowest tender.
It is not surprising that such a system of tender would sooner
or later be also used for the designs of buildings, and indeed,
architectural competitions have been in existence for a long
time. However, whilst the system of tender is not regarded as
controversial, the opposite is true of competitions, which are
almost always accompanied by gossip, backbiting, arguments,
quarrels, reproaches and vilification.

This book deals with such architectural competitions. After an
introductory essay on various aspects of the concept in
general, fifteen of the more important competitions from the
last two hundred years are examined in closer detail; all of
these are 'open' competitions - that is to say, those in which
anyone was allowed to participate - the winners of which were
commissioned to execute the building in question. The choice
fell on open competitions because potentially these offer the
greatest surprises. Here every competition organiser has a
chance to see his dream come true: to discover the architect
who can create 'the most beautiful building in the world'.

As it was also our aim to offer the richest possible picture of
architecture over the last two hundred years, we tended to
choose competitions from counties where interesting
developments were taking place at that moment. Ultimately,
however, the choices were somewhat arbitrary: one important
factor was the availability of sufficient material from
participants other than the winners. It was frequently found
that the organisers of a competition had kept only the winning
designs. Other entries were at best returned to their senders,
but usually destroyed. This may be understandable for reasons
of privacy - who would wish to go down in history as a loser? -
but it does not satisfy our curiosity.

The various competitions are mainly described in the
narrative form. For this reason, Dennis Sharp and Kenneth
Frampton have been asked to explore a number of separate
aspects in more depth.

*Junzo Sakakura: competition entry
for the International Congress
Building, Kyoto, Japan; 1962.*

COMPETITIONS, THE TREASURE HOUSES OF ARCHITECTURE

WHEN IN 448 BC, after the Persian wars, the Council of Athens wanted to erect a war memorial on the Acropolis, it decided to play safe. Several artists were invited to submit designs, and these were put on display for ten days. After that, the citizens of Athens were allowed to make a definitive choice by means of a public vote.

It is entirely understandable that the Council acted in this way. Putting up a building, especially a large one, is a radical step; it will influence the environment for many years, thereby arousing emotions, particularly when it has symbolic value, such as the seat of a government, a temple, a church, a town hall, or, of course, a monument. The shape of the building will also determine the image of the 'symbol', and more than with 'ordinary' buildings, people will want to become involved with the design at an early stage in the proceedings.

For this reason the Council of Athens guarded itself in advance against possible criticism by allowing the citizens to express their opinion on the possible form of the war memorial beforehand. To the organiser, a competition seems the ideal means of choosing the right designer, especially as a number of different entries offer a greater chance of being pleasantly surprised.

The war memorial on the Acropolis is not the only example from the distant past. In 1401 a competition was announced in Florence for a pair of bronze doors for the cathedral of Santa Maria del Fiore. It is known that the goldsmith, Fillippo di Ser Brunellesco di Lippi Lapi - Brunelleschi for short - took part. But without much success; the winner was Lorenzo Ghiberti. Later, in 1419, a competition was announced for the dome of the same cathedral. This time the winner was Brunelleschi, who was by then engaged in architecture. The dome, which has since become world famous, was built between 1421 and 1436. If the inhabitants of Athens were able to take a decision, the Florentine parishioners were given less say in the matter. A jury was appointed to judge the designs.

That juries can be unpredictable is obvious. In the second half of the sixteenth century, King Philip II of Spain announced a competition for the building of the monastery at Escorial, northwest of Madrid. Twenty-two architects were invited to take part and the Italian architect, Giacomo Barozzi da Vignola, would judge the entries. Vignola, however, combined the entries he liked best into a new design which he showed to King Philip, who was impressed and commissioned Vignola to build the monastery. Nothing came of it, in the event, but the story does illustrate the problems that may arise. Clearly, a competition is not quite so ideal for all the parties concerned.

ANYONE DELVING INTO THE HISTORY of architectural competitions is bound to come across some disreputable tales. Take, for instance, the competition for the extension to the Louvre in Paris. Louis XIV wished to surround himself with magnificent buildings, and in 1664 appointed his minister of finance, Jean

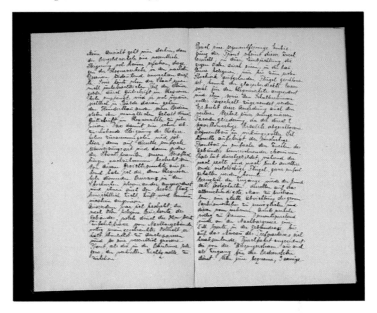

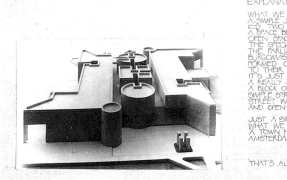

Head office of the Hongkong and Shanghai Bank in Hongkong, the result of a closed competition in 1979 between seven famous architects' offices. Winner Norman Foster Associates from London also contructed the building. See also pp. 14-19.

How many explanatory notes should accompany a design? Competition programmes are often very precise about this; sometimes an architect does what he thinks best. In the 1903 competition for the Austrian Savings Bank, one of the entrants, Ferstel, filled a complete exercise book with explanations. An anonymous entrant in the 1967 Amsterdam Town Hall competition preferred to be brief and succinct.

9

Baptiste Colbert, to 'Ordonnateur général des bâtiments'.
One of Colbert's first decisions was to have the Royal Palace of the Louvre completed.

Work had been in progress on the palace since 1546, but the east elevation still had to be finished off with an imposing façade. Colbert organized a kind of competition which resulted in a number of suggestions being sent to Rome to be assessed by Italian architects. They responded by returning him their own designs, whereupon Colbert decided to invite Gianlorenzo Bernini to come to Paris to complete the Louvre.

One can imagine the French architects did not take kindly to this, especially Claude Perrault - who had taken part in the competition - and who took it upon himself to slate Bernini's design, supported by many other French architects. The attack was successful; Louis XIV rejected Bernini's plans and the commission for the east wing of the Louvre was given to a trio of French architects: Louis Le Vau, Charles Lebrun and - naturally - Claude Perrault.

It is not surprising, therefore, that in the world of architecture the idea of competitions soon became associated with wrangling, quarrelling and controversial decisions, which later became worse. Paradoxically, despite the bad name that competitions were rapidly gaining, more and more competitions were being organized.

In Great Britain, for instance, competitions were held for the Bank of England (1788), the National Gallery (1832), and the Houses of Parliament (1835), all in London. During the reign of Queen Victoria there were sometimes more than a hundred competitions a year, resulting in buildings like the town halls of Cardiff, Glasgow and Manchester, Liverpool Cathedral, and the Victoria and Albert Museum, London. In the United States the number of competitions was also gaining ground. In 1792, competitions were held both for the White House and the Capitol in Washington D.C. and later, in 1848, for the Washington Monument. In 1871 the city of Philadelphia organized a competition for a new town hall.

These fairly random examples demonstrate that competitions deal mostly with public buildings which, to many people, also have symbolic value. But competitions can be used, too, for other purposes.

In the 1860s, housing for the lowest paid was an urgent priority in New York City. True, regulations existed for the building of dwellings, but these were widely disregarded. In 1879 the State of New York prescribed that every bedroom should have a window. This gave the journal *Plumber and Sanitary Engineer* the idea of organizing a competition for a 'model tenement' for large families; the winning design being the one which combined maximum safety and comfort with maximum profit for the builder.

There were 209 entrants, and James E. Ware won first prize with his design 'Light, Air and Health', which has since had much influence on tenement housing, especially in New York City. The dwellings were mockingly referred to as 'dumbbell houses' because of their ground plan, 7.5 metres wide and 27 metres deep, with two small courtyards in the middle, on either side of a narrow passage.

THE COMPETITION ORGANIZED BY *Plumber and Sanitary Engineer* could be described as an ideas competition. The object was not, in the first place, te realize a specific building but rather to solve an architectural problem. In fact the competition for the dome of Florence Cathedral in 1419 was also an ideas competition: here, too, the aim was to solve an architectural problem. An even older example exists; after Canterbury Cathedral was almost burnt down in 1174, ideas were invited for the restoration of the ruined choir.

Closely linked to the ideas competition are study competitions, held especially among students and within the architectural community. In this context the Prix de Rome has become a byword in many countries. This prize was instituted by the Ecole des Beaux Arts in Paris in the nineteenth century; the winner received a grant to study in Rome for several years. Later many other countries adopted the idea.

Ideas competitions to solve everyday practical problems have become increasingly common in the twentieth century, especially for housing projects and new buildings. In the nineteenth century they were still relatively rare, apart from the 1889 competition for a tower at the World Exhibition in Paris. Superficially, the problem was how and where a tower of this kind could be built; in fact, there was quite a different motive behind this competition - it was already a foregone conclusion that the design by Gustave Eiffel was the only right one. It was more the intention to find an elegant way to allow Eiffel to execute his design without offending too many others. Similar ulterior motives lay behind the 1860 competition for the new Paris Opera. Baron Hausmann, who had pushed through the idea for a new opera house, had picked the architect, Rohault de Fleury, to the displeasure of the Empress Eugénie who wanted to give the commission to her protégé, Viollet-le-Duc. Hence the decision to hold a competition, although the jury did not, in this case, allow itself to be influenced by the ulterior motives of the organisers. Neither

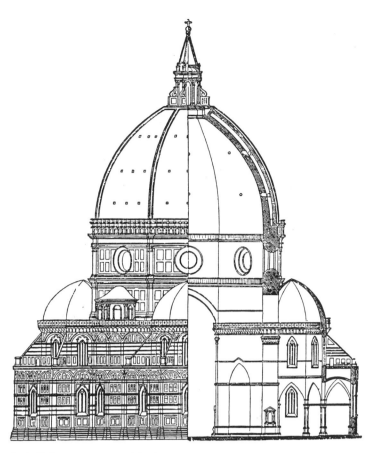

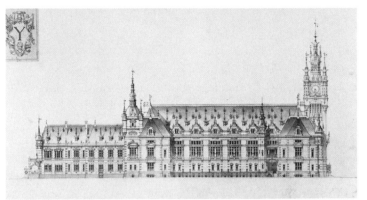

In 1419 there was a competition in Florence for a seemingly insoluble problem: to design a dome for the half-completed Santa Maria del Fiore Cathedral. Brunelleschi had a brilliant plan - instead of one massive dome wall there should be two thin walls that would combine to support the structure. He had been inspired with this idea when studying the arches built by the Romans. This construction of his was copied far and wide.

The 1884 competition for an Exchange building in Amsterdam produced many elegant designs, such as that of L. Klingenberg and E. Tauschenberg, above.

But this competition was not a success: winner L.M. Cordonnier was accused of plagiarism and his design, centre, was not used.

With the above Neo-Renaissance design, 'Mercurea', H.P. Berlage and Th. Sanders gained third place in the Amsterdam Exchange competition. This design bore no resemblance to the Exchange building that was completed in 1903 to a design by Berlage, and that came to be seen as a watershed in Dutch architecture. The fact that Berlage's design was used had little to do with his winning third prize some time earlier, but much to do with his friendship with Alderman M.W.F. Treub. In 1896, ten years after the unfortunate competition, Treub approached Berlage about building the Exchange in Amsterdam.

Rohault de Fleury nor Viollet-le-Duc were among the winners. A young, little known architect, Charles Garnier, got the award.

BUILDINGS THAT ARE PLANNED in the 'normal' way can also lead to intriguing incidents. There are quarrels, plagiarism, angry confrontations between sponsor and architect, and the final product often bears little resemblance to the early designs on the drawing board - if it is built at all, for many designs die a premature death. But such goings-on usually remain within four walls and only the finished building is judged.

In competitions, however, the entire process is staged in public. Another important feature is that there is usually only one winner, so that the other participants are, per definition, losers. Jealousy flares up with a fierceness equal to the number of entrants minus one. And once emotions are aroused, so is nationalism.

Architecture has always been internationally orientated. Architects travel far and wide to acquire ideas in other countries. At the time of the Renaissance, Italy was a popular destination; in later periods cultural capitals such as Paris, London and Vienna were preferred.

It is not surprising, therefore, that architectural competitions are often international; either - as in the case of the Escorial and the Louvre - the jury is composed of foreigners, or the competition itself is open to foreigners. But woe betide if one of those foreigners actually wins the competition.

Then jealousy joins forces with nationalism and the result can be petty-minded behaviour.

In 1884 Amsterdam city council announced an international competition for a new Exchange in the city centre. 199 entries were received, including one which was disqualified. Initially, the international jury was unable to agree; ten prizewinners were therefore selected of whom five were invited to take part in a follow-up competition in 1885.

A year later the jury came to an agreement and proclaimed the Frenchman, L.M. Cordonnier, as winner. After the result was announced a great commotion broke out, and age-old arguments as to whether or not a new Exchange was even necessary were raked up. Moreover, Cordonnier was accused of plagiarism: one part of his design was alleged to be a copy of the town hall at La Rochelle; an accusation which the architect refuted by saying he had been 'inspired' by the town hall in question.

For many months Amsterdam was in the throes of disagreements, until, early in 1886, the city council decided to award the prizes in accordance with the jury report after all,

The 1927 competition for the League of Nations Building in Geneva is often taken as the prime example of just how much can go wrong. The final building is the result of complicated compromises. Seven teams tied for first prize, after which a committee of diplomats had to appoint a team of five architects from these winners. See also Kenneth Frampton's essay, pp. 192-203.

but with the clause that the council was under no obligation to have the award-winning design carried out.

At this, tumult erupted in earnest: the second prizewinner made a fiery plea for his own design and many outsiders submitted new ones. The affair dragged on for a long time, until finally the city council decide to abandon the idea altogether. Ten years later, the architect, H.P. Berlage, was asked personally to design a new Exchange and he designed, in all secrecy, a building which even today remains one of the most important in the entire architectural history of the Netherlands.

A simlar disheartening affair was to occur in Amsterdam some eighty years later, around the competition for a new town hall. After his victory, the winner, the Austrian, Wilhelm Holzbauer, was fiercely criticized by Dutch architects, one of whom reproached him in all seriousness for speaking German. Once again the affair dragged on for years and once more the project was temporarily abandoned. Eventually Holzbauer was allowed to build a town hall, but in a form no one could ever have foreseen.

Such absurd situations are not confined to the Netherlands. Witness the results of the competition for a National Centre for Art and Culture in Paris. In 1971, when the jury awarded first prize for this building at the Plateau Beaubourg to an Italian, Renzo Piano, and an Englishman, Richard Rogers, this hardly met with the approval of French architects.

The competition was intended to break with the existing French system of choosing architects for state commissions; but to have foreigners picked as winners proved to be the last straw. French architects - united under the banner 'Le Geste Architectural' - tried six times to contest legally the building of the Centre Beaubourg. Their attempts were in vain.

THE RUMPUS AROUND COMPETITIONS may make entertaining reading for the general public, but it should not be allowed to blur the issues. Competitions are held with the purpose of obtaining the best possible building.

Sometimes the organiser is magnanimous enough simply to want a sensational building, dreaming secretly that his competition will discover a great, as yet unknown, talent that will raise architecture to new heights. But often he has a less idealistic, more pragmatic aim, and is simply out to get the best, most reliable, design. In either case, a competition is a good means to gather designs from which to make a choice, but everything stands and falls with the jury. Choosing a building (or a town-planning project - also the subject of competitions) is delegated to the jury; it is placed in the hands of people who are assumed to be experts. This is why people of diverse backgrounds, such as politicians, civil servants and building contractors have always been brought together in juries. And over the years architects began to play an increaingly important role. The question is, which architects? It is often hoped that really good architects will themselves take part in the competition, so they should not always be invited to sit on the jury. And besides, a competent architect is not necessarily a good judge. A good jury member must be able to judge as part of a team. Experience has shown that many jury members are unable to do this. It often happens that a jury cannot reach agreement because the opinions of its members are too divergent. On the other hand, a jury whose members share exactly the same views on architecture may not be open to designs which express different ideas from their own. In brief: the choice of the future building is, in effect, already made when the jury is selected.

For the competition for the Centre Beaubourg in 1971, a jury

Winning design of Austrian Wilhelm Holzbauer for the Amsterdam Town Hall competition, 1967. Despite conscientious adjudication, this design evoked such an outcry in the Netherlands that it was decided not to implement it for the time being. About 20 years later a new town hall was built in Amsterdam, to a completely new design by Holzbauer and Cees Dam.

P & T Architects and Engineers Hongkong (formerly Palmer & Turner) built several office blocks for the Hongkong and Shanghai Bank. No winner was appointed for the 1979 competition for a new head office. According to this plan the new building would be completed in two stages. First one tower - that qua design fitted in with the 1935 buildings - was to be built, see above. Later the old building was to be replaced by a pyramid-shaped structure and a second tower, see below.

was appointed, almost half of which consisted of liberal-minded architects, and for the rest of experts from the world of museums and libraries. This choice guaranteed an open-mindedness towards the submitted designs, although it was still a gamble whether or not these experts were capable of working together.

A jury always remains unpredictable. During the competitions for a new building for the League of Nations in Geneva, in 1927, the jury had to assess 377 entries. The design by Le Corbusier and Pierre Jeanneret seemed all set to win first prize, until one of the more conservative jury members pointed out that this design had not been drawn in ink (as prescribed by the programme) but was mechanically reproduced. Because of the obstinacy with which this one person stuck to his point of view, the atmosphere was spoilt; the jury was unable to make a unanimous recommendation and merely awarded nine money prizes. No glorious winner in this case. True, Le Corbusier and Jeanneret received one of the prizes, but that was poor comfort.

Anyone taking part in a competition would be well advised to look carefully at the list of jury members, assuming this list is available in advance. Over the years many guidelines have been set up for the organization of competitions, including one which insists that the composition of the jury should be known beforehand, but it still happens that the jury is not appointed until after the entries have been received.

When a list is available, an analysis of the composition of the jury gives an indication of the type of designs the sponsors have in mind. When, in 1922, the *Chicago Tribune* newspaper announced a competition for a new office building, the jury was known beforehand and anyone with knowledge of the facts would have realised that these jury members were fairly conservative; they could not be expected to have open minds towards avant-garde designs. However, the *Chicago Tribune* competition was an international one which received much publicity in the international editions of the paper. To many foreign architects, the names of the jurors did not mean much, and in their ignorance they thought they would be taking part in a competition in which every design stood a fair chance. American architects received an additional clue which made it clear that the paper was decidedly not looking for epoch-making architecture. Although this was an open competition, the *Tribune* had also invited, for a fee, a number of American architects favoured by the sponsors, to participate. In all correctness, the programme mentioned these architects by name, and from this, observant Americans could conclude what kind of building the organisers wanted: a

The closed competition of 1979 for Hongkong and Shanghai Bank produced several innovative designs for skyscrapers. Above left: Plan from American architects Skidmore, Owings & Merrill: a 38-storey office tower supported by pillars at the sides. There would be a public square underneath the tower and an oval-shaped entrance hall immediately above this. The design by Harry Seidler Associates of Australia is shown below, with its enormous covered inner courtyard - between a glass façade curving inwards - which would be reached through a spacious entrance hall; see also the façade detail, below right. Above right: Design submitted by the English architects, Yorke, Rosenberg & Mardell, whose plan proposed a two-stage building. First a tower with 27 storeys would be built, a spacious loggia on the south side; later the old building would be replaced with two equally tall towers. But this same architects' office also developed an alternative plan to incorporate into the new block the façade of the existing office. In this case only one skyscraper would be added to the original building, below.

skyscraper in neo-style, in the tradition of the Beaux Arts which was fashionable in America at that time. Misunderstandings of this sort can be avoided when the sponsor decides at the outset to have a closed competition; a format to which more and more organizations resort. In that case only a limited number of architects are invited to take part in the competition. If all the invited architects are paid in full from the beginning, this is called a 'multiple commission'. A closed competition is certainly not a new phenomenon. While little is known about the earliest history of architecture, it may be assumed that the first competitions were confined to architects and artists who were specifically invited to take part. This was already the case with the competition for the war memorial on the Acropolis and for the Escorial.

Many present-day competitions do not have juries, but the sponsor simply decides for himself, even though he may take architectural advice. Recent examples of this are the closed competitions held for various new West German museums and for the new buildings of the Hongkong and Shanghai Bank in Hongkong. In 1979 the Bank decided to enlarge its offices, choosing from a number of designs, and sought the expertise of the agency, P.A. Management Consultants Ltd. Seven firms of architects were invited to take part: two from Great Britain, two from the United States, two from Australia and one from Hongkong.
On 11 July 1979, all the architects were invited to head office where the plans, wishes and objectives of the Bank were explained. Afterwards the architects could put questions to the

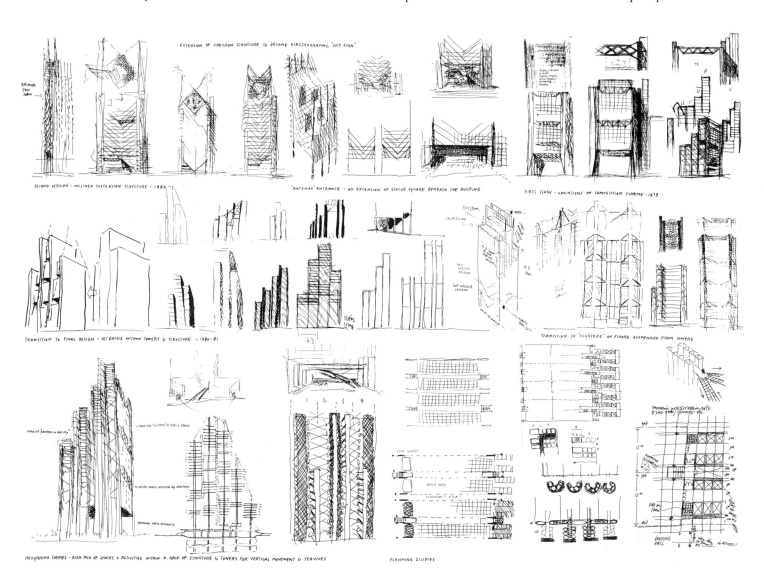

Foster's winning design for the head office of the Hongkong & Shanghai Bank, 1979, consisted of a square block with five hollow supporting towers on each side, fitted with lifts and other conveniences. Between these towers there would be horizontal linking structures in three places, which would span the 48 metres between the five towers. This construction provided maximum

flexibility for designing the floors and the façades. It also left the ground floor free for open public space. The shape of the skyscraper altered radically, but the principle was retained. These sketches by Foster show the main developments.

Top now, right: Design for the competition, with to the left,

Intermediary stage in wich the three heavy connecting steel structures are replaced by many lighter, V-shaped ones.

Centre: Development of the final concept - block shapes of varying heights and floors suspended per cluster from the towers. This definitive design is further elaborated below. Foster said of it:

'Recurring themes: rich mix of spaces and activities within a grid of structure and towers for vertical movement and services.'

directors and advisers. It was also decided that the designs would have to be in the possession of the Bank by 8 October, that same year. The eventual choice was made by the directors in collaboration with the firm of consultants, and with Gordon Graham of the British architects' organization, RIBA, as architectural adviser.

It seems likely that in future, private companies will increasingly operate along these lines. Much bother can be eliminated in this way, but the chance of discovering unknown talent is also diminished.

ORGANIZING A LARGE OPEN COMPETITION is an undertaking that only government bodies can tackle successfully nowadays. And only then if they are strongly motivated and in search of the 'best available talent'. The hundreds of entries alone make a competition into a nerve-racking event which makes high demands upon the organisers.

The French president, François Mitterand, is thus motivated. He wants to restore Paris to its international stature and regards it as the duty of the French government to aspire to the best of the best. For this reason, some large open competitions have been organized for buildings in Paris, two of which were highly successful, even though they were accompanied by a great deal of argument. In 1982 an international competition was announced for the Parc de la Villette, where a 'Park of the 21st century' was to be realized. There were 471 entries, from which the jury eventually appointed the one by Bernard Tschumi as the winner.

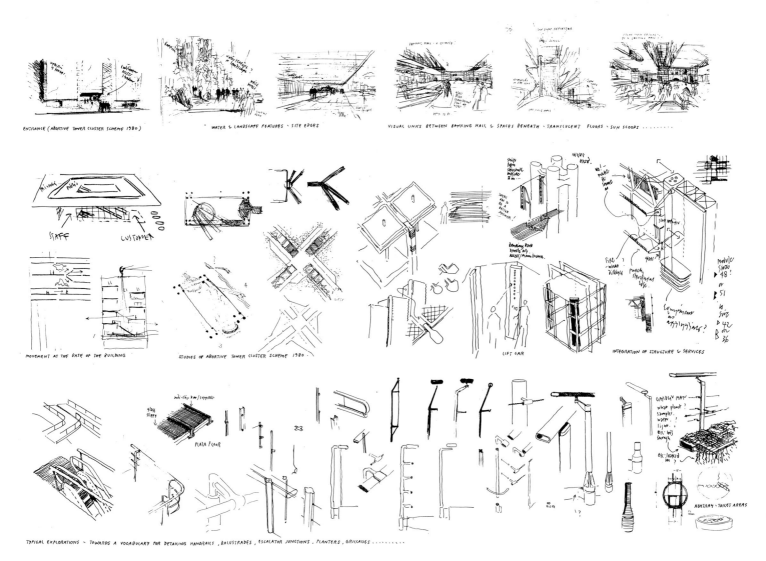

Design sketches by Foster.
Above: Entrance, view, immediate surroundings and glass floor between the public square and the basement.
Centre: Various technical solutions such as integrating the support structure with the technical services and siting the traffic movement.
Below: Designs for developing a vocabulary to describe the details of handrails, balustrades, escalator

junctions, indoor plant and flower boxes, and grilles.

Norman Foster's definitive design for the Hongkong & Shanghai Bank: a 200-metre high, 47-storeyed superstructure in a steel frame. Total floor area 100,000 square metres, spread over many more or less independently operating units, nicknamed by Foster 'villages in the sky'.

The international competition for the completion of the axis between Louvre and La Défense (Tête Défense) in 1983 elicited 424 entries. The Dane, Johan Otto von Spreckelsen, became the winner.

But a third competition proved more troublesome. When, in 1983, entries were invited for a new opera house at the Place de la Bastille, 756 designs were received; some three to four kilometres of panels had to be erected to display them all to the jury. Yet none of the designs impressed the jury sufficiently; only after much argument was it decided to show six designs to the president, who picked the one by the Canadian, Carlos Ott, as being the best.

In view of the large number of entrants, it is clear that open competitions on this scale have become huge undertakings. And however sound the organization, with however much care the jury has been selected, and however well everything proceeds according to the guidelines set up by national and international bodies, the real success of a competition always rests on the quality of the entrants. And that cannot be made to order.

During the 1980s the climate has been relatively favourable for competitions. In many Western countries the post-war building boom, which kept most architects so busy that they had no time and no need to take part in voluntary competitions, has come to an end. Now that there is no longer an abundant supply of work, architects have enough time to take part in competitions, all the more because there is always the hope of an important commission and besides, their designs may well give them useful publicity.

The 1980s are also proving fruitful in another respect. Architecture is passing through a phase of transition. Many new ideas and forms are being tried out. This tends to make sponsors hesitant and leads them to opt for an open or closed competition which will enable them to make their choice from a number of specific designs. Designers, for their part, use competitions to propagate new ideas.

Yet there are architects who deliberately never take part in competitions. The Dutch architect, J.J.P. Oud, wrote in 1954: 'It is precisely the incessant to-and-fro between the wishes of the sponsor and the ideas of the architect which make building into a living embodiment of society's needs. It is in this respect that competitions are hopelessly inadequate; because of this permanent lack of contact they lead to a cut-out architecture, not to realities of steel and stone . . . Because the contact between life and design is so minimal in competitions, it is best to use them sparingly.'

Oud never took part in a competition. And he is not the only one; other great architects can be named who have never, or only rarely, done so, including Frank Lloyd Wright, Gerrit Rietveld, Louis Kahn and Willem Dudok. But on the other hand there are architects who have taken part in competitions all their lives, out of a feeling of conviction: Alvar Aalto, who must have participated in at least 58 competitions (he won 25); Eliel Saarinen who sent entries to a good 20 (he won at least 12 first prizes); and Arne Jacobson who probably took part in just under 20.

HOWEVER MUCH CRITICISM there may be, however much trouble every competition entails, they will probably always continue to be held. Competitiveness runs in the blood of Western man, and mutual envy drives him to greater achievements. Organisers know this only too well, and in their search for the

The final result of the closed competition for the Hongkong & Shanghai Bank, in 1979, shows in many aspects a new approach to building. It is generally the technical innovations that are discussed, though architect Foster stresses that these should not be seen unrelated to the general aim, and that the contents, too, make this a completely new type of large building. This can be seen, for example, if you look at the public area on the ground floor and probably even more in the open and flexible interior that makes a complete break with traditional office towers, where every floor is identical. The connection with outside is also unusual, affording magnificent views and generous supplies of natural light. An example of this is the atrium in the photograph: this is a covered courtyard at the heart of the building, between the third and eleventh storeys. Daylight showers inside, refracted by mirrors: this is done in such a way that light pours right through the atrium from the eleventh floor to the public square at ground-floor level.

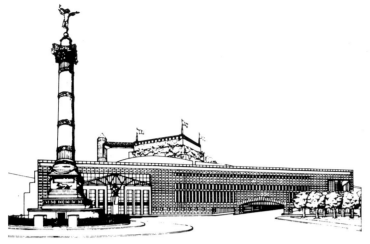

In 1983 there was an international competition for a new opera house in Paris on the Place de la Bastille. There were 756 entries, from such internationally famous figures as Richard Meier, Henri Ciriani, Harry Seidler, Kisho Kurokawa, Charles Moore and Christian de Portzamparc. The competition was won by an unknown Canadian, Carlos Ott - many suspected this was a pseudonym for Richard Meier.

Another competitor was the Austrian, Wilhelm Holzbauer, whose design resembled the one he had made for the Town Hall-Muziektheater in Amsterdam, see pp. 156-167.

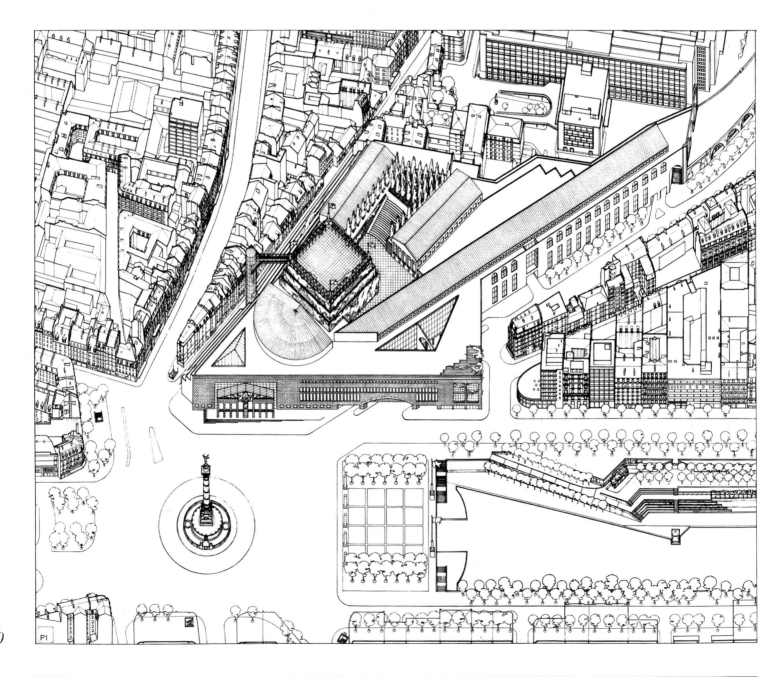

best of the best they will, time and again, decide to hold great architectural competitions.

But apart from a future there is also a past. For art- and architectural-historians, competitions are a yardstick. They can observe the state of architecture at a given moment and see how at a particular time different architects have responded to the same assignment. Especially at a time when architecture is undergoing change, competitions prove - with hindsight - to be real treasure houses in which one can feast one's eyes. But just as in the treasure vaults of dead kings, many of these treasure houses are virtually empty. Much material has disappeared, often destroyed at the instruction of official guidelines. This makes a tour of the remaining full treasure chambers all the more fascinating.

The 1983 competition for the completion of the axis Louvre-La Défense had 424 entrants and a great variety of designs. The Amsterdam architects' office, A. Alberts, offered a plan for a giant public building that would appear to arise organically out of the ground. Winner was the Dane, Johan Otto von Spreckelsen, with his plan for a second, mammoth Arc de Triomphe.

THE WHITE HOUSE IN WASHINGTON

ARCHITECTURAL COMPETITION TO DESIGN A RESIDENCE FOR THE PRESIDENT OF THE UNITED STATES.

PUBLISHED: March 1792; result: 17 July 1792; number of entrants: 7

JURY: President George Washington in consultation with the Government Commission for the District of Columbia.

WINNER: James Hoban; honourable mention: John Collins.

CONSTRUCTION: 1792-1830 (James Hoban, Benjamin Henry Latrobe)

IN MARCH 1792, a modest advertisement announced a prize of 500 dollars for the 'best design for a presidential dwelling'. Eighteen lines contained all the information felt necessary for the participants. They would have to submit floor plans, drawings of elevations, cross sections, estimate the amount of masonry needed, and it would also be an advantage, if the main part of the dwelling were to be a separate building which could be added on to, as and when required.

The competition was published by the government commission for the District of Columbia, but who exactly would be on the jury was not considered worth mentioning. Nor was there any reference to the drama concealed behind the advertisement. In fact one person had been working on a presidential house for over two years. Or rather, creating its environment - the future city of Washington - on his drawingboard. He was confident that he would be asked to design the most important buildings. This man was the French-born architect, Pierre Charles l'Enfant.

The decision to found this new city had not been reached without difficulty. In 1783 when the Peace of Versailles was concluded, whereby the thirteen United States of America became officially independent from Britain, it was immediately clear that there would have to be a new capital. But for a long time no agreement was reached about its location.

Philadelphia stood the best chance: delegates from the thirteen states had been meeting here since 1774, and it was also the place where in 1776 the Declaration of Independence, drawn up by Thomas Jefferson, had been proclaimed. Moreover, the city occupied a central position, was easily accessible and was well provided with amenities. But Philadelphia spoilt its chances when in June 1783 it did not react promptly to a mutiny of soldiers gathered in front of the State House where Congress was at that moment in session. Members of Congress felt so threatened that they took refuge in Princeton, and for their future sessions preferred Annapolis and Trenton rather than Philadelphia. At the end of 1784, Congress found a

Distant view of The White House - or at least how Pierre l'Enfant imagined the official residence of the president would look when he designed the new city of Washington in the 1790s. Sketch is by Elbert Peets, based on l'Enfant's preparatory studies.

satisfactory nome in New York, where it remained until the question of a permanent residence had been resolved.

This did not happen until 1790. The constant travelling had not benefited Congress' ability to take decisions, and the question of the new capital was now overshadowed by other problems. The tide turned in 1787, when in a short time, agreement was reached about the Constitution. Two years later George Washington was unanimously elected president and the decision about the new capital could no longer be delayed.

A solution was reached mainly through the diplomacy of Jefferson, appointed by Washington as minister for foreign affairs. Through his efforts a compromise proposal, put forward by finance minister Alexander Hamilton, obtained a majority. According to this proposal, Philadelphia would be the seat of government for the first ten years, whereafter both government and president would move to a new city to be built near Georgetown on the river Potomac.

This city would not be within one of the thirteen states but in an-as-yet-to-be-formed federal district of Columbia, on land given up for the purpose by the states of Virginia and Maryland.

No sooner had the location of the new capital been decided in 1790, than preparations for building got under way.

The astronomer and topographer, Andrew Ellicott, was entrusted with preparing detailed maps of the area, and Pierre Charles l'Enfant was asked to make drawings indicating the most advantageous siting of buildings, streets and amenities.

L'Enfant, in fact, was given the task of designing the new capital.

The first eighteen months that l'Enfant worked on his project passed more or less uneventfully. Washington was full of praise for him and on one occasion wrote that 'from the moment he first made l'Enfant's acquaintance he was convinced that he was not only a man of science, but also someone who knew how to couple good taste with craftsmanship, and that he was for that reason better qualified than anyone to do the work required of him'.

But l'Enfant was an individualist. This was all right as long as he only had to deal with the president and with Jefferson, with whom he had frequent and intensive consultations. These two actually held very divergent ideas about the future capital. Jefferson envisaged a city of modest proportions and of a somewhat rural character. Wahington, on the other hand, thought in terms of a metropolis that would have to stand comparison with London and Paris, cities of respectively 800,000 and 600,000 inhabitants at that time. L'Enfant self-confidently followed his own ideas, although he naturally had to take the wishes of the two statesmen into account.

He tackled the project with thoroughness, and first studied the town plans of many American and at least twelve European cities - 'not in order to copy them but to study details such as the location of public buildings, arsenals, markets, ports etc'. His final plan for the city of Washington was grand and monumental; a formal geometric pattern in which the important buildings occupied dominant positions. The most striking features were the rigid rectangular grid and the broad diagonal avenues linking all the important centres with each other and aimed, according to the designer, 'to make the real distance look less from place to place by giving them reciprocity of sight and making them thus seemingly connected'.

THE GRAND DESIGN HAD MANY CRITICS, and Jefferson, too, had difficulty with the Versailles-like character that the French l'Enfant had given to his city. But President Washington approved it and saw the design as a worthy capital for a new world state.

In December 1701, l'Enfant's solitary existence came to an end: his plan was ready and presented to the government commission. Then the problems began. It all started when l'Enfant had a recently built house, belonging to relatives of a commission member, pulled down, even though it could have been spared for several years. The commission's anger increased when l'Enfant proved not open to criticism of his plan. On the contrary, he even made a request to President Washington to be appointed director general, a post that would make him independent of the established hierarchy, and answerable only to the president. When this request was rejected, l'Enfant steadfastly refused to hand over his plan. Washington and Jefferson made several efforts to make him change his mind, but by the end of February their patience was exhausted.

Quick action was important in those years; personal whims were not tolerated, hence the harsh decision to relieve l'Enfant

of his function. His plans were adapted and completed by Andrew Ellicott, and an architectural competition announced for the most important buildings: the Capitol and the presidential residence. On 27 February 1892 Jefferson wrote a letter of dismissal to l'Enfant, and by 14 March the text of the advertisement had already been drawn up. The competition, too, was treated with urgency: the entries had to be submitted by the middle of July.

IN THE EARLY SPRING of 1792 the members of the commission were not exactly flooded with designs for the most important building of the new state. Eighteen people took part in the two competitions, of whom only eight made designs for the president's house, including one who was disqualified because his plan arrived after the closing date.

It was not really a poor score. In those days the architectural profession was not held in great esteem and was practised by relatively few people. In the higher social circles there were some amateur architects, of whom Thomas Jefferson was one of the best known, and sometimes carpenters and builders taught themselves architecture. But only a few enjoyed proper professional training, which in those days meant Europe. L'Enfant was such a person and moreover he had succeeded in making a living, while other trained architects could only practise in their spare time. The designs for the president's house reflected this situation, and the ways in which the various participants prepared their designs were as divergent as their professional backgrounds.

There is, for instance, a stack of unsigned designs by Jacob Small. It is unclear whether these should be attributed to Small Senior, a builder and architect in Baltimore, or to his son, a carpenter, architect and timber merchant from the same city; or possibly to both. In any case the drawings are typical of what can be expected from a self-made architect. Even the quantity is remarkable: at least four designs for the president's house and three for the Capitol points to a practical, almost opportunistic approach. And then the style of the drawings: simple and straightforward, with an uninhibited application of detail that had proved successful elsewhere. Admittedly, the chosen models were not bad: the state building of Annapolis, dating from 1772, and the turret of the state building of Maryland.

The design submitted by Andrew Mayfield Carshore was quite different. This amateur architect was an Irishman by birth, who had enjoyed a good education and earned his living as a teacher. He gave full rein to his imagination in his drawings, which had beautifully executed details. The main drawing of the front elevation was in perspective - what was for those days most unusual in architecture, and used only in paintings or in illustrated books on urban beauty. It explains perhaps why Carshore, a true artist, signed his work with his full name. He was also inspired by picturesque English and Irish country homes from the end of the sixteenth century.

There was one design that stood out and was submitted under the pseudonym AZ. It was not discovered until 1915 that this was submitted by no one less than Thomas Jefferson. This was not just the work of any amateur; he knew his classics and was

The design of Andrew Mayfield Carshore attracted attention because of its distinct artistic style. The façade was in grey tones, and he made a perspective study clearly indicating how the central house could easily be enlarged by adding wings to each of its four corners. Right: Carshore's ground plan with the wings of the house drawn in with a fine pen.

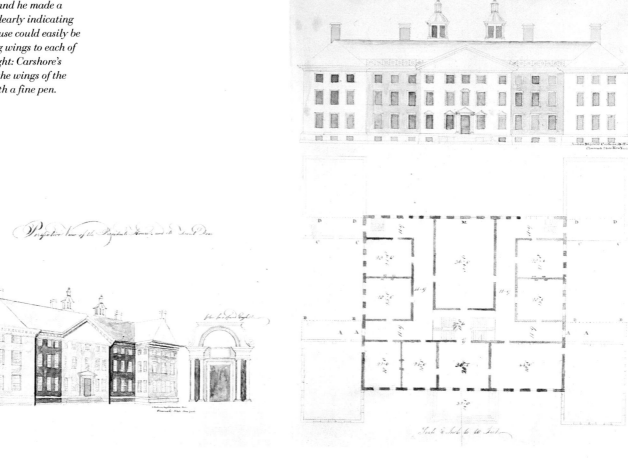

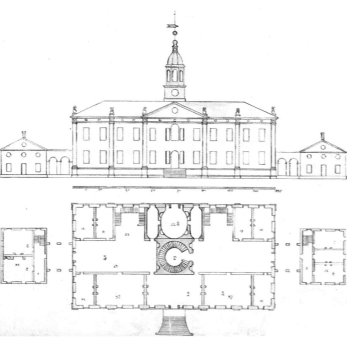

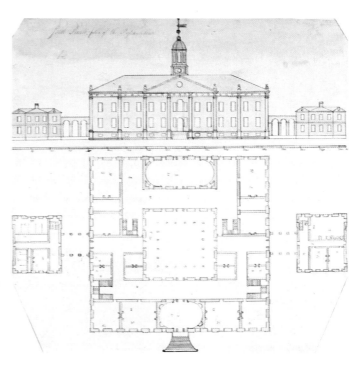

Jacob Small submitted several designs for the presidential residence and all quite similar. Each had the main entrance, with a window above it, flanked by smaller windows; a forefront embellished at regular intervals with massive pilasters; and oval rooms - fashionable at the time - were incorporated into his floor plans.

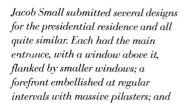

25

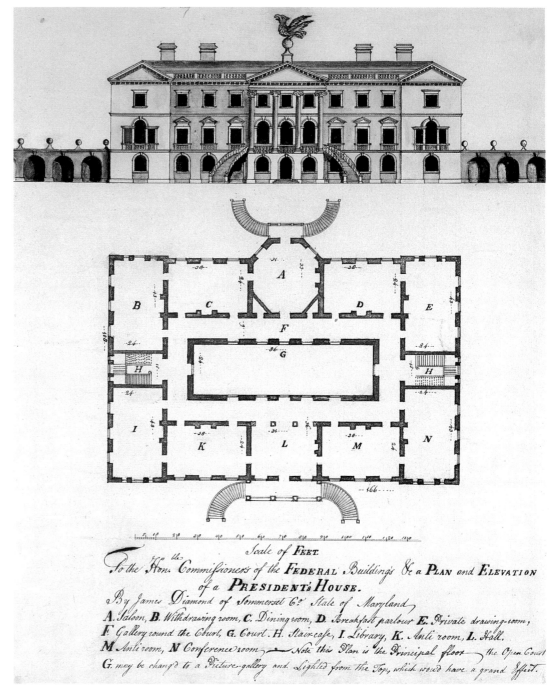

To the Honble the Commissioners of the FEDERAL Buildings &c a PLAN and ELEVATION of a PRESIDENTs HOUSE.

By James Diamond of Sommerset Co. State of Maryland

A. Saloon, B. Withdrawing room, C. Dining room, D. Breakfast parlour E. Private drawing-room, F. Gallery round the Court, G. Court, H. Stair-case, I. Library, K. Anti room, L. Hall, M. Anti room, N. Conference room — Note this Plan is the Principal floor — the Open Court G. may be chang'd to a Picture-gallery and Lighted from the Top, which would have a grand Effect.

familiar with recent developments in architecture. His design was virtually a copy of the *villa rotunda* by Andrea Palladio, the sixteenth century Italian architect who in the eighteenth century was inspiring much of Europe and whose influence was now reaching America. But a spectacular cupola had been added to the copy, with a roof of glass and closed segments arranged alternatively. Such a design had hardly been shown before, except in Paris when in 1782 the Halle au Blé had opened with a similar cupola. A novel curiosity in that city, it had attracted a great deal of attention, including that of Thomas Jefferson, American envoy from 1783 to 1789.

ONLY TWO PROFESSIONALLY trained architects took part in the competition: Stephen Hallet from Philadelphia and James Hoban from Charleston. Hallet's design has unfortunately been lost. His contribution to the competition can only be deduced from a few sentences in old documents, unlike the design by James Hoban, who eventually won the competition. The most remarkable aspect of Hoban's entry was not his design but the way in which he personally accompanied it. As soon as he heard of the competition, he immediately travelled to Philadelphia, where he had himself introduced to the president by an old friend of Washington's. There is no doubt that the ensuing conversation concerned the competition and that Washington himself made his wishes known.

Moreover, the president gave Hoban a letter of introduction to the government commission, so that he could inform them of his plans or gather information that might be useful to his design. With this letter in his pocket, as well as several more from prominent figures, Hoban visited a number of commission members, and not without success. A letter from

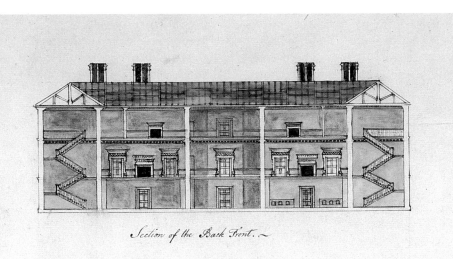

Section of the Back Front. —

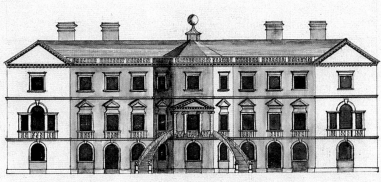

Back Front. —

Scale of FEET

To the Hon.ble Commissioners of the FEDERAL Building's &c.
An ELEVATION and SECTION of the Back Front of a PRESIDENT's HOUSE
By James Diamond of Somerset County —

the commission to Thomas Jefferson, dated 5 July 1972 states: 'Mr Hoban applies himself closely to a draft of the president's house. He has made a very favorable impression on us.'

ON 16 JULY, WASHINGTON JOINED the commission in Georgetown to judge the designs, and the next day the results were made known. James Hoban won the commission and the prize money. An unexpected honourable mention went to the New Yorker, Collin Williamson. Unfortunately, not a single drawing by him has been preserved, and little can be traced about him as a person.

Did Hoban deserve to win both the prize and the permission to build the presidential house? Anyone studying the competition through modern eyes is bound to be horrified by its injustices, yet in those days things were regarded differently. Hoban was indeed cunning, but he did not disobey any

regulations. His design, too, shows evidence of thorough craftmanship, which later enabled him to lead a reasonably prosperous life as an architect; unusual for the time.

There is, however, a basis of truth in the reproach aimed at Hoban immediately after the competition, that his design was plagiaristic. Architect Benjamin Henry Latrobe, acting architect of the presidential house during the years when Hoban was working elsewhere, expressed this in the most bitter terms in 1806: 'It was not even original, but a mutilated copy of a badly designed building near Dublin.' Latrobe was referring to the palace of the Duke of Leinster and he was not the only one to see the connection. All the same, it would be fairer to say that Hoban had taken elements from existing buildings and combined them into a new whole, which was common to architecture of the day. Moreover, Hoban, like Jefferson, knew his classics, and was even more sophisticated in the application of this knowledge. For instance, he based the proportions of the floor plan on the mathematical design of Palladio's villas, so that the proportions and mutual distances of all the elevations complied with the laws prevailing in classical architecture.

AFTER HE HAD FIRST MADE several radical modifications to his design, as specified by the president, Hoban was able to start building almost at once. These included more ornamentation on the façaades, and enlarging the whole building by a fifth. The commission calculated that this would increase the cost far too much, but a solution was found in October 1783 when it was decided to have a building of two rather than three storeys. By that time construction was already well under way. Time was pressing. By 1800 the entire city of Washington had to be so far completed that the government and president could take up residence there. A frenzied construction fever must have raged on the Potomac during those ten years, whereby various priorities repeatedly ousted one another. Hoban was soon not only working on the president's house, but also on a hotel, several government buildings and even for a while on the Capitol. A confusing entanglement of interests often hampered the building activities, and the supply of money did not always flow smoothly. It must be regarded as a miracle that on 1 November 1800, the president of the day, John Adams, moved into the house, with only a few rooms more or less habitable. After Adams left the house, in March 1801, his successor, President Thomas Jefferson, initially refused to live in his new official residence unless certain essential amenities were first put in.

Once Jefferson was in the house he had a great many improvements made. After Hoban's contract terminated in 1802, he appointed the architect, Benjamin Henry Latrobe, for this purpose. Even though Jefferson bequeathed a reasonably comfortable home, in 1809, to his successor, Madison, the building was still by no means complete. By 1814 it seemed that building was definitely at an end. In 1812 war had broken out again between America and England, and in 1814 the English troops reached Washington, where they first set fire to the Capitol, completed in 1811, and then to the president's house. The damage seemed virtually irreparable, but the opposite turned out to be true. In retrospect it has often been said that this fire made many people realize the importance of the capital city. Be this as it may, the repair works were tackled energetically and in 1815 Hoban himself was appointed to restore the president's house. During the next fifteen years he was allowed to enlarge it;

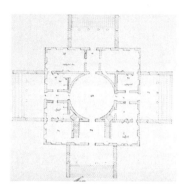

Statesman Thomas Jefferson could not resist taking part in the competition even if he was one of its organisers. He had more success at keeping his name out of the competition than with his Palladian design: it was 1915 before anyone discovered the real indentity hiding behind motto 'AZ'.

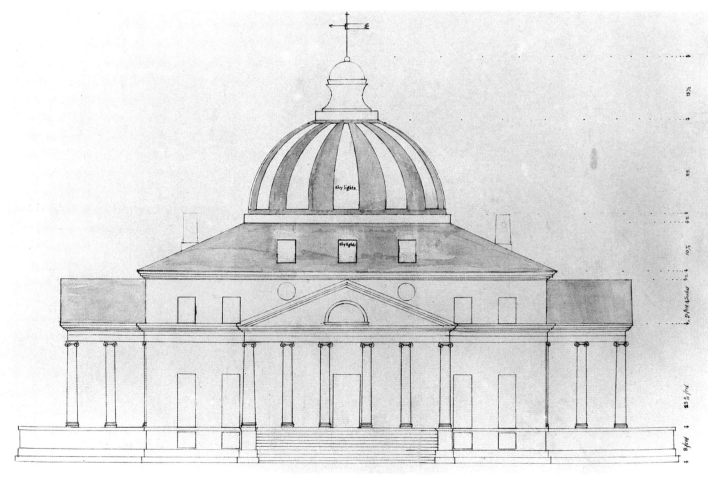

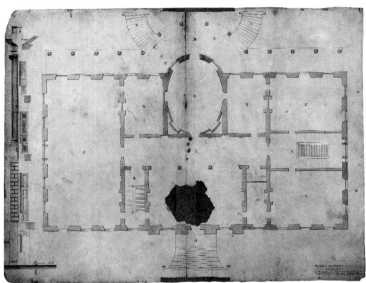

James Hoban made numerous drawings for the presidential house, but only a few have been preserved. The drawing, above, reputedly from Hoban, dates from the eighteenth century, although it is unlikely that it is one submitted for the competition, but made shortly afterwards. Research shows that Hoban initially designed a three-storey house which later, in 1783, became a two-storey one.

The floor plan, left, comprises one of several studies Hoban submitted. On the left-hand side is a cross-section of the façade at the main entrance, when the house was to have three storeys, and includes the exact positioning of the pilasters for the two upper floors.

wings were added, as well as the huge porticoes that still adorn the north and south elevations today. Great care was also lavished on the gardens and on the interior of the rooms. In short, Hoban was given the chance to give style to the presidential house, a chance he would probably have missed if it had not been for the fire.

OFFICIALLY, the completion date for the president's house is usually given as 1830, a year before Hoban's death. Both the interior and the exterior were then completed according to plans drawn up by Hoban himself, although volumes could be written on the alterations that were carried out later. The name 'The White House' came into use only after the civil war, 1861-1865. It was at this point that the House became a living legend.

HOUSES OF PARLIAMENT, LONDON

NATIONAL ARCHITECTURAL COMPETITION FOR THE HOUSES OF PARLIAMENT IN LONDON, SEAT OF THE HOUSE OF LORDS AND THE HOUSE OF COMMONS.

PUBLISHED: June 1835; result: 31 January 1836; number of entrants: 97

JURY: Charles Hanbury Tracy, Thomas Liddell, Sir Edward Cust, George Vivian.

WINNERS: 1 Charles Barry; 2 John Chessell Buckler; 3 David Hamilton; 4 William Railton.

CONSTRUCTION: 1836-1870 (Charles Barry in cooperation with Augustin Welby Pugin)

SELDOM WAS A DISASTER so welcome as the fire that reduced the London Houses of Parliament to ashes in October 1834. Of course, the country was deeply shocked by the 'terrible fire' that raged for two days and set the whole of London talking. But no sooner had the fire been put out than the daily and weekly papers began saying that now was a unique opportunity to build Houses of Parliament worthy of the British Empire.

The old accommodation had been far from satisfactory. The Palace of Westminster was a mishmash of buildings, added in the course of the centuries to the Royal Palace in which Parliament used St Stephen's Chapel as its assembly hall. Altogether an impractical and inconvenient conglomeration, suffering from bad smells, poor ventilation and appalling acoustics.

Renovations were constantly taking place and in 1831 a committee, led by Colonel Trench, had asked architects Robert Smirke, Benjamin Wyatt and Sir Jeffry Wyatville to examine what further improvements could still be made. Their ideas had hardly been committed to paper when they were once more superseded.

With the passing of the Reform Bill in 1832, the problem became far more urgent: the number of boroughs was increased and more than 600 MPs now confronted with the building's disadvantages. Improvement plans became immediately more ambitious. A new committee, this time under the chairmanship of Joseph Hume MP, consulted thirteen architects who were virtually unanimous in their opinion that no further renovation could bring relief; demolition and rebuilding were the only chance. They did think, however, that the beautiful St Stephen's Chapel should

The interior of the Parliament buildings is designed in a richly decorated Gothic style, as can be seen in the House of Lords. In 1844 architect Barry employed Pugin, 'maestro of British Gothic art' for these designs. Pugin, a then unknown artist, had previously worked with Barry on his competition entry in 1835, and had also made the illustrations for another entrant. The House of Lords that Pugin drew for Gillespie Graham can be seen on p.39. Barry himself worked on all the details of his building, continuously changing his design up until his death in 1860.

The illustration of the south front on p.30 was made in 1842. If you compare this with the present appearance of the Houses of Parliament, you see that the tower of Big Ben -- in the background, delete in the drawing, and in the picture, far right -- was to alter its appearance considerably.

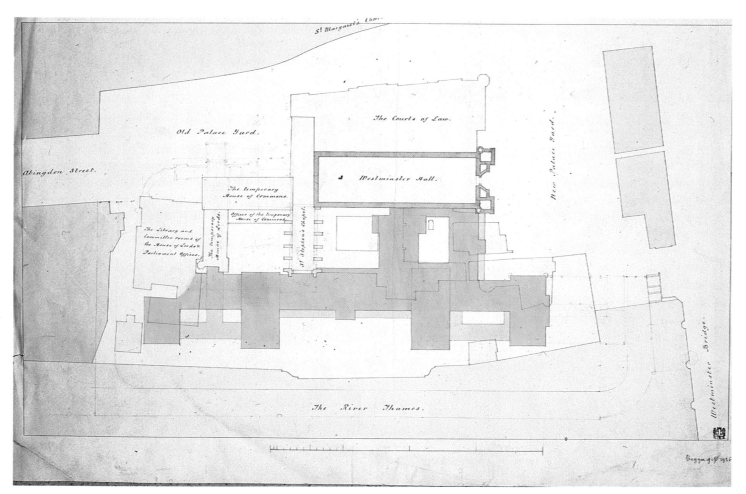

In 1835 Sir Robert Smirke, commissioned by the government, designed a building to replace the Houses of Parliament that had largely been destroyed by fire; a great deal would be restored but there would be little impressive new building. This plan led to violent reactions; many felt that the British parliament should have a more imposing home. The protest resulted in cancellation of Smirke's commission that same year. Nevertheless, Smirke's plan was not without its good points, and would have made a considerable improvement to the former parliament buildings. This can be seen from the drawing, where Smirke has sketched in his suggestions in red.

be spared, to be incorporated in the new building complex as entrance hall, library or chapel.

Progress was slow; the government was in the throes of economic recession. But as it happened, this very recession turned out to be useful: it created the need for office space where bankruptcies could be handled. An area inside the parliamentary buildings where disused wooden tallies were stored was selected for this purpose. These tallies were therefore burned, on 17 October 1834, in the stoves of the House of Lords, causing so much heat that 'it could be felt through the floor matting that the stone floors became warm'. All unsuspecting, the workmen left for home at five o'clock, and an hour later the fire broke out. It was not immediately clear what should be done. Parliament was first offered the almost completed Buckingham Palace, but after considerable discussion it was decided that this building was really much better suited to be the royal palace. Then there were suggestions to restore the burnt building as far as possible, and just before leaving office, government Lord Melbourne's commissioned architect Robert Smirke to design a 'modest reconstruction' of the Houses of Parliament.

But when this leaked out, public opinion protested. A press campaign was mounted, urging the construction of a building that would do justice to 'Britain's important position in the world'. The new Houses of Parliament would become the largest and most important building complex in the country, and would stand comparison with the 'splendid monuments in St Petersburg and Paris'. Popular pressure was so powerful that the commission given to Smirke was withdrawn, and it was decided to organize an open architectural competition for a palace for the British Parliament.

ACHITECTURAL COMPETITIONS were not unfamiliar in Britain in those days. But since they often led to abuses, they were much criticised. For this reason, the competition committee, set up in 1835 - with members from both the Lords and the Commons - did everything in its power to organize the competition so that no fault could be found with it. The programme was carefully planned down to the finest detail, and described minutely in what form the many drawings would have to be submitted. For instance, the use of colour was not permitted in the drawings, as this might possibly mislead the jurors. Only sepia tinting for the three-dimensional drawings (the angle of vision was precisely stated) was allowed. Furthermore, all entrants were to be anonymous - using a motto or pseudonym - and it was settled in advance that a maximum of five prizes of five hundred pounds each would be awarded. The winner of the first prize

The competition for a new Houses of Parliament presented no easy task: never had such a large-scale design been required by architects - the front of the building was more than 90 metres long. Many tried, above all, to avoid monotony. Lewis Nockalls Cottingham, above right, chose his own interpretation of the Elizabethan style; Thomas Rickman, above left and left, produced an eclectic design containing many Gothic elements.

would receive an additional thousand pounds if his design were not executed. And yet the competition aroused discontent, especially among architects. For one thing, only designs in the Gothic or Elizabethan styles were allowed to be submitted, which amounted to taking sides in a vehement controversy that was raging among architects in those days. At that time, the classicist movement was reaching its zenith in Britain, which meant that the majority of architects closely followed the precepts from Greek and Roman antiquity. A revaluation of Gothic architecture had begun as early as the 1750s and hesitant attempts at Neo-Gothic were on the increase, but this was a trend mostly confined to church building.

The Elizabethan style was even more controversial. It referred to an even more recent, marginal trend in architecture which derived its examples from the time of Elizabeth I (1558-1603), a period of flourishing artistic growth in England. The term 'Elizabethan', however, was more often used with reference to painting, music and literature than to architecture, and no guidelines existed for building in such a style. There were some examples to which the name was applied, but these were all country mansions. The anonymous architect, Candidus, expressed a typical view on these mansions when he wrote in the *Architectural Magazine* that 'some of these undoubtedly display a certain stateliness and old-fashioned sumptuousness, that please, as uncommon and curious, even while they show themselves almost entirely devoid of grace and real elegance'.

THE COMPETITION COMMITTEE had strong reasons for precisely stipulating these two architectural styles. Unlike Classicism, Gothicism was regarded as a national style, and the new Palace of Westminster was intended to be the pride of the British nation. Besides, it was pointed out that a special bond existed between Gothicism and Parliament; both found their origins in the Middle Ages. A final point in favour of Gothicism was that it was a style with Christian origins, in contrast with pagan Classicism. The only real point in favour of the Elizabethan style was that it was specifically British, but it was probably only offered as an additional option in order to give the designers a little more freedom.

However, these were emotional considerations, which by no means convinced all architects. But as the idea of winning the

Second prize was awarded to the delightful design by John Chessell Buckler. Later there was much criticism of Buckler's pseudonym, which, it was said, was not 'pseudo' enough, and people complained that it was only thanks to his friendship with juror Hanbury Tracy that he won his prize.

competition was so appealing, most of them set aside their objections. A further point was that the Gothic style was popular with the public at large. So much so, indeed, that in 1819, the classicist façade of a new extension to the old Houses of Parliament, the High Court (designed by architect John Soane) had to be demolished immediately after completion and replaced with a Gothic façade. The chief argument advanced at the time was that it was more in keeping with Westminster Hall, another Gothic building.

Another point that rankled many architects was the composition of the jury. It consisted entirely of ex-members of parliament because these were allegedly best able to judge what were the 'ambitions of the day'. Architects were not considered capable of this, and moreover they were suspected of being biased against professional rivals. It cannot be denied that parliamentarians have a finger-tip feeling for what is vital in a particular period, but it was an equally reasonable assumption that members of the jury also had their architectural prejudices. Chairman Charles Hanbury Trace and Thomas Liddell were both well-known adherents of Gothicism, and both had, as amateur architects, designed the occasional country home in that style. Sir Edward Cust had never himself practised architecture, but his personal friendship with architect Charles Barry was common knowledge, particulary after he had taken Barry's advice in an attack on the classicist National Gallery, designed by William

Wilkins. George Vivian had published a number of pamphlets about new buildings in London, showing a clear preference for the picturesque architecture associated with the Elizabethan era.

These objections, however, withheld few architects from taking part in the competition. Ninety-seven designs were submitted; a very large number considering the short space of time allotted for this huge undertaking.

IN JANUARY 1836 the result of the competition was published, which at once set all tongues wagging. So many people - both within and outside Parliament - felt involved with the new Houses of Parliament, that it was decided to publish all the designs. An exhibition was organized where initially 78 non-winning designs were shown, and later also the designs by the four winners: Charles Barry, John Chessell Buckler, David Hamilton and William Railton.

For weeks the papers overflowed with comment. The new Palace of Westminster had clearly stirred the imaginations of the architects; there were the most magnificent drawings to be seen. In the trade press, however, reactions were far more reserved, and opportunity was often taken to vent much pent-up anger. For instance, the authoritative *Architectural Magazine* declared: 'We would have preferred the Hellenistic style, or a variant such as Ancient Roman; for the beauty of these styles is less subject to local and contemporary

Scottish architect D. Hamilton gained third prize with his Elizabethan design - though not everyone recognized it as such. At any rate, it was certainly not Gothic. Hamilton later - see text on p.35 - expressed in no uncertain terms his feelings about 'Gothic barbarism'.

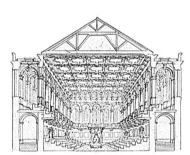
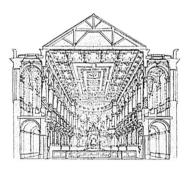

preferences than is the Gothic style. A public building, intended to last for centuries, must not owe its beauty to a whim of fashion.'

And the Scottish architect, David Hamilton, - himself the winner of the third prize for his Elizabethan design - wrote lamentingly that 'Gothic barbarism is again to be allowed to triumph over the masterpieces of Italy and Greece', and 'When our architects begin their studies . . . they learn the distinctive characters of the Greek orders, the proportions between the height and diameter of a shaft, those of the echinus, the mutulus and the abacus, those of the entablature and the pediments . . . Let it not be said then that we run away from our own principles, when an opportunity is offerd of placing before the eyes of Europe what we can effect . . . Gothic architecture having, in truth, no strict rules of proportion, size, height, mouldings, decoration being all arbitrary, you will there indeed be safe from criticism . . .'

It was also remarked that most of the Gothic entries were all too ecclesiastical in character, and that virtually no one had succeeded in creating an harmonious whole. The Elizabethan designs - which in fact numbered fewer than ten - were chiefly noted for their lack of clarity.

'The general impression which the whole has left on our minds', declared the *Architectural Magazine*, 'is regret that so much exertion was fettered . . . by the style. It appears clear to us that the greater number of the authors of these designs are deficient in what we call a reasoning taste. Many have taken precedent as a guide for bringing together certain forms; and a still greater number seem to have had no other aim than that of producing a grand, rich or picturesque effect in the exterior, without reference to what is within, to use, or to practicability. While we state this, we would not hesitate at £100,000, more or less, on the exhibition of a design worthy of the nation, whether Gothic, or Grecian; but a number of those in the exhibition we should be sorry to see executed at any price.'

All this criticism, however, was weakened by the fact that even the most rabid critics agreed with the award of the first prize to the design by the London architect, Charles Barry. At the time of the competition he was already an architect of high repute, who had designed impressive buildings such as St Peter's church in Brighton and the Travellers Club in London. He was also one of the first to have broken with the 'slavish following' of the classics, although he had not found his new examples in Gothicism but in the Italian Renaissance. He had struck lucky when making his Gothic design, in engaging the services of a young, unknown draughtsman: Augustus Welby Pugin. This young man proved a master at drawing Gothic detail, a love for which he had imbibed since childhood. Barry carried sole responsibility for the design, but it is certain that Pugin made a substantial contribution. All the more so since the jury praised the design especially because 'the drawing of the elevations gave evidence of a feeling for and thorough

The design by William Railton that gained fourth prize was striking for its artistic drawing; this could not, however, conceal the fact that the façade along the river Thames lacked unity.

SPEAKERS RESIDENCE   COMMONS BUILDINGS AND

NORTH FRONT OF THE SPEAKERS RESIDENCE

The jury was unanimous in its decision to award first prize to Charles Barry. Hanbury Tracy said that Barry's design was far superior to all the other entries. What made Barry's work particularly distinctive was that he had succeeded in producing one majestic unity. He was one of the few architects who had not been daunted by the prospect of one long façade along the Thames. His plan was extremely clear, though in fact much was altered during building. For although the main design was unchanged - with its central hall between House of Commons and House of

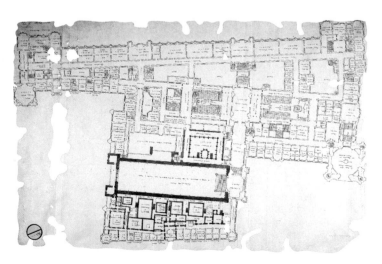

corridors, numerous courtyards, characteristic corners and countless committee rooms and libraries on the river side - the original main ground-plan was replaced by a rectangle.

WESTMINSTER HALL IN ITS PRESENT STATE.   NEW FRONT TO LAW COURTS.

FRONT TOWARDS NEW PALACE YARD

knowledge of Gothic architecture'.

The magisterial main plan of the design was Barry's own work, though, and this also weighted heavily. That the beautiful Gothic details did not in themselves tip the balance is shown by the fact that Pugin had at the same time worked on the design submitted by James Gillespie Graham, a less successful competitor.

RARELY HAS A COMPETITION led to such a fine building as the new Houses of Parliament in London. It became a 'dream in stone', as the Russian Czar Nicholas I said, and as early as 1899 the *Architectural Review* remarked with admiration that the building had won the hearts of all England.

Rarely, too, did so many obstacles have to be overcome before a building was completed. Immediately after the jury's verdict was made known, stubborn rumours about jury favouritism were thoroughly investigated, and Barry's design was exposed to much criticism. But the architect had sufficient political support and enough flexibility to steer his design - in slightly adapted form - past all objections. Moreover, he proved to be someone who thrived even when sailing against the wind.

In addition, the very difficulties and the constant criticism - inevitable in the case of an enormous building with which so many people, are involved, such as an entire parliament and changing goverments — led him to unprecedented achievements. For if everything had gone according to plan, the building would have been completed in 1842. As it was, in 1844 Barry still found himself with a building that was nowhere near completion, with fully worked out plans but without detailed designs for the interior, and with a

37

RIVER FRONT OF M^R. GILLESPIE GRAHAM'S
Intended to Harmonize with

dissatisfied government that would tolerate no delays beyond 1845. Barry therefore once again called on the help of Pugin and this time it proved an even luckier stroke of luck than before.

Pugin, meanwhile, was no longer unknown. Not only had he accomplished a number of much discussed buildings, but he had also - in word and deed - become one of the most fervent advocates of Gothicsm. Particularly after becoming a Catholic in 1835 and making a tour of the great French cathedrals, he had become brilliant at handling Gothic forms. In this renewed cooperation Pugin's contribution still remained confined to the execution of details, for which he received meticulous instructions from Barry. But Barry had enough good sense to give Pugin the opportunity of expressing himself as the 'maestro of Gothic'.

There were other fortunate side effects, too, to the delays. The end of the 1840s marked the beginning of a forceful

revaluation of craftsmanship, and the new Houses of Parliament were used to show what British craftsmen were capable of achieving, in areas such as woodcarving, ornamental iron-work, and joinery. When finally in 1852 both the House of Lords and the House of Commons were in use, the building - though still not completely finished - had indeed become what the British nation - and the competition committee - had envisaged in 1835: a Palace that was their national pride, and made by the best of British talent.

FOR THE NEW HOUSES OF PARLIAMENT;

Chapel, & with Westminster Hall & Abbey

The Edinburgh architect, James Graham, called in the services of Augustus Welby Pugin for his competition entry. The style of Pugin, who also worked for Barry, is clearly recognizable both in the perspective drawings and in the interior drawings for the House of Lords: the Gothic detail is executed with care and precision. Apart from this, Graham's design had little in common with Barry's.

The central concept is quite different: Barry conceived the Houses of Parliament as a unity, while Graham designed many separate elements.

THE PARIS OPERA

COMPETITION FOR A NEW OPERA HOUSE (ACADÉMIE NATIONALE DE MUSIQUE) IN PARIS, FRANCE.

PUBLISHED: 29 December 1860; closing date: 31 January 1861; result: February 1861, with the proposal that a closed competition be organized among the five prizewinners. This was announced at the beginning of March 1861; closing date: early May; result published: end May 1861; number of participants: 170 (171 designs)

JURY A. Comte de Walewski (Minister of State), chairman; architects: Cardeillac, A.N. Caristie, S.C. Constant-Dufeux, J.F. Duban, H.A. de Gisors, E.J. Gilbert, H. Lebas, J.I. Hittorf, J.B.C. Lesueur, H. Lefuel, L. Lenormand, and Ch. A. Questel.

WINNERS OF THE FIRST ROUND: P.R.L. Ginain, Botrel and A. Crépinet, A.M. Garnaud, J.L. Duc, Ch. Garnier. Winner of the closed competition: Charles Garnier

CONSTRUCTION: 1861-74, after a design by Charles Garnier

IN 1885 there was an attempted assassination of the French emperor, Napoleon III, just outside the entrance to the Salle Le Peletier in Paris. The emperor was unhurt, but the incident had other repercussions. Georges-Eugène Baron Haussmann, prefect of Paris, a protégé of Napoleon, took the opportunity to urge the emperor that the Paris Opera deserved something better than the cramped premises it then occupied. The Salle Le Peletier had never been intended as more than temporary, and the site in Rue Le Peletier, surrounded by narrow streets, was totally inappropriate. Paris, Haussmann said, should have a spaciously situated opera house. This would at the same time make it more difficult to execute any attempted assassination.

The emperor was interested. He agreed that the present accommodation was unimpressive and totally out of keeping with his own notions of imperial grandeur. Moreover, discussions had been taking place for some time about a new opera house in a new location. Several architects had already made designs in the hope of receiving this prestigious assignment.

THE PARIS OPERA had stood near the Palais Royal, once the

palace of Cardinal Richelieu (1585-1642). On the site of the right wing of the Palais, Richelieu founded a theatre where until 1763 not only plays but also operas were performed. After this theatre was destroyed by fire, a new theatre was built nearby, in Rue St Honoré, but in 1781 this also burnt down. In the same year a temporary opera house opened on Boulevard St Martin, the 'Théâtre de la Porte St Martin'.

At the same time there were discussions about where to build the permanent opera house. A number of architects had a clear preference for Place du Carousel, between the Louvre and the Tuileries. In 1781, architects François Bélanger and Joseph Peyre each made designs for an opera house on that site. Later, other architects were to follow their example.

But not everyone thought this was the most suitable place for an opera house. In the same year, 1781, Etienne-Louis Boullée made a plan for Terrain des Capucines, just north of Place Vendôme. In 1789 another architect, B. Poyet, preferred Place Louis XV (now: Place de La Concorde) for his opera house site. All these architects made their designs without having received a specific commission. Everyone agreed that the opera house should be given suitable, impressive premises as soon as possible, since opera formed an important aspect of Parisian entertainment. And what architect would not be delighted with the privilege of building such a temple of culture? With their unsolicited designs some were already making a bid for a possible commission.

In vain, as it turned out. France had other worries at that time. In 1789 the Revolution broke out, and dominated both home and foreign politics until 1795. Nevertheless, there was a consensus that the Théâtre de la Porte St Martin was not the ideal place for an opera house. So in 1794, the Opéra National was moved to the new Salle Montansier, opposite the Bibliothèque Nationale. As this was still only a temporary arrangement, many architects continued to produce designs. In 1800, J.Ch. Huet had the idea of moving the opera back to

the Palais Royal, but like so many others, his design got no further than the drawingboard.

In 1809, however, the question was considered more seriously. A competition was announced for a building to fill the gap between the Louvre and the Tuileries. The competition was won by the team of Charles Percier and Pierre Fontaine, whose plan incorporated a new opera house opposite the Palais Royal. But the politicial situation in France was not yet stable enough for building to begin, and opera performances continued to be staged in the Salle Montansier.

Risk of fire was a constant threat - not surpisingly, since two theatres had already been reduced to ashes. The Salle Montansier was also alarmingly close to the Bibliothèque Nationale. The building was therefore demolished in 1820 and the Opera was transferred, temporarily once again, to a new building in Rue Le Peletier. This 'Salle Le Peletier' had been designed by architect F. Debret, who had been instructed to incorporate the auditorium of the Salle Montansier, in its entirety, into his plan.

For a long time this remained the home of the Opéra National, although this building, too, was destined to go up in flames. But by then it was 1873, and much water had flowed under proverbial bridges.

Operatic art, with its spectacles in which realistic flares and impressive light effects - obtained by oil lamps, torches and later gas lamps - were freely used, has always constituted a fire risk. It is not surprising that so many opera houses have perished in flames.

In 1841 when fire broke out in the Salle Le Peletier (on that occasion not ending in total destruction) the discussion about a definitive home for the Opéra National started once more. The minister for internal affairs, Ch.M.T. Duchatel, proposed a competition for architects. Initially, this met with a lukewarm response, but the minister persisted. In the years that followed he continued to lobby for his idea, and in January 1847 the government announced its decision to organize a competition. The time was ripe. Many architects had been preparing designs on their own initiative, of which those by Hector Horeau, J.B.A. Couder and L.A. Lusson found particular favour with the press.

A competition would clearly be a good way of selecting the best architect. The only question still to be solved was where the site should be. A study of the designs submitted to date showed that not everyone had the same preference. Architect Charles Rohault de Fleury had made nine designs for opera houses at different locations in the city. This interesting project was important in the eventual choice of site. But the competition that Minister Duchatel proposed did not take place. The government abandoned the idea because of lack of funds.

It was imperative that something be done about the unsatisfactory accommodation of the Opera and in 1850 Charles Rohault de Fleury was intructed to make alterations to the Salle Le Peletier.

ALTHOUGH THE OPERA was important to the Parisian entertainment world, plans for a permanent musical theatre had difficulty getting off the ground. After the renovation of the unsatisfactory Salle Le Peletier, there was a lull in activities. It looked as if everyone had lost interest in the project. But in 1852 President Louis Napoleon had himself proclaimed Emperor. France was an empire once more and if the new Emperor Napoleon III were to have his way, would be an empire of the same grandeur as that experienced during the reign of the first Napoleon.

One of the emperor's ideals was to make Paris into the 'plus belle ville du monde', the most beautiful city in the world. His uncle and predecessor, Napoleon, had had the same ideal and Napoleon was determined to achieve this. As a start, he appointed Georges-Eugène Baron Haussmann as prefect of the Seine Department. Haussmann would further the ambitions of Napoleon III and bring the French capital new grandeur and style.

One of Haussmann's priorities was the radical improvement of the Paris street plan. He wanted to get rid of the over-populated districts and the endless narrow streets; he wanted wide boulevards conveniently linking all the main points of the city. This would also achieve the happy aim of preventing the Parisians from barricading the narrow streets as had been done all too often in the recent past. In this new, spacious street plan the emphasis would be on striking and impressive buildings.

In 1857 Napoleon became personally involved with a possible new opera building. The Russian architect, A. Cavos, had sent him a design which he must have examined closely, and about the same time Rohault de Fleury also prepared a design. No decisions were taken. Then, on 14 January 1858, the attempt on the emperor's life was made in front of the Salle Le Peletier.

IN MARCH 1858 HAUSMANN decided that the new Opera should be located at Boulevard des Capucines, just north of Place Vendôme, at the intersection of six boulevards, three of which were still to be built. He played his cards cleverly. In 1860 he asked a commission to investigate the possible sites for a new opera house. Less than two months later the 'Commission d'Enquête', the Commission of Enquiry, published a report listing the various possibilities. And indeed, a preference emerged for the site that Haussmann already had in mind. The decisive factor was that this site lay in a neighbourhood where many opera-goers lived, and that it was possible to build there without having to demolish many valuable old buildings.

In September 1860 the government approved the commisson's conclusions and gave the go-ahead to build the new Opera. Haussmann, meanwhile, had not been idle. In 1858 he started building Avenue Napoléon III - today Avenue de l'Opéra - and

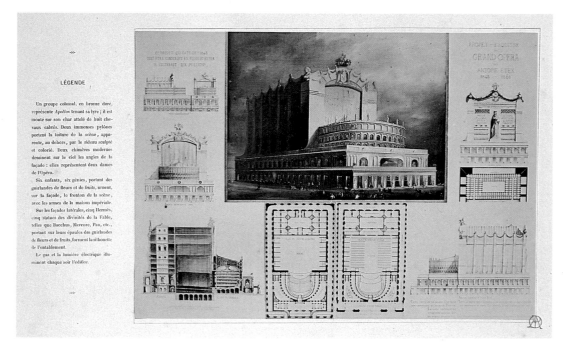

Almost all Paris' large opera buildings ended up in flames: the old Opera in the Palais Royal burnt down in 1763, the same fate befell its successor in Rue St Honoré in 1791, and the Salle Le Peletier was reduced to ashes in 1873. Previously, in 1841, there had been a fire there, which had been caught in time; but it prompted action to design a new Opera House. In 1844 Auguste Lejeune spontaneously designed such a building, see p.42. He probably chose the edge of the Bois de Boulogne for the location. The following year Antoine Etex designed a 'Grand Opera' from brick and iron, see this page. This was the design he displayed at the 1861 Salon, claiming he had made it in 1843, intending it to be a 'cathedral for art'.

in 1860 construction began on new blocks of houses around the future site of the Opera. These houses were designed by Rohault de Fleury and Henri Blondel. In April 1860 Haussmann displayed a map of his proposed city plan, showing the outline of an opera house based on the design of Rohault de Fleury. In December that year Rohault de Fleury improved the design. He was clearly the most likely candidate for the much-coveted commission.

However, on 29 December 1860 the government suddenly announced a competition for the new Opera House. It was rumoured that the Empress Eugénie was the main driving force behind the idea. She wanted to prevent Rohault de Fleury getting the commission; her preference was for her protégé, architect Eugène-Emmanuel Viollet-le-Duc, whom she and her husband greatly admired.

The days in which an emperor, still less a prefect, could high-handedly force through his own ideas, had passed. In 1860 Paris was the city of the bourgeoisie, and the Opera was to be their monument in the renovated city. Not without cause the commission of enquiry Haussmann's new location so suitable; it was in the centre of a typically bourgeois neighbourhood. If the emperor and empress wished to impose their own choice of architect, they would be wise to make it appear as if they had nothing to do with it. Just as Haussmann had for his definitive location invoked the aid of a commission, so the imperial couple had to put up with a competition and a jury, even if this should release a genie from a bottle, impossible to tame.

THE COMPETITION PROGRAMME was extremely succinct. Anyone, regardless of nationality, was allowed to take part and the participants were given barely a month: all entries had to be submitted by 31 January 1861. Minister of State Count de Walewski justified this short period by saying that only draft designs were required. Each participant had to submit three drawings: a ground plan, a lengthwise cross-section and an elevation, all accompanied by brief notes. Entries had to be submitted under a motto, and a sealed envelope had to be enclosed, containing the name and address of the architect. The design programme was equally precise: as regards the exterior, it was stated that there should be a coach drive, a separate entrance for holders of season tickets, and several vestibules at the front of the building, as well as a box-office and areas for the service staff. Near the vestibules there should be staircases offering convenient access to the floors above. There had to be a separate entrance for the emperor, and the auditorium should be able to seat an audience of 1800 to 2000. The stage should be 14 metres wide, 32 metres deep,

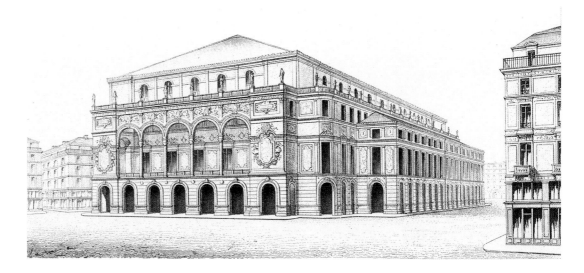

The competition for a new Opera House was announced in 1860. All entries were exhibited - anonymously - in January 1861 in the Palais de l'Industrie, and were seen by the press, who seized the opportunity to make scathing cartoons of some entries, see below. Who exactly took part in this competition is not known, though later designs of some entries were published, for example that of Jules Charles Simonet, p.44 below. Tipped to win by the press was Eugène - Emmanuel Viollet-le-Duc, whose design, right, is interesting because it is one of his few modern architectural works. His influential writing shows that he was a strong supporter of a rational and scientific approach to building, and was especially fond of the Neo-Gothic style. In 'Le Moniteur Universel', of 11 February 1861, Théophile Gautier, a fervent supporter of Garnier's, described Viollet-le-Duc's design as 'the most individual of the whole exhibition'. In it, Viollet-le-Duc paid great attention to the surrounding building plans of Ch. Rohault de Fleury and H. Blondel. Inside, careful thought is paid to efficiency of movement, and the emphasis is placed on the design of the hall, see also p. 49.

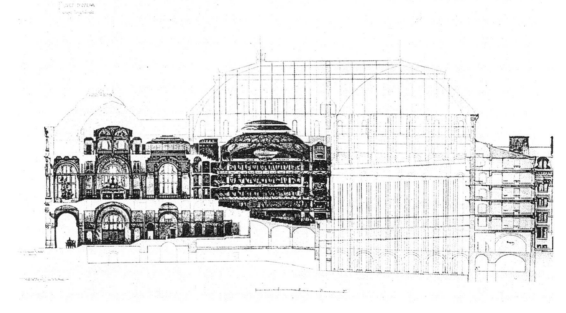

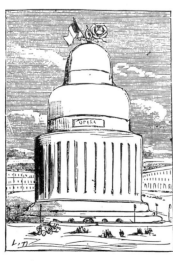

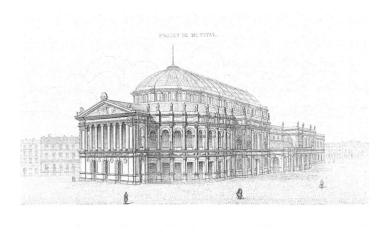

PROJET DE M. TÉTAZ.

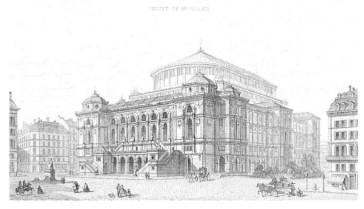

PROJET DE M. HALLER

Vue perspective.

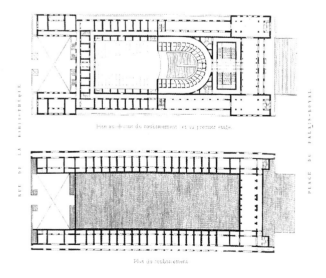

Plan au-dessus du soubassement et au premier étage.

Plan du soubassement.

and be able to hold 400 people. In addition there were specific requirements regarding foyers and boxes, and storage space for costumes near the stage.

It has been said that this precise programme, emphasizing the efficient functioning of the theatre, was attributable to Viollet-le-Duc, whose work stresses functionality. But a competition is not made merely by its programme. The jury is also important.

Minister of State Walewski, who announced the competition, became chairman of the jury. The other twelve members were all architects, of whom eight were delegates from the Department of Architecture at the Académie des Beaux Arts (Caristie, Duban, De Gisors, Gilbert, Hittorf, Lebas, Lefuel and Leseur) while the other four represented the Council of Civil Building Works (building experts Cardeillac, Contant-Dufeux, Lenormand and Questel). It was certainly a jury of professionals.

By the end of January 1861, 171 entries had been submitted, among which - as would later appear - many came from architects who had already been working on plans for the Opera. However, many designs came from younger architects trying their luck for the first time.

All entries were exhibited in the Palais de l'Industrie on Champs Elysées, where not only the jury was able to inspect them but where the press also had free access. Even before the jury announced its decision, a discussion arose in newspapers and trade journals about the, still anonymous, designs.

The press was virtually unanimous that the design which everyone suspected, with almost total certainty, to be by Viollet-le-Duc, had the best chance of winning.

If Viollet-le-Duc were tipped as winner, this was not so much because of the quality of his design but more because of his relationship with the empress. The trade press were enthusiastic about the design of Botrel and Crépinet, which was said to have 'a clear ground plan and highly successful ornamentation'.

The press was less pleased with the general standard of the designs. It was noted that the strict division between the 'Classical school' and the 'Gothic school' had been abandoned, but that unfortunately this had given way to a rather insipid mishmash garnered from many past styles. Voices were raised in plea for a new style, appropiate for an opera house.

The fact that the Englishman, E.M. Barry, son of Sir Charles Barry, was among the entrants, shows that the competition drew attention even outside France.

The jury examined all the entries and began a process of elimination. After the first ballot 43 projects remained. After

In 1861, the magazine 'Revue Générale de l'Architecture et des Travaux Publics' published several entries from the first round of the competition. Top left: Design by Jacques Martin Tétaz, thought by many to stand a very good chance of winning. Under: Design of the then 26-year-old Martin Haller. Left:

Perspective and ground plans for the designs by Amadée Gouder.

There was a second, closed competition won - to the surprise of many - by Garnier, then 36 years old. He had been trained at the Ecole des Beaux Arts where jury member H. Lebas had been his teacher. In 1848 he won the Grand Prix de Rome travelled to Italy where he lived until 1858.

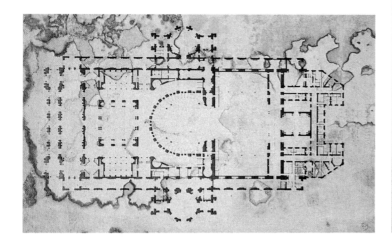

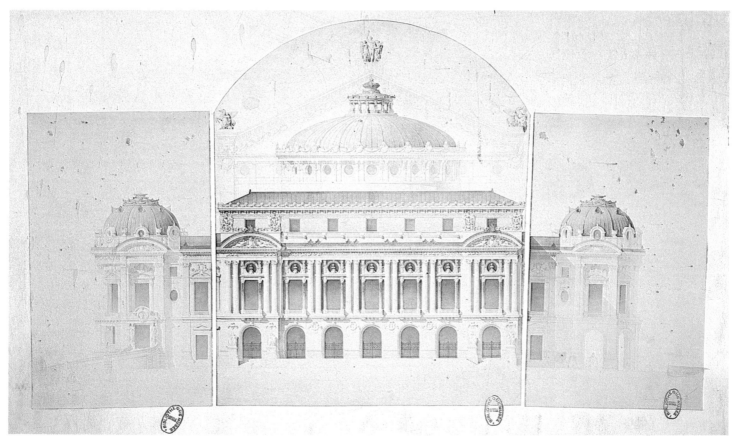

Garnier's first design for the competition has probably been lost; we have no record of it. The opera archives contain many drawings by Garnier, probably all designs that he made after he had won the competition. The original design for the second round is probably also lost. Above left: Floor plan showing the first balcony. Above right: Imperial entrance in Rue Auber on the west side of the building. This entrance was planned with an eye to the safety of the royal visitor - in 1858 there had been an attempted assassination of the French emperor when he was going to attend a performance in Salle Le Peletier. In this drawing Garnier has sketched in a possible plan for the raised entrance drive. The story goes that this raised driveway for coaches was required because of Napoleon III's aversion to lifts. It was a very complicated procedure to contruct, since very little space was available. Garnier made a sketch and later constructed a lifesize model using sandy ground; he had a coach and four try out the bend, and then made alterations, guided by the tracks they left in the sand. Above: Early design for the front façade, see also p.40. Left: Royal pavilion with the driveway just visible.

Above: Rear view of the Opera House
on Boulevard Haussmann.
The Emperor's Pavilion with its
raised driveway is on the right, see
also p.47.

Right: Cross-section of the Opera
House.
P. 49: Impression by E.E. Viollet-le-
Duc of the opera foyers - straight
lines, classical design. Further
illustrations of Viollet-le- Duc's design
on p. 45.

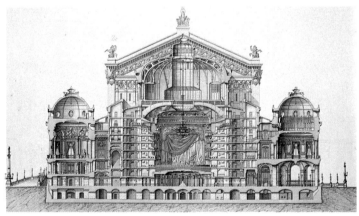

the second this number was reduced to 16. At this point all the
leading candidates such as Barry, were still in the race,
Viollet-le-Duc, Rohault de Fleury and J.M. Tétaz.
In view of the jury's professional expertise, it seems likely that
most of its members had a fairly clear idea of the identities
behind the various mottos. The methods and drawing styles of
Viollet-le-Duc and Rohault de Fleury, in particular, were well
known.
Apparently, the jury felt that a new opera house offered a
welcome opportunity to make a fresh, rather more unorthodox
choice. Perhaps it was felt that the Second Empire ought to
produce a building style of its own. This must remain
conjecture, but how else can we explain that at the third ballot
the jury eliminated the two major candidates, Viollet-le-Duc
and Rohault de Fleury. Only seven projects remained,
incluiding the one by Tétaz. Yet, he too fell by the wayside.
At the fourth ballot only the designs of Ginain, Botrel and
Crépinet, Garnain, Duc and Garnier were left. Yet, Ginain and
Garnier were both young architects who were not widely
known among the general public, although Monika
Steinhauser writes in her study *Die Architektur der Pariser
Oper* that they cannot have been unknown to the jury. Both
had once been students of jury member and vice-chairman
Lebas.

After due consideration the jury reached the unanimous
conclusion that none of the five entries was worthy of the
'Grand Prix'. We can only guess their reasons. Was the standard
of the entries still considered inadequate? Had the
succinctness of the programme provided too little insight into
the abilities of the remaining five? Or was it simply impossible
for such a large jury to reach agreement? Finally, awards were
made as follows, and not three prizes - as had originally been
decided - were awarded.
The first prize, of 6,000 francs, went to Ginain. Second prize of
4,000 francs went to Botrel and Crépinet. Garnain, winner of
the third prize, received 200 francs and Duc, winner of the
fourth prize, 1,500 francs. Garnier came last; he was awarded
fifth prize: 1,000 francs.
The real first prize, the commission to build the Opera, was
not awarded. Although the competition programme stated that
in such a case the government was free to take its own
decision, it accepted the jury's advice to organize a closed
competition.
This was announced at the beginning of March 1861.

Viollet-le-Duc had had enough, and did not take part.
The team of Botrel and Crépinet split up and took part
separately. Later, in 1925, Garnier's widow revealed that her
husband had at the time suggested to Ginain, the first
prizewinner, that they prepare a joint project; a proposal
which Ginain apparently rejected.

This time the participants were given two months, though the
programme was much more extensive and detailed than the
first one. It was even described as an exceedingly complicated
briefing. After the entries had been received, the jury needed
almost a month to reach a verdict, but at the end of May it
decided unanimously that Charles Garnier should be invited
to build the new Opera. The jury praised the remarkable
aesthetic qualities of Garnier's design and the felicitous layout
of its ground plan. The monumental façades were also
considered most impressive.

It was decided. On 6 June 1861 Count de Walewski officially
appointed Charles Garnier as architect of the Paris Opera and
commissioned him to prepare the definitive design.
Garnier's Opera was accomplished, though not without
difficulty. Garnier himself was not happy with the site. He was
particularly bothered by the newly built houses around the

square, designed by Rohault de Fleury and Blondel.
Viollet-le-Duc had taken these buildings fully into account (he
adapted his opera house to its environment), but Garnier
concentrated exclusively on his own creation. He would have
preferred to have built it elsewhere, where it would be seen to
better advantage. However, the site could not be changed.
On 27 August 1861 building was started, but it was to be
almost a year before the first stone was laid. When the site was
being prepared, a small underground stream was discovered
which caused many headaches. In 1863 there were further
delays, this time due to political problems. Napoleon III
thought it desirable - for political reasons - to give the
building of the Hôtel Dieu hospital - diagonally opposite
Notre Dame - priority above the prestigious and costly opera
house. The emperor expressed deep concern for the social
problems in Paris, hoping in this way to get into the good
books of the working classes.
Nevertheless, progress was made, however slow. In 1867 the
façade was unveiled and in 1870 the main structure was
complete. The completion of the interior could then be started.
Unfortunately, the Franco-Prussian war broke out and the
Second Empire came to an end.

The previous two pages show Garnier's design for the staircase which applied, he said, a 'system of oppositions' or contrasts.
This achieves a remarkable effect, particularly because of the space beneath the main staircase, scarcely noticed by the visitor who ascends these stairs, see bottom of p. 53, while from the side a totally different effect is achieved, see right.

Initially, the government of the new Third Republic had no wish to put money into Garnier's creation. But when in 1873 the Salle Le Peletier went up in flames, there seemed no alternative. The new opera was quickly completed and on 5 January 1875, President M.E.P.M. MacMahon officially opened the building.

The emperor and empress saw the construction of the Opera but not its completion. Napoleon died in England in 1873; Eugénie stayed in England until the summer of 1875 and then left for Switzerland. It is doubtful whether she was sorry never to have seen Garnier's work; she had been strongly against the jury's decision and is said to have been furious on learning that Viollet-le-Duc had not been chosen. Yet she did meet Garnier once, and asked him, 'What style is your Opera? Is it Louis XIV or Louis XV?' And the story has it that Garnier replied, 'Neither, your Majesty; it is in the style of Napoleon III'.

INDEED, GARNIER'S OPERA and the Second Empire are indissolubly linked. Yet we do not speak of a 'Napoleon III' or a 'Second Empire' style. The great diversity among the entries for the first competition shows how attitudes and ideas were already shifting. Architects no longer clung to one favoured style, but followed a more eclectic approach: looking for what was best in a variety of proven styles.

Young Garnier - 35-years-old when he won the competition - was not unfamiliar with this phenomenon. His Opera is primarily a Neo-Baroque creation, but it also contains elements from the French and Italian Renaissance. Perhaps most striking is the manner in which he designed his building: with self-assurance, a youthful élan and great vivacity. Garnier believed in what he wanted to build: a palace for the citizen in which to enjoy a delightful prelude to an operatic performance for which he had paid his money.

Garnier designed a 'temple de la Bourgeoisie triomphante',

hence the imposing façade and the overwhelmingy staircase in the vestibule. Garnier's rival, Viollet-le-Duc, abhorred this excessive pomp. He felt the building should have been more sober, more efficient, and that greater emphasis should have been placed on the interior of the auditorium. Garnier found the auditorium of secondary importance; it was the actual building where operas were performed that the public came to see, and an impressive entrance was what mattered to him. Garnier did not become the father of a new architectural style, as perhaps he had hoped. But his Opera House is unique; he made it a palace, not for courtly nobles, but for free citizens. Small wonder that many architects of opera houses since his time have studied his work closely.

It is greatly to the credit of the jury that it recognized the self-assurance in Garnier's design. It was an even greater credit that this jury had the courage te reject the obvious favourites, despite the imperial displeasure this aroused. It is hard to avoid the conclusion: the architects on the jury counted themselves among the self-assured, victorious bourgeoisie.

Garnier thought the imposing staircase should act as an overture to the opera the visitor was about to enjoy, like a roll of drums, a crescendo of strings or a trumpet blast.
Above left: View of a first-floor foyer.

Centre: Southern entrance from the Imperial Pavilion at the end of the driveway, see also p. 47.
Above right: Rich decoration on the ceilings of the foyers, recalling the interiors of castles and palaces from the 17th and 18th centuries.

The Reichstag in the 1980s makes a very different impression from how Paul Wallot imagined it 100 years before, see p.62. During building, considerable changes were made, and after completion in 1894 - 11 years after the competition - much more was to change.

The Reichstag was often the centre of important events in Germany.
Below: Protest of thousands against the killing in 1919 of Rosa Luxemburg and Karl Liebknecht, leaders of the communist Spartacus group.
Centre: The Reichstag in 1930.

THE REICHSTAG IN BERLIN

NATIONAL ARCHITECTURAL COMPETITION FOR THE REICHSTAG IN BERLIN, SEAT OF THE PARLIAMENT OF THE GERMAN EMPIRE

PUBLISHED: 2 February 1882; result: 24 June 1882; number of entrants: 189

JURY: Architects F. Adler, J. van Egle, Martin Haller, G. van Neureuthen, Persius, Franz Schmidt and Vincent Statz; the painter, Anton von Werner, and 13 members of Reichstag and Bundesrat

WINNERS: 1. Paul Wallot, Friedrich Thiersch; 2. Cremer and Wolffenstein, Kayser and Von Grossheim, Heinrich Seeling; 3. Giese and P. Weidner, Hub. Stier, L. Schupman, Busse and Franz Swechten, Hermann Ende and Wilhelm Bockman

CONSTRUCTION: 1883-1894 (design: Paul Wallot)

EARLY IN 1882 a competition was published in Berlin asking for designs for a building to house the Reichstag, or German parliament. Never before had such a large sum of money been offered to the winners, and few competitions had ever been set up for so important a building. No wonder a large number of architects entered, and that this competition gives us such a comprehensive picture of the Germany of that time, and not only in the field of archtiecture.

In 1882 the German empire had been in existence for exactly 11 years. Its creation had produced, for the first time since the Middle Ages, a unity combining virtually all the German-speaking states in Europe. The inception of this empire was in the first place due to Otto Eduard Leopold von Bismarck, who in 1862 had been appointed chancellor by King Wilhelm I of Prussia, to help him, against the wishes of the aristocracy, to strengthen the army. Bismarck succeeded not only in making the Prussian army, within an extremely short time, the most powerful in Europe, but he also, by means of a number of tactical wars, managed to unify all the German states. On 18 January 1871 King Wilhelm I was crowned in Versailles as Emperor of the German Empire, of which Berlin became the capital.

The empire was ruled by an authoritarian government in which, next to the emperor, Bismarck held great power.

Recent photograph of the Reichstag on the Platz der Republik, formerly Königsplatz, West Berlin. Immediately behind the building is the Berlin Wall that since 1961 has divided the city into East and West.

Below: the definite design of Wallot.

The 1882 competition was the second organized for the Reichstag; ten years earlier there had also been a competition resulting in a winner, but no building. On that occasion all the winning designs had been published.

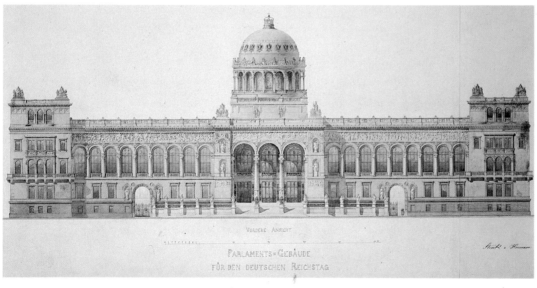

VORDERE ANSICHT

PARLAMENTS=GEBÄUDE
FÜR DEN DEUTSCHEN REICHSTAG

Above: After ample consideration, the jury for the 1872 competition awarded first prize to Ludwig Bohnstedt, from Gotha. This plan was never executed, and Bohnstedt's almost identical entry for the 1882 competition did not gain an award. Below: The 1872 design by Heinrich Strack and Heinrich Hermann.

The large assembly room as designed
by Martin Gropius and Heino
Schmieden in 1872. Paul Wallot
worked with these architects from
1864 to 1868 and had specialised in
applying white primer in drawings to
produce the effect of depth. After
Wallot left them, Gropius and
Schmieden continued to use this
technique.

The 1872 competition had a truly international character: beside the 70 German entries there were 15 British, seven Austrian, four Dutch, three French, two Italian and one American. People were especially curious to see the British entries: how would an Englishman design a German parliament building? Right: The design made by George Gilbert Scott and his son, John Oldrid, remained in the running until the last round.

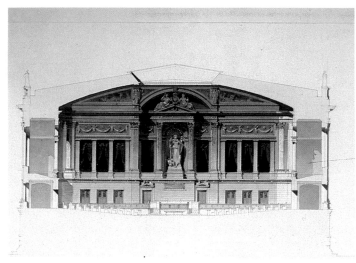

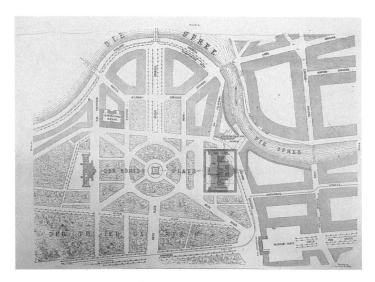

Cross-section and site sketch made by Emil von Lange and Joseph Bühlmann from Munich in 1872. This design did not gain a prize, and only Bühlmann - again unrewarded - took part in the 1882 competition.

But several states kept a measure of autonomy, Prussia being 'primus inter pares' or, first among equals. There was even a whiff of democracy: the Reichstag. This was a representative body whose members were elected by universal male suffrage. The emperor had scarely been in function for two months when the ministry of trade published his plan to erect a new parliamentary building to accomondate both the Reichstag and the Bundesrat (the consultative body of appointed - not elected - deputies of all Federal states). It soon became clear that the Reichstag was held in great esteem by the German people. The German architectural press - in particular the *Deutsche Bauzeitung* - objected strongly to the idea that the erection of such a building would be merely a matter of bureaucratic routine. It wanted a better location to be found and an international competition to be organized. Only then would a building be produced 'worthy of the representative governing body of the German people'. The architectural press had the support of the Reichstag and Bundesrat deputies. The government agreed to a competition. The programme was published in 1872 and the competition closed in that same year.

Although there were 102 entries, including 17 foreign ones, no building resulted. The main reason for this was that the competition programme had been rather vague, so that none of the designs offered enough basis for a new building.

Not even the plan submitted by L. Bohnstadt from Gotha, to which the jury, consisting of 19 members, had awarded first prize.

To make matters worse, the site promised by Bismarck - a piece of land on the Koningsplatz belonging to a certain

Right: Perspective and ground plan of the 1872 design by Hermann Ende and Wilhelm Böckmann from Berlin. This did not remain in the running for long, but in 1882 almost the same design by these architects gained third prize. Their motto was 'Finally'.

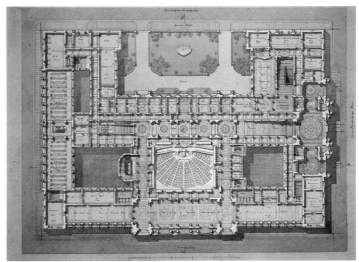

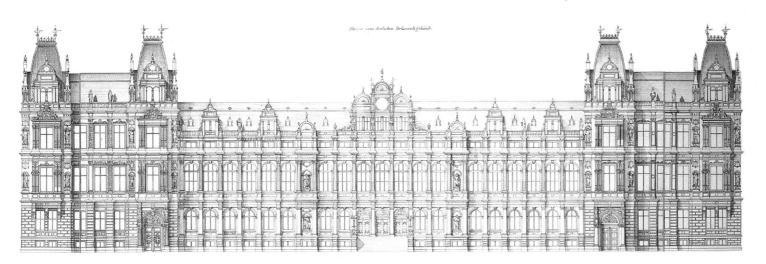

Design in Renaissance style, from 1872, by Robert Cremer of Aachen.

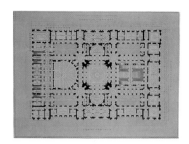

Prince Razcinsky - was no longer available by the time the result was published; the prince had suddenly changed his mind about the sale.

FORTUNATELY, IN 1871 a temporary building had been hastily erected to house the Reichstag (based on a design by Friedrich Hitzig). This made it possible to spend ample time in planning a better and, it was hoped, more successful competition. Members from Reichstag and Bundesrat, as well as members of the Berlin Academy of Architecture, worked on the preparations.

In February 1882 when the new competition programme was made public, even the critical *Deutsche Bauzeitung* declared itself reasonably satisfied. The programme was described as 'thorough and comprehensive', and strangely enough the decision that this time the competition should only be open to Germans met with approval - national consciousness had grown considerably during one decade of empire. The amount of prize money also attracted favourable comment; more than 100,000 German marks was made available (in 1872 it had been 30,000 marks). The winners of the earlier competition were specially invited to take part again, for a generous fee. Surprisingly, the *Deutsche Bauzeitung* did have objections to two terms of the competition which others regarded as improvements on the earlier one: the compulsory anonymity of the participants and the fact that entries would not be made public until after the verdict. The journal said: 'We regret this for the sake of our younger colleagues who will now have less opportunity to have their talents published'. Finally, there was some indignation at the composition of the jury: with seven architects as against thirteen members of parliament, the journal considered the experts to be too much in the minority.

'IT IS MUCH TO THE CREDIT of the German architectural community that it has pursued a solution for the greatest national task with such earnestness and devotion,' concluded the architectural critic, Hermann Eggert, after the result of the competition had been published in June 1882.

'The competition has yielded an unexpectedly large number of praiseworthy designs, and the general standard is . . . admirably high. Several among the designs give evidence of a splendid approach and daring creativity on the part of the designer, while at the same time displaying total command of architectural expression and brilliant presentation techniques.' Although Egger thought that no single design was directly suitable for execution, he attributed this chiefly to the cramped building site. This site was in fact the same one as for the competition of 1872 - the plot at the Konigsplatz belonging to Prince Razcinsky. The authorities had vainly tried for eight years to find a better site, but unexpectedly returned to the old plot when it became once more available through the death of Razcinsky.

Together the entries formed a fairly faithful reflection of German architecture of the time. Eclecticism was trumps, many older buildings styles reappeared. Renaissance-style designs were in the majority, imitations especially of the Italian Renaissance being popular all over Europe at that time. There were far fewer Classicist designs; at the beginning of the nineteenth century ancient Greek architecture had stood model for many architects, but had lately begun to lose favour.

Gothicism, on the other hand, had recently become a popular source of inspiration, although Gothic entries were under-represented (only six). Imitations of German Renaissance style, which had been increasing in popularity, were also clearly in evidence.

The shared first prize went to Friedrich Tiersch from Munich and Paul Wallot from Frankfurt am Main, the latter having been chosen by a large majority of votes. There were only two votes against; the journal *Der Baumeister* sneered: 'and naturally, both from laymen'. Wallot's designs met with almost universal acclaim also outside the jury, particulary because of his clear and effective floor-plan. The external shape of his design also appealed to many, even though it was not easy to classify. At all events it was a highly personal design, which contained many typically German features. The Dutch art historian, E. Gugel, described it as 'a variety of High Renaissance, in which the ornamentation shows great personal imagination, and a wealth of national elements'. The journal *Centralblatt der Bauverwaltung*, published by the Ministry of Public Works, found that Wallot had not 'followed the broad, well-trodden path of Italian Renaissance but had found his models in the German Renaissance'. This journal also praised Wallot's design for its 'forceful masculinity in contrast to the weak, smooth, graceful elegance of the Neo-French and Viennese Renaissance'. Impressive it certainly was.

Viennese architect Otto Wagner submitted a design under the motto 'Res publica, res populi'. It was to be one of his last classical designs: a few years later he became a leader of the new architectural movement in Vienna from which the Sezession developed.

CLEARLY WALLOT WOULD BE GIVEN the commission to build the Reichstag. Before this point was reached, however, the architect met with several objections. The main one came from the Bundesrat who objected, among others, to the location of the assembly hall on the first floor 'only accessible by a staircase with almost seventy steps'. But when Wallot altered his design to make the assembly hall on ground level, the Academy of Architecture objected that the transparent dome now towered so high above the assembly hall that not enough light reached the area below. Wallot then removed the dome from the assembly hall altogether and placed it further forward, this now being the only means of retaining this 'landmark' for the general public' in his design. But this involved several architectural complications which appeared almost unsurmountable.

THE CONSTRUCTION OF THE REICHSTAG took ten years. The building was first used in 1894. Over the years, the design had acquired more and more typically German features, which culminated in the text on the imposing façade: 'Dem Deutschen Volkes' (To the German People). The dome, once again moved to its previous position above the assembly hall, was now lower than it had been in the original plan, but the façade was much larger than could ever have been anticipated in 1882. The German Empire had experienced a great economic boom over the previous decade, and although Bismarck had been dismissed in 1890 by the new Kaiser, Wilhelm II, wealth and prosperity seemed limitless. Small wonder that at the opening ceremony the Reichstag was welcomed as a new national monument.

The architectural journal *Der Baumeister* in 1903,

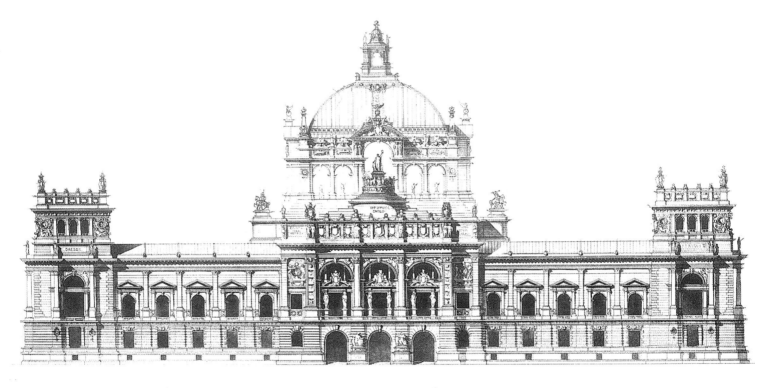

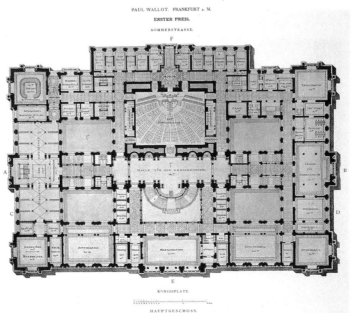

Paul Wallot's winning design from 1882. Much was to be altered in the following years, for example, the entrance - compare p. 54 - and the ground plan. Almost the only part unchanged was the large assembly hall.

pronounced this building as the most important monument of the Bismarck era: 'A wonderfully faithful reflection of that tremendous popular movement and strength which had led to the foundation of the German Reich, which was not the work of one person but that of a whole nation, which was the result of a thousand years of development, and which met not only the needs of the present but would also form the basis for the existence of countless future generations.'

Bombastic words in a bombastic time, whose echo could not last long. Even under Kaiser Wilhelm II the foundations were being laid for the first world war, which would plunge Germany into bitter debt. And when in the early 1930s Germany was about to enter the darkest period of its history, the Reichstag building also suffered, almost symbolically. The legendary fire, for which the Dutchman, Van der Lubbe, was declared the culprit, heralded the beginning of the downfall of an empire. And it transformed the 'monument of German self-awareness' into a ruin, whose proud golden dome even today has still not been restored.

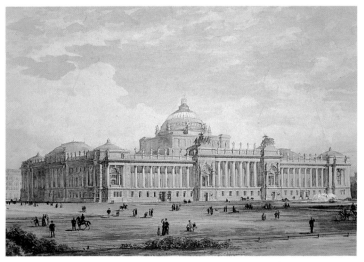

Designs from 1882. From above:
Wilhelm Cremer from Aachen; Oskar
Sommer from Frankfurt am Main;
Heinrich Jozef Kaiser from Berlin;
and an anonymous entry.

THE EIFFEL TOWER

COMPETITION TO DESIGN A WORLD EXHIBITION IN PARIS, INCLUDING A FEASIBILITY STUDY FOR AN IRON TOWER AT THE CHAMPS DE MARS, WITH A BASE DIAMETER OF 125 SQUARE METRES AND A HEIGHT OF 300 METRES.

ANNOUNCED: 1 May 1886; closing date: 18 May 1886; number of participants: 107.

JURY: Chairman: J. Alphand, director of the Exhibition.
Other jury members were politicians, scholars, architects and engineers, including H. Brune, Ed. Collignon, V. Contamin, Hersent, Molinos and Admiral Mouchez.

WINNERS: Eiffel and Sauvestre; Jean Camille Formigé; Ferdinand Dutert.

CONSTRUCTION: 1887-1889 after a design by Eiffel's office.

Almost immediately after winning the coveted commission in May 1886 to build a 300-metre-high iron tower, Gustave Eiffel, partly prompted by a tight budget — he had to fund most of the tower himself — made a second, more constrained, design. The second floor, in particular, was less grand, and to accommodate the lifts, the feet of the tower had to be reconstructed.

MANKIND HAS ALWAYS BEEN fascinated and impressed by tall
buildings. Time and again, people have tried to make
buildings higher than any other in existence. The ancient
Egyptians achieved a height of about 146 metres with the
Pyramid of Cheops; medieval Europeans were no less
successful. Many cathedrals and churches received gigantic
towers; the church of Our Lady in Antwerp (1352-1616) was
120 metres high, and Cologne Cathedral was planned to have
two towers, each 156 metres.
In the nineteenth century there was an upsurge of interest,
especially in Europe and the United States, in yet taller towers.
In 1863 the Mole Antonelliana in Turin was completed, a
tower of 170 metres, which for several decades remained the
tallest in the world. In 1848 work was started in Washington
D.C. on a stone obelisk in memory of President George
Washington. It was intended that this stone needle would
eventually be 183 metres high, but this proved technically
impossible. The building was not completed until 1885, and
its total height was 169 metres.

THE TRUE FIGHT FOR THE tallest tower was fought on the
drawingboard, rather than in reality. The magic limit was the
tower of 1000 feet or a little over 300 metres. For about sixty
years, architects and engineers dreamed of breaking this
architectural sound barrier.
In 1831 the Cornish engineer, Richard Trevithick, designed a
tower of a 1000 feet on the occasion of the Reform Bill to
reform the franchise in Britain. The monument was envisaged
as a round, tapering column made of cast iron, with a base
diameter of 30 metres narrowing to about four metres at the
top.
The tower would be made of 1500 pieces of cast iron, each
roughly three metres square, in the middle of which there
would be a round hole just under two metres in diameter, and
in each corner another round hole of about 45 centimetres.
These holes would make the structure lighter and lessen wind
resistance. The plates would be five centimetres wide and
weigh about 3000 kilos each. Within the cast iron structure
there would be a round shaft, three metres in diameter, to
accommodate a lift by which visitors could reach the top. And
at the top a gigantic cast iron statue was envisaged. However,
Trevithick died in 1827 and with him the driving force behind
the project. In 1852 the Great Exhibition closed in London, a
world exhibition where Crystal Palace had been the great
attraction. Its closure raised the question of the future of this
gigantic glass palace. Although parliament decided to have the

*During the 19th century, the
constructing of high towers caught
the imagination of designers
worldwide and the most fascinating
designs began to appear on paper. In
1876 Clarke and Reeves designed a
tower, the top of which would be
festooned with light bulbs to brighten
up America's centenary celebrations.
Inspired by this on his trip to*

*America, the Frenchman, Sébillot,
designed a similar 300-metre-high
iron 'Tour Soleil', right, wich he
redesigned with Bourdais three years
later in stone.*

building demolished, some people tried to find a new destination for it. In the journal *The Builder* the architect, C. Burton, suggested using the material from the exhibition halls to build a tower of a 1000 feet of iron and glass on top of Crystal Palace. The idea of such a tall tower clearly continued to fascinate, even though Burton's plan stood no chance at the time.

In the early 1870s America was preparing to celebrate the centenary of its independence. This called for a majestic monument, and one of the most spectacular projects was that by engineers Clarke and Reeves. They proposed a round, iron tower, again 1000 feet high. For the construction, they were thinking of round wrought, iron columns such as were manufactured in their own factory for the building of bridges. These columns would stand vertically and be interconnected by means of diagonally placed smaller iron tubes. The designers proposed to locate the tower at the Centennial Exposition in Philadelphia, which was to take place in 1876. At night the tower would be illuminated by many lamps. The most striking aspect of the design was that Clarke and Reeves concerned themselves solely with the construction of the tower. There was no architectural ornamentation, it was a purely technical construction, with a shaft in the middle for the lift to the observation platform at the top. Although the project received much praise, no one made any great effort to have it realized.

In 1881 the Frenchman, Sébillot, designed a 'Tour Soleil', no doubt inspired by the idea of Clarke and Reeves during a visit to the United States. He proposed to build an iron tower of 300 metres from whose pinnacle Paris could be lit. The idea was not sufficiently thought out and, three years later, Sébillot produced a new design, this time in collaboration with architect Jules Desiré Bourdais; a stone tower, also 300 metres high, and richly ornamented in the style of the Tower of Pisa. The fact that Sébillot and Bourdais came up with such a spectacular design should be seen in the light of the approaching centenary of the French Revolution. Both must have thought that the occasion called for something grand.

THIS WAS THE OPINION, TOO, of engineers Emile Nouguier and Maurice Koechlin who worked at the office of the French engineer, Gustave Eiffel. In May 1884 they suggested designing a tall tower for the world exhibition that was to take place in Paris in 1889. Early in June they produced a sketch: a large, iron tower 300 metres high, consisting of four legs, made of girders riveted together, joining at its peak. The idea for the future Eiffel Tower was born.

On 6 June 1884, two engineers from Monsieur Eiffel's bureau, Emile Nouguier and Maurice Koecklin, completed a study for a 300-metre-high tower for the approaching world exhibition in Paris. Their boss was unimpressed, but allowed them to work on the idea further. Architect Sauvestre was called in to give form to the design and when it was exhibited in September, Gustave Eiffel, won over by the new result, immediately patented the design under his and his employees' names. Later that year, on 12 December, he bought the two out of the project for one per cent of the projected building costs, and promised to mention their names in connection with the tower at all times.

The new drawings were displayed in the Palais de l'Industrie in Paris. Eiffel was surprised but on closer reflection considered his subordinates' project worthwhile. On 18 September 1884 he applied for a patent for the design which was entered under the names of Eiffel, Nouguier and Koechlin. The three men were much in the public eye, which gave other people ideas too: more and more proposals for a tall tower were submitted, including a construction of wood and brick by Neve and François Hennebique. It was a contest of tall 'paper' towers.

AT THAT TIME EIFFEL WAS ALREADY a renowned engineer, many of whose executed designs — mostly bridges and viaducts — were greatly admired by the public. So when Eiffel dismissed the design by Sébillot and Bourdais as impracticable — the stone construction would be too heavy and it would take too long to build — most people took his word for it. One of these was Edouard Lockroy, and his opinion was to have far-reaching consequences. For in December 1885 Lockroy was appointed minister of trade, and one of his many duties was to oversee the organization of the forthcoming world exhibition. On 1 May 1886 he announced an ideas competition among French architects and engineers for the world exhibition of 1889. The competition included a study into the feasibility, location and shape of an iron tower 300 metres high, covering 125 square metres of the Champs de Mars. Without any doubt the minister had Eiffel's design at the back of his mind. Although the closing date was 18 May, there were 107 entrants, many of whom had made a joke of the whole affair. The jury, under the chairmanship of J. Alphand, director of the exhibition, looked at the entries, but a special subcommittee of the jury — comprising Philipps, Ed. Collignon and V. Contamin — were instructed to study them in detail. Apart from Eiffel and Sauvestre's design, eight others were considered worthy of examination. Bourdais had replaced his stone tower by an iron one, clad with copper plates, and there were also designs by Boucher, Henry, Marion, Pochet, Robert, Rouyer, and Speyser. Apart from Eiffel, none of these received a prize. When the jury announced its verdict there were three first prizewinners, including the design by Eiffel and Sauvestre. Like the other two winners, Formigé and Dutert, they received 4,000 francs. Three projects were awarded second prizes of 2,000 francs each, and seven received third prizes, of 1,000 francs. In addition the jury gave honourable mention to six designs. The winners of the first prizes were given the most important commissions for the exhibition: Eiffel was allowed to build the tower — although he had to

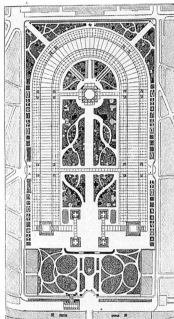

On May 1, 1886, Minister Edouard Lockroy launched a competition to find the best concept for the actual layout of the 1889 world exhibition. The exhibits would be shown later in and around the Palais de l'Industrie; along the Esplanade des Invalides and the Champ de Mars; and between these two points, along the banks of the Seine. Adventurous entrants were free to enclose a design for a tower — height 300 metres, surface area 125 square metres — which would eventually loom above the Champ de Mars.

Above: Design submitted by Eiffel and Sauvestre for the 1886 competition. The arch of the tower would give access to the exhibition, while wrapped halfway around it an iron and glass exhibition hall was planned. The exact location of the tower — indicated by four small squares — can be seen in the area plan, centre. Between the Seine (at the bottom) and the tower are gardens, while behind is the imposing horseshoe-shaped exhibition hall and enclosed gardens, culminating in two dome-roofed pavilions, either side of the tower. The design is almost the same as the one Sauvestre made in 1884, except for a less impressive glass roof on the first floor, and a missing third floor, and arch from directly under the second floor.

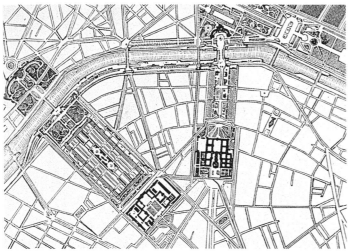

Architects Cassien-Bernard and Nachon, not following the competition rules too rigorously, moved the tower — Eiffel and Sauvestre's version, as they knew it would win — from the exhibition altogether and straddled it over the Seine at Esplanade des Invalides. With the tower out of the way, they could devote their attention to the development of the exhibition site. Placing the tower in its new site was not such a bad idea as it would involve the Palais de l'Industrie, top right-hand corner, far more in the proceedings. Left, in the same drawing, is the Esplanade and above it the fine straight lines indicating the Champ de Mars.

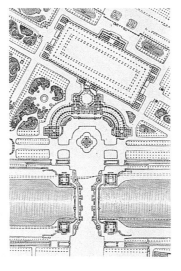

Centre: Site of the exhibition complex. Left, at a diagonal angle, the Champ de Mars, and, almost centre, the Esplanade des Invalides with the Palais de l'Industrie across the other side of the Seine.
Right: Detailed study of the tower, straddling the Seine at Pont Alexandre III.

find a better solution for the lifts; Dutert was commissioned for the Galeries des Machines; and Formigé for the Palais des Arts Libéraux.

As for the tower, it was a foregone conclusion. The competition served only to obtain greater certainty as to the technical feasibility of a tall tower, and to find an elegant way of pushing Eiffel's design forward among a host of others. In its final report the jury stated unambiguously that it had wanted 'an original masterpiece of the French metalwork industry' and that 'only Eiffel's design met this condition'.

Immediately after the result was made known, a storm of criticism broke out, not so much aimed at the manner of assessment as at the design itself. Now that the dream of an immensely tall tower was about to be realized, primeval conservative instincts seemed to be breaking loose. In the journal, L'Illustration, Paul Edel got into a rage about the exhibited designs: 'Even on entering the hall where the drawings of the lucky winners are displayed, one is struck by the paucity of imagination and the lack of ideas on the part of the participants.'

What galled him particularly was that most of the entrants had blindly copied Eiffel's tower. 'Ah! that tower, so useless, so irritating, so undecorative, twice as high as the Pyramid of Cheops and six times higher than the column at the Bastille, it must have been a real nightmare, giving those poor architects sleepless nights.'

After the result was announced, the French professional journal La Construction Moderne made a belated plea for Bourdais' project and argued that it was impossible to put lifts inside the curved legs of Eiffel's design.

Initially, Eiffel took little notice of the criticism. All that mattered to him was the fact that he could start building the tower, although there were still some problems to be solved, including the financing. In the end, Eiffel gave his personal guarantee for the shortfall of three-quarters of the costs.

Work had scarcely begun when the daily newspaper, Le Temps, ran a 'Protestation contre la Tour de M. Eiffel', signed by many prominent names from the French art world, including Guy de Maupassant, Alexandre Dumas Fils and Charles Gounod, who were scornful of the tower. The architect, Charles Garnier, of L'Opéra, wanted it demolished and the poet, Paul Verlaine, called it a 'squelette de beffroi', or skeleton tower. The story goes that Verlaine, for the rest of his life, never set foot in that part of Paris where the Eiffel Tower stood.

Eiffel did not let the critics have their way, and in an interview in the same paper he hit back: 'I believe that this tower will have a beauty of its own. Do people believe that just because we are engineers we do not care about beauty and that, whilst we concern ourselves with soundness and durability, we do not attempt to make our buildings elegant? Do the true functions of strength not always concur with the underlying principles of harmony? Which principle have I taken most into account when building this tower? Wind resistance. Well then! I claim that the curves of the four legs of this building, as they follow from the calculations, will create a great impression of strength and beauty.'

Thanks to Eiffel's self-confidence and technical know-how, the work progressed steadily. After 26 months the Eiffel Tower was completed and the world possessed its long-awaited 'tower of 1000 feet' at last. A dream had come true.

Above: Charles Dutert's studies were popular with the jury and he was among the first prizewinners. He envisaged two-thirds of the exhibition site as a landscaped area, dotted with small buildings, and bordered by the larger exhibition halls. The central focal point would be the tower — Eiffel and Sauvestre's, of course.

Right: Architect Raulin's design also took Eiffel and Sauvestre's tower as starting point, but he had the imagination to adapt it more to his own vision. He, too, created a vast, horeshoe-shaped exhibition palace of iron and glass, but glassed-in the front of the tower, between its main arch and base, and added huge glass halls either side. His idea was to make the tower less distinct in appearance, in order to give a more coherent overall impression to the site. For his efforts Raulin was awarded second prize and 2,000 francs, as were his fellow architects, Cassien-Bernard, Nachon and Perthes. Third prize went to Ballu, Fouquiau, Hochereau and Girault, Paulin, Pierron and Vaudoyer.

The design of Raulin, above, is a richly decorated Eiffel tower with an added imposing glass palace, reminiscent of London's Crystal Palace, built in 1851. The side of the hall facing the Seine was trimmed with two rows of ornate arches and the main tower flanked by two smaller ones — or at least small in comparison; each was hundred metres high.

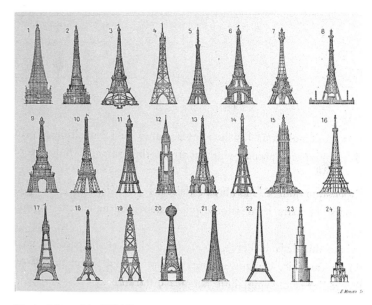

The building of the Eiffel Tower stirred the imagination of many. An even taller tower was suggested as a tourist attraction for an important exhibition in London's Wembley Park. A competition was duly organized and the race was on. Above: 24 of the entries, many similar to the Eiffel Tower, but all at least 350 metres high. While foundations were dug for a tower, Wembley Park never got around to actually building one.

Jean Camille Formigé won first prize in the 1886 competition. The jury thought his design for the exhibition halls 'outstanding' and words like 'pure elegance' and 'grandeur' were dropped. His reward was to design the Palais des Arts Libéraux, but even he didn't think twice about shifting the tower; it was placed on the Champ de Mars in the centre of gardens, and surrounded on three sides by his halls. Above: View of his design from the Seine, with the tower omitted. Right: his site plan with, from left, the Seine, the Quay, the gardens, and the tower — its base indicated by four squares — and behind it the main entrance to the exhibition halls.

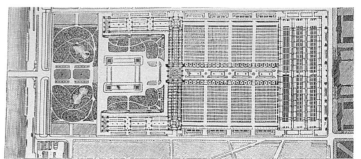

In 1887 work finally started on Gustave Eiffel's tower. In June the foundations were laid and a month later the construction of the actual tower began. A few statistics: 40 designers masterminded the tower's 12,000 parts, which were manufactured by Levallois-Perret, and accurate to within less than a tenth of a millimetre. Up to 300 construction workers put the components together using no fewer than 2,500,000 rivets. The tower took 26 months to build and cost one man his life.

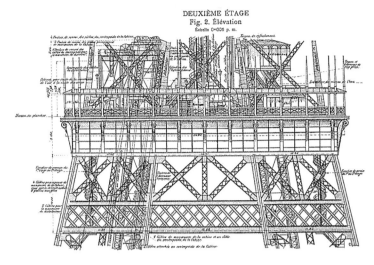

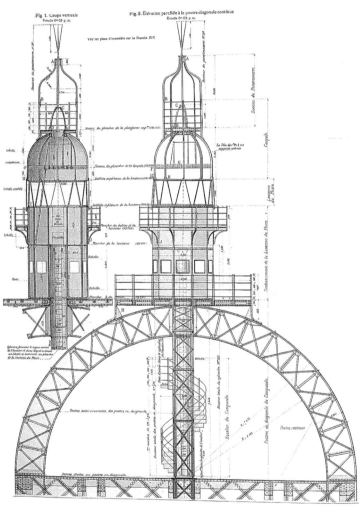

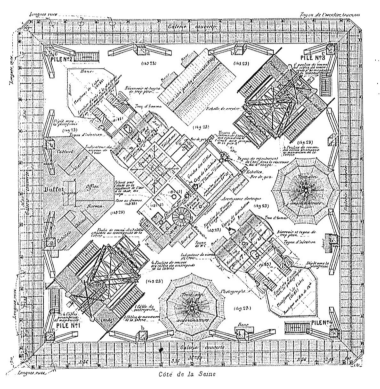

On this page a handful of the thousands of studies needed to construct the Eiffel Tower. Above: an overview of the tower's second floor. Below: Ground plan of the second floor with the liftshafts by 'Pile no. 1', bottom left, and 'Pile no. 3', top right-hand corner. Left: Pinnacle of the tower, the cause for a long time of much scientific observation.

THE AUSTRIAN SAVINGS BANK IN VIENNA

COMPETITION FOR A NEW BUILDING FOR
K.K. POSTSPARKASSE (SAVINGS BANK) IN VIENNA.

PUBLISHED: 25 January 1903, result 10 June 1903;
number of participants: 32.

JURY: Dr Mansuet Kosel (director of the Savings
Bank), chairman; Gustav Bamberger (architect and
painter); Leopold Bauer (architect); Emil van
Foerster (director of public works at the Ministry of
Internal Affairs); Michael Koch (architectural
administrator); Josef Künstler (director general at
the Ministry of Finance); Franz von Neumann
(architect); Georg Niemann (professor at the
Academy of Fine Arts in Vienna); Andreas Streit
(architect); Christian Ulrich; Alexander Wielemans
(architect); Karl von Wiener (director and chief of
the Arts Council at the Ministry of Culture and
Education).

WINNERS: Eugen Faszbender, Otto Wagner, Von
Ferstel, F. von Krausz and Josef Tölk, and Theodor
Bach. The design by Wagner was recommended for
purchase.

CONSTRUCTION: July 1904 – December 1906 (in
1910-1913 an extension was built at the rear using a
design by Wagner).

VIENNA AT THE TURN OF THE CENTURY. As this century has
progressed, this phrase has acquired more and more a
legendary ring to it, being associated with names such as
Freud, Wittgenstein, Kokoschka, Klimt and Schönberg. Vienna
was the city of the Sezession, the city of the Vienna Werkstatte,
and the city of the Vienna School.

But above all it was the capital of a large empire with more
than 50 million inhabitants, which extended over Austria,
Hungary, Bosnia and Herzegovina.

Although the dual monarchy had little internal unity, this was
hardly evident in Vienna. The city grew in size, became
industrialized on a large scale, and changed radically in
appearance. After Kaiser Franz Josef I decided in 1857 to have
the fortifications demolished and to designate the land on
which they had stood for the building of the Ringstrasse, or
Ring road, the city looked quite different. Each of the
pracht-bauten (beautiful buildings) on the Ringstrasse was a
separate monumental expression of power, grandeur and
self-confidence.

In 1883, a savings bank was founded for the kingdoms and
lands represented in the Reichstag, the Kaiserliche and
Königliche (Imperial and Royal) Sparkasse. It was designed for
the 'little man' and it has sometimes been said that it was
intended to be a counterweight to the Jewish-dominated
banks. This bank proved a great success. Initially housed in a
Dominican monastery, the savings bank had to be transferred
in 1885 to the old university library at numbers 7-9, Postgasse.
The university had moved into an imposing new building on
the Ringstrasse a year earlier.

The activities of the bank grew steadily, while the number of
staff, who had to work in ever more cramped conditions, also
rose. It is said that staff complained about mice eating their
packed lunches, and that both clients and staff used to spit on
the floor, thus creating a breeding ground for TB bacteria.
Ventilation was a major problem. In some departments the
windows were never opened, because the slightest breeze
caused havoc among the many papers lying on the desks. In
1906 there was great anxiety among the staff because a
32-year-old employee, Olga Hahnel, died. In spite of this
genuine unease, the management ignored the grumbling, since
a new savings bank building was nearing completion at that
time, the design of which paid great attention to industrial
hygiene.

These new offices were going up on the premises of the former
Franz Josef barracks. They were situated on the edge of the
inner city and had been pulled down in 1898 to make room
for the final section of the Ringstrasse. In 1902 the Austrian
Savings Bank bought the plot and in early 1903 a competition
was officially published among architects, who had to be
residents of the 'Kingdoms and lands represented in the

View of the Austrian Savings Bank in the 1980s. A building architecturally ahead of its time, with little decoration, very restrained in style. The entrance to the bank has aluminium columns under the porch; it is clearly visible from the Ringstrasse. Below: View from the ringroad, in the foreground the square with bust of the founder of the Austrian Savings Bank, Georg Coch.

Reichstag' (the Austria of that time, excluding Hungary or Bosnia).

In the competition programme much attention was paid to maximum possible efficiency and hygiene. It was stipulated: 'The basement must comply with the demands of modern living and must be suitable for office work; it must be designed in such a way that good access of daylight and good natural ventilation are ensured.'

Of course, the competition stipulated more. For instance, the entrance had to be in the Bibergasse; to be precise: in that section of the street which, by way of the Lisztstrasse (the later Georg Coch Platz), was visible from the Ringstrasse.

The architectural style was left to the discretion of the designer but 'the building must, both by its simple and dignified layout and by the avoidance of excessive external and internal ornamentation, bear the character of a state building. In the planning of any ornamentation, great attention must be paid to durability and low maintenance costs'.

The programme emphasized the need for good communications between departments; it spoke of 'reliable, easy and quick connections between all office areas. All parts of the building must therefore have good links with each other, so that it will not be necessary to cross courtyards and office areas'.

One further aspect of the specifications must be mentioned, since it was to play an important part in the aftermath of the competition. Behind the main entrance in the Bibergasse a spacious lobby was envisaged with entrances to the management offices and the banking halls. Further on in the programme there were detailed descriptions of the conditions these banking halls would have to meet. There would have to be one hall for cheque traffic and another one for savings traffic, in addition to a central banking hall. For each of these there were precise specifications given about how large it should be, how many tills it should have, how much space the staff would require, and so on.

THE DEADLINE FOR ENTRIES WAS April 1903. The architects had more than three months to work out and send in their designs. By that time, 32 designs had been received.

A week later the jury — under the chairmanship of the director of the savings bank — met for the first time. Immediately a minor problem arose: six projects had arrived without the name of the designer, which was not permissible in the terms of the programme. A discussion ensued about what should be done, and after much deliberation it was decided to appeal in the press for the names of the anonymous participants. When the jury met for the second time, on 6 June 1903, this proved to have worked and all the anonymous participants had made themselves known.

During this meeting the jury made a first selection from the designs. On the basis of considerations such as overall impression, spatial layout, lighting, the location of staircases and the construction of the building, each project would be subjected to a vote, and finally the aesthetic aspects of the design would be considered.

In the two-and-a-half hour meeting, all 32 designs were reviewed, and 14 were unanimously rejected: six were unanimously recommended to go on to the next round. In the case of 12 projects the decision was passed by a majority vote: eight were rejected and four went on to the next round. In the jury report the reasons for rejection were outlined briefly. Four days later the third jury meeting took place. First, at the suggestion of the chairman, those four projects were discussed that had not reached this round with unanimity. They were discussed at length and there was another vote; none of them was eventually considered good enough.

There were then six designs left. As there were five prizes to be awarded, this meant that only one would have to be dropped. Again, all six designs were discussed at length, and it can be deduced from the jury report that the longest time was spent on project number two, by Otto Wagner. In general terms, this project was judged favourably. There were some reservations about the placing of the stairs to the management offices, which were not considered to be in the right place, and about the possibly insufficient lighting in some of the office areas. There were further reservations about the second glass roof, and the fact that its surface area was too small by some 4000 square metres. 'As for the aesthetic aspect, this design cannot be defended.'

But the real controversy arose over the fact that Wagner combined the banking halls into one great hall. It was noted that this contravened the conditions of the competition, even though it was admitted that Wagner's solution had certain advantages. The chairman, who was director of the bank, said that the project complied entirely with the spirit of the

The interior of the building is also very restrained. Wagner concerned himself with all the architectural details, and also designed the furniture - black laquered wooden chairs, and cupboards with aluminium fittings. This photograph shows a committee room; background: Painting of Emperor Franz Joseph.

programme, and Karl von Wiener, from the Ministry of Culture and Education, stated that the programme did not expressly stipulate a strict separation of the various halls. After all the designs had been discussed, a vote was taken. Only one design — by Von Krausz and Tölk — was unanimously recommended for an award. Design number 18, by Brang, received only two votes and was therefore rejected. The other four designs were recommended for an award, albeit not unanimously.

After the chairman had published the result (the designs by Faszbinder and Tremmel, Wagner, Krausz and Tölk, Von Ferstel, and Bach each received 3000 crowns), architect Von Neumann requested that his dissenting vote should be explicity recorded in the jury report. In his opinion, Wagner's design was contrary to the programme and was for that reason not eligible for an award. In addition, he wished it to be

buildings in an historically conscious, somewhat classical style, which seemed fairly appropriate in the Vienna of the second half of the nineteenth century, in about 1890 his views changed. It has been said that because of his upbringing, Wagner consciously sought security, both financially and socially, as an architect-cum-speculator. Once he had, in his own view, acquired this sufficiently, he felt free to develop his own ideas.

In 1893 he won a competition for further development in the city of Vienna. In this case he used the flow of traffic as the basis for his design. The Ringstrasse had by that time been built — a visual reminder of Viennese power and architectural skill — and Wagner took this road as his starting point for a new traffic system in Vienna.

Between 1894 and 1897 he devoted himself to part of this new communication plan: he was asked to build the Viennese

The main hall — Wagner planned many ventilation shafts here to stop it from becoming stuffy. The floor is composed of glass tiles, allowing light through to the basement. This hall is almost universally recognized as one of the first examples of modern architecture in the 20th century.

recorded that the design should nevertheless be recommended for purchase by the savings bank.

FIVE WINNING DESIGNS, of which the one by Otto Wagner was considered for realization. Although with hindsight it is easy to say, this was quite understandable. But Otto Wagner — already over 60 at the time — was at that stage in his career fascinated by the idea of communication.

Whereas during the first decades of his career he had designed

Stadtbahn (Municipal Railways). At the same time he was appointed professor of architecture at the Viennese Academy. From then on he placed increasing emphasis on a functional view of architecture. He took as his motto 'Artis sola domina necessitas', or 'Art is governed solely by necessity'.

A second concept that began to play an ever greater part in Wagner's thinking was that of the *Nutzstil*, or Utility style; the design of a building must not be determined by its beauty but by its utility.

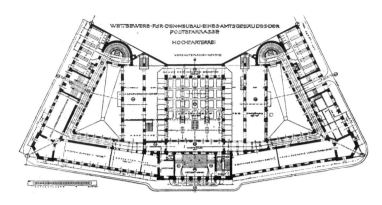

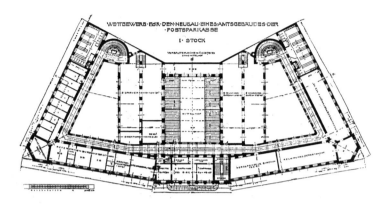

Top: Wagner's ground plan for a mezzanine, which would house the administration in the heart of the building.

Centre: Wagner's ground plan for the first storey.

As Wagner saw it, art should be dominated by the necessities of modern life, particularly modern metropolitan man's increasing desire to move around from place to place.

It does not do Wagner justice merely to give a general outline of his ideas. Nor is it true that he expounded these views in a very radical way. In the 1890s and during the first years of the twentieth century he was strongly influenced by the ideas of the Sezession, a group of mostly young artists who — like the Art Nouveau movement in France and Belgium and the Arts and Craft movement in Scotland — were searching for a new means of artistic expression.

A great influence on Wagner in those years was his pupil and assistant, Joseph Olbrich. But around 1903 it seemed as if Wagner were beginning to detach himself from that influence and becoming more able to let his *Nutzstil* govern his thought and action.

The competition for the savings bank enabled him to express the essence of a bank according to his own ideas, even though this appears to be in conflict with the specifications laid down in the programme. In his design for the exterior of the building he moved further than ever from ornamentation.

WAGNER'S IDEAS MAY HAVE FALLEN on fertile ground as regards the director of the bank, but elsewhere they remained a matter of controversy. The exterior of the building was particularly criticized. Conservative Viennese tried to have Heinrich von Ferstel's design adopted — which was in the familiar Renaissance style. In vain. Wagner's design was carried out, although the staff grumbled that the building looked like 'a tarnished post box', and a few months after the inauguration

the newspaper, *Neue Freie Presse*, called it 'a hideous design with its marble slabs attached like shingle to the walls with nails or screws'.

The international architectural world took a more favourable view and in due course the building began to be regarded as one of Wagner's greatest achievements and one of the most important models for the new, functional style.

However, Wagner was about to suffer a defeat. Or rather — the chairman of the jury was forced to bite the dust. For the competition had a fierce aftermath.

Architect Peter Paul Brang — contributor of design number 18, which was the last one to be rejected — disagreed with the jury. In November 1903 he wrote a letter to the Trade Group for Architecture and Public Works of the Austrian Engineers and Architects Society. In this letter he requested that the competition committee of this society should express its opinion on the procedures followed in the affair of the savings bank. Brang felt he had been passed over and did not consider that Wagner should have been given an award — in which case he himself would still be eligible. In December 1903 a subcommittee of the society met in order to give its verdict. In the ensuing report, the course of events was dealt with at length. The committee first stated in general terms that a jury should in all circumstances be allowed to subject designs, turned down because they were contrary to the rules of the programme, to a fresh assessment after the publication of the result; it should still be possible to recommend such a design for purchase.

In order to ascertain correctly whether a design contravened the programme, the subcommittee referred to the rules laid

Wagner's design included a glass roof immediately over the office area and two glass domes rising majestically above, but the jury was somewhat dubious. Not only would it be costly; it might later prove an irritation to the houses planned for this area. The domes disappeared. Wagner designed a new cornice with eight wreath-like decorations which also adorns the rear of the building in such a position that from the street it appears to be part of the front façade; see also photograph p. 73.

The Austrian Savings Bank competition was not anonymous — architects were to send in their entries under their own name. However, several entrants thought it was an anonymous competition and sent in their plans under a motto. Drawings by architects Franz von Krausz and Josef Tölk arrived in a styleful box with their two names neatly on it and sealed with sky-blue tape. The small square containing their names was repeated in the bottom right-hand corner of each drawing. Their design was praised by several jurors for its simplicity; though it was felt that the domes at the corners should discreetly vanish — see also p. 79 above. These two architects were influenced by ideas of the Sezession, as can be seen in their design of the arched porches above the entrance; in other ways they were affected by 19th century eclecticism. The jury was right in stating that the domes on the corners of the building did not fit the design.

The jury found the plan by Franz von Krausz and Josef Tölk both clear and uncluttered, but they had reservations about the position of the central reception area. The main hall where cheques would be negotiated was placed in the heart of the building, a large semicircular area with counters all round it; in the right wing there are three more halls, see ground plan below. Despite criticism, this was the only design unanimously recommended for a prize.

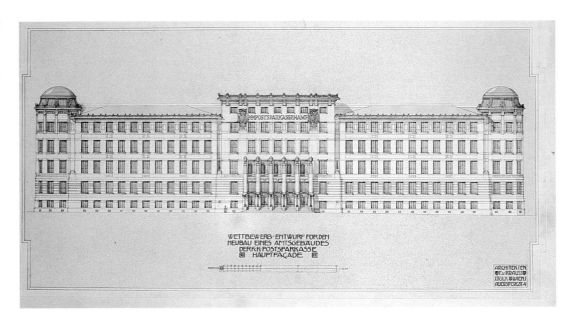

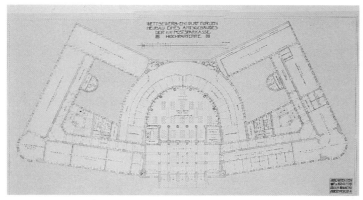

Theodor Bach's entry, which also gained an award, was praised by the jury for its clear and simple design and the efficient connecting lines. The façade 'met all the requirements, although it would have to be somewhat simplified'.

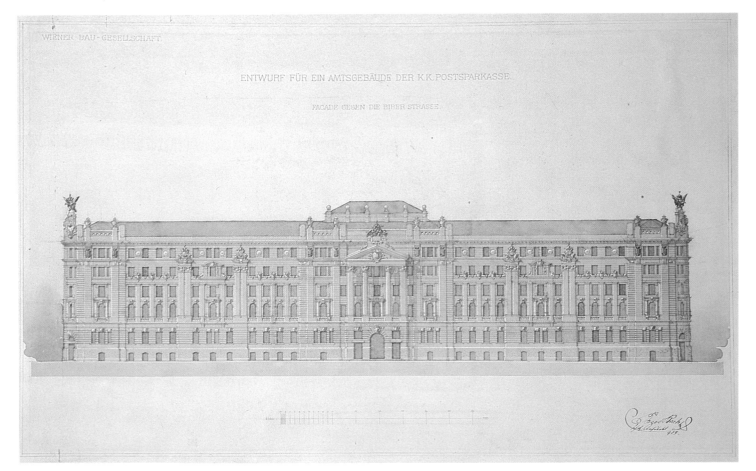

down for competitions by the Society. These rules stipulated that the majority of members of every jury should be professionals, in order to prevent them from being outvoted by laymen. Moreover, the committee referred to the condition that a jury may judge the entries only in the spirit of the programme.

In connection with this last point, the report referred to the competition for the Reichstag in Berlin, where one of the foremost architects of the time was excluded from the competition because he did not keep to the programme. The committee described this as exemplary policy. They did not mention the name of the entrant, Heinrich von Ferstel (1828-1883), nor added that Von Ferstel's design was later bought by the Berlin jury.

The committee saw it as a 'basic mistake' that the jury of the Savings Bank competition had not made a careful assessment as to whether the entries contravened the rules of the programme. The question still remained whether design number 2 — by Otto Wagner — should be regarded as being in contravention of the programme.

First, the programme was examined and analysed in detail. Partly because the programme stipulated a lobby from which entrances should lead to the management offices and the banking halls, the committee felt that in view of the use of the plural, it could not be concluded that the drafters of the programme had envisaged an amalgamation of these halls. If this had been the case, they could easily have added a phrase to the effect that 'these halls could be either separate or combined'. The conclusion was therefore that design number 2 was 'definitely in contravention of the programme'.

At the end of the report the committee stated: 'Design number 2 is in contravention of the programme and should not have been awarded a prize. We further feel that design number 18 by architect Peter Paul Brang should have been awarded a prize after being judged by the jury.' A third point made by the committee was that no objections could be made against the purchase of design number 2 — and the decision to carry it out.

Architect Brang was vindicated, although it has not been possible to ascertain whether he belatedly received any money from the savings bank. To be vindicated by one's own professional organization is satisfying, but one cannot do much with it in practice. To architect Wagner, the verdict made little difference. He remained the real winner on all fronts.

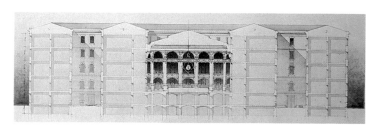
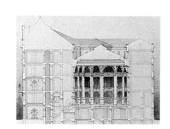

One of the architects who submitted, using a motto, was Skowron; his name was sent in a separate, sealed envelope, and does not occur on the drawings. See also p. 3.

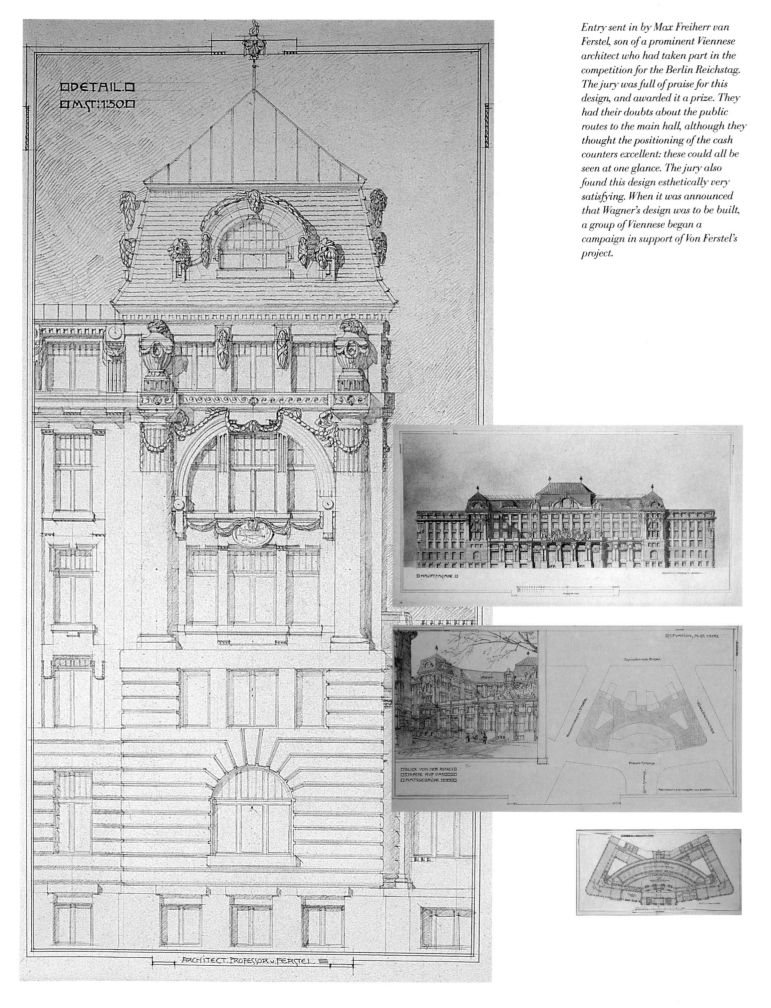

□DETAIL□
□M ST:1:50□

ARCHITECT: PROFESSOR v. FERSTEL

Entry sent in by Max Freiherr van Ferstel, son of a prominent Viennese architect who had taken part in the competition for the Berlin Reichstag. The jury was full of praise for this design, and awarded it a prize. They had their doubts about the public routes to the main hall, although they thought the positioning of the cash counters excellent: these could all be seen at one glance. The jury also found this design esthetically very satisfying. When it was announced that Wagner's design was to be built, a group of Viennese began a campaign in support of Von Ferstel's project.

STOCKHOLM TOWN HALL

The Blue Room in Stockholm Town Hall: an exuberantly designed covered couryard with marble tiles, stairs and balcony; a most impressive staircase, graceful pillars and a wooden roof of palest blue.

NATIONAL ARCHITECTURAL COMPETITION FOR A NEW PALACE OF JUSTICE IN STOCKHOLM, SWEDEN.

PUBLISHED: First round: Autumm 1903; result: 26 March 1904; number of participants: 25; second round: 21 October 1904, result: March 1905; number of participants: 5

JURY: Junker G. Tamm, former governor of Stockholm; Carolus Lindhagen, burgomaster of Stockholm; Judge Richard Öhnell, secretary to the City Council Committee; Professor I.Gustav Glason, president, building section of the Swedish Society of Architects and Engineers; Gustav Wickman, Swedish architect; M.Nyrop, Danish architect.

WINNER: 1. Ragnar Östberg; 2. Ivar Tengbom/Ernst Torulf; 3. Carl Westman; Carl Bergsten; Charles Lindholm (shared third prize)

CONSTRUCTION: 1911-1923 (Ragnar Östberg).

Det nya rådhusförslaget på "Eldkvarnens" plats.

Even before a competition was announced, Östberg had made several designs for a new Town Hall. Above: Design published in the daily newspaper Aftonbladet on 15 November 1901.
Centre: Design made at the request of Judge Öhnell in 1902. Below: Part of the competition design, 1904.
Plans were anonymous, but this clearly resembles the above design, and city councillors on the jury could probably easily guess the identity of the architect.

THE STORY GOES that when as an old man, Ragnar Östberg was walking along the banks of lake Malar in Stockholm, he sighed: 'I no longer have a soul; I have put it into that building'.
And he pointed to the town hall, on which he had worked intensively for twenty years.
Architects are not always able to estimate how future historians will evaluate their work. Östberg, however, predicted their response quite accurately. For the town hall of Stockholm is now commonly referred to as 'the idiosyncratic creation of Ragnar Östberg', or as 'a very personal building where a conscious attempt has been made to reproduce all that is noble in Swedish architecture'. When speaking of Stockholm Town Hall one is therefore speaking of Östberg. Yet he had to travel a long and difficult road before he achieved his life's work. And it was a road full of unexpected turns, which initially seemed to be leading to somewhere quite different.

THE STORY OF THE TOWN HALL began in about 1890. Stockholm city council had been busy for years with plans to replace the old town hall. This was both an administrative centre and a district courthouse. This mixture of legal and administrative powers could be traced back to the medieval city law of Stockholm, according to which it was the same group, the *rådmän*, who governed the city and administered the law. The process of separating city administration and legal affairs was long and tedious. There would have to be two separate buildings: a town hall and a court of justice. But there were endless discussions about a suitable site for these two new buildings - discussions that were followed with great interest by the people of Stockholm. The young Ragnar Östberg also followed these developments with keen interest. During the

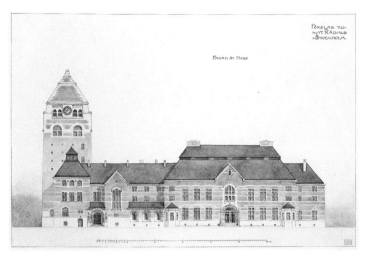

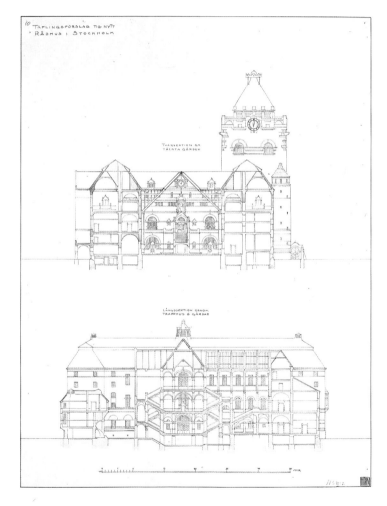

Tipped to win for the first round was Carl Westman, whose building was placed at the end of the peninsula, a position highly recommended by jurors, since it left plenty of free space.

The jury was not enthusiastic about Westman's first design, finding it lacking in balance. The tower, though stumpy, proved acceptable, since it was to serve as a prison. In his design for the second round, right, Westman's tower is slimmer and the front of the building is symmetrical; but this only secured him third prize.

1890s he was working for an older architect, I.G. Clason, and was, as he said, delighted by the impressive task of designing a town hall, a task that would free the imagination from daily routine. In 1901, when the Stockholm Art Society for the first time invited architects as well as painters and sculptors to take part in their annual exhibition, Östberg seized his opportunity. He submitted a sensational design for a town hall, situated in the old city centre, that combined administrative and judicial functions. He approached this task with great seriousness: in drafting the programme he held lengthy consultations with a local representative, *rådman* Öhnell, which were later to stand him in good stead.

IN 1902 THE CITY COUNCIL decided to give priority to building a court of justice. Öhnell was at that time secretary to the city council committee that was making preparations for both buildings. He immediately contacted Östberg, 'since he had previously shown interest in the matter'. Together they examined possible locations for the new courthouse and finally decided to propose the 'Steam Mill site' (Eldkvarnen) to the council. This site was not actually on the island of Staden that forms the old city, but close to it. It is, moreover, one of the finest locations of Stockholm - a slightly projecting corner of the island of Kungsholmen, strikingly situated on lake Malar.

Östberg immediately started designing a monumental court of justice for this site. In order to persuade his fellow councillors of the suitability of the location, Öhnell showed them his designs. This proved successful: by 27 October that year the city council had decided to purchase the Steam Mill site. However, they did not yet want to decide who was to design the new court of justice: an architecture competition would determine the issue.

The competition was organized quickly and with attention to detail. The task of drafting the rules was given to none other than Östberg's former employer, I.G. Clason, president of the building section of the Swedish Society of Architects and Engineers. The rules were published in the autumn of 1903. The competition was to consist of two rounds, the first of which was open to all Swedish architects, with no money prizes attached. Six participants in the first round would be chosen to take part in the second round, and would all be paid the sum of 1,500 Swedish crowns each, plus a chance to win either the main prize of 3,500 crowns, or a share of the 5,000 crowns that was to be distributed among the other five competitors. The winner of the first prize would probably also be asked to build the court of justice.

The competition programme was both detailed and comprehensive. It stated precisely what kind of drawings would have to be submitted, on what scale and - for the drawings of the façades - from what angle. The use of colour was permitted. The entries were to remain anonymous, until the end of the second round. The favourites of this round would be referred to only by their mottos. The entries, it was stated, would be judged 'on the basis of their practicality, their artistic merit and their financial feasibility'. The names of the members of the jury - and possible replacements - were also announced in advance. Architects and civil servants were represented equally.

BY 15 MARCH 1904, the closing date for competition entries, 24 designs had been submitted. Among them was Östberg's - anonymous like all the rest. Within a week the jury had chosen the six participants in the next round. When the mottos of their designs were announced, on 26 March, Östberg found that his was among them. His design was called 'Malardrott' which means King of lake Malar - a nickname for Stockholm is Malardrottningen, Queen of lake Malar. Östberg's biographer, Elias Cornell, was probably right when he wrote in 1965 that it must have been difficult for the jury not to recognise the authorship of Östberg's entry straight away.

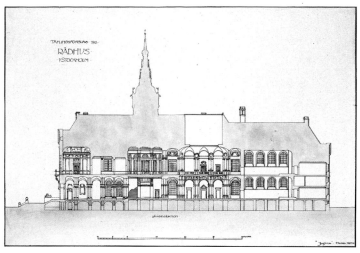

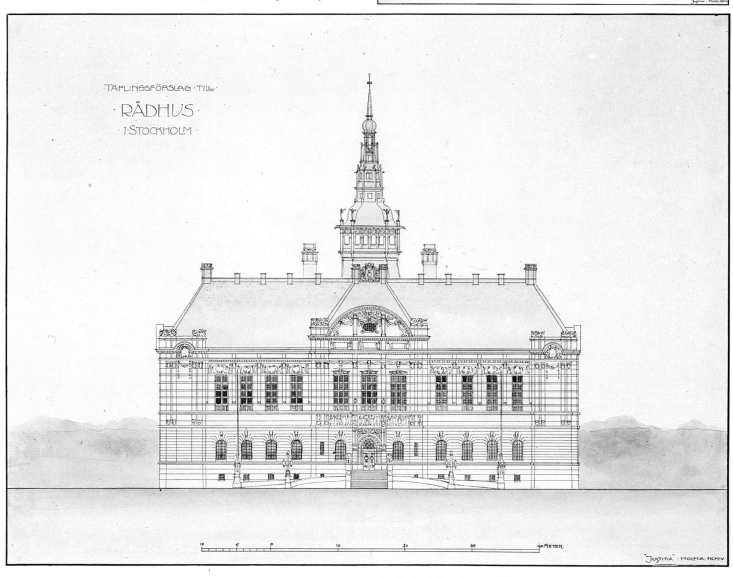

Lindholm designed a graceful building for the first round, described by the jury as "well-proportioned, imposing architecture". But they regretted that the striking position on a peninsula had not been exploited and that even the corner overlooking the beach received no special accent. Lindholm took these criticisms to heart, witness his second design on p. 90.

85

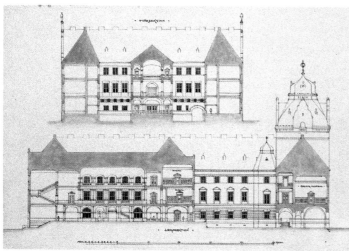

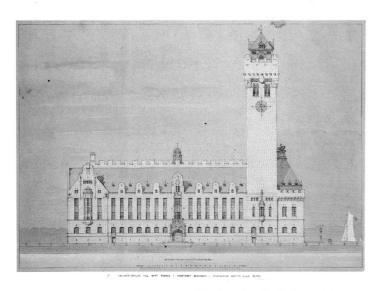

The jury thought the front of the building in Tengbom and Torulf's first design uninteresting, while 'the major façade is compressed by a tower-like structure, too low and squat for a tower but too high to be part of the building'. The second design, below, differed considerably, but the jury remained critical.

His design for a court of justice on Eldkvarnen must have been known to all the jury members. But there is no evidence of any bias: in the jury report 'Malardrott' was not praised more than the other five.

The jury's report was completely businesslike. In the case of all six designs the site, the ground plan, the façades and the perspectives were discussed as objectively as possible. However, this was preceded by an introduction in which the jury declared its dissatisfaction with the general standard of the entries. Few competitors, they said, had succeeded in producing a well-balanced design in which ground plan, cross-section and façades formed a harmonious whole. Many had failed to provide easy communication between the various sections: their corridors and inner courtyards were impractical, somber and unattractive. The six designs selected compared favourably with the rest, but each of these was also criticised. Two entries, motto 'Hörne' or 'Corner' by Carl Westman, and motto 'Malardrott', were judged slightly more favourably than the other four.

Hörne was noteworthy because of its situation: Westman shifted the building to the corner of the quayside, which 'made it possible to create a fine square by the entrance to Kungsholmen, and provided more space both for the northern façade with the main entrance and for the eastern façade'. But the jury was less happy about the exterior: 'The architect strains too much after effect and inclines towards the picturesque, while the top of the tower in particular could be greatly improved.'

In the case of 'Malardrott', it was chiefly the ground plan that was praised. All six assembly rooms surrounded a central hall, although 'the shape of this hall seems to separate the rooms rather than unite them, and moreover receives too little light'. The jury also appeared impressed by the draughtsmanship, though here too it remained critical: 'The tower, which appears so attractive in its interplay of lines, would perhaps be of more practical use if the city archives were housed in it.' In other words, a building should not only be beautiful but also functional.

THE SIX FAVOURITES were not given much time: the second round was not officially opened until 11 October and their new designs had to be in by 25 January 1905. The competition programme was more detailed than it had been for the first round and it was noticeable that the jury allowed the participants in some ways more and in some ways less freedom. For instance, it expressed a clear preference for a ground plan like Östberg's, in which 'all the assembly rooms were grouped around a central hall'. But possibilities were left more open with regard to site. Even the bridge to Kungsholmen could be shifted 'or projected in another corner, should this prove desirable'.

Not until March 1905 did the jury reach its final decision. The first prize went to Ragnar Östberg. It is unlikely that he had been given preferential treatment by jury members such as Öhnell and Clason, for once again the records show the jury to have been unbiased. For instance, the jury ordered precise calculations to be made of the total costs of each design, as

well as measurements of the surfaces of the coutyards in each entry. Based on the result of these calculations, plus their judgment of practicality and artistic merit, the committee decided unanimously to award 'Malardrott' the first prize. Once again all the designs received extensive analysis according to the same formula: sites, ground plan, façades and perspective. And once again all the projects were both approved and criticised.

Third prize was shared among Carl Westman, Carl Bergsten and Charles Lindholm. The jury said of Westman's design: 'Many parts of the building receive insufficient light and the bridge leading across the courtyard is very poor in practical and aesthetic terms.'

TÄFLINGSFÖRSLAG TILL RÅDHUS I STOCKHOLM. MOTTO: "NON SENZA DIGNITÄ".

The entry 'Non senza dignità' (by an architect whose identity is unknown) was so well drawn that the jury overlooked several weak points such as the strange additions at each corner and the superfluous boiler house.
Architect Axel Ahlberg, though invited, did not take part in the second round. The design seen above is by an unknown architect.

Like 'Stockholms äldsta sigill' (the oldest seal of Stockholm) by Lindholm and 'Ett öres frimarke' (a 1 öre postage stamp) by Bergsten, Westman's design was said to display a number of weaknesses. Bergsten's design was the one that the jury least knew how to respond to. He was the only person to submit a design influenced by the international avant-garde and the Vienna Sezession. The jury wrote: 'This entry, both in its exterior and its interior design reveals a foreign character: it is difficult to imagine it in this city. Nor is the form of the ground

TÄFLINGSRITNING · TILL · RÅDHVS · I · STOCKHOLM

plan well adapted to the stipulated site.' The jury presumably realised that the design was not really mature and that its young creator was still searching: in the first round he had submitted a design with a totally different style.

The second prize went to Ivan Tengbom and Ernst Torulf for their design 'Lilleputt', awarded to them chiefly because of the 'simple, clear ground plan with its fine open forecourt by the main entrance'. Then the jury went on to explain in great detail why this plan, both practically and aesthetically, could not

In the first round this romantic design was submitted by Bergsten, but the jury was not impressed and described the façades as 'unacceptable'. However, the ground plan was pronounced excellent and Bergsten passed through to the second round, in which he produced a completely different style of building, *see p.91.*

compare with 'Malardrott'.

The jury expressed great enthusiam for Östberg's design. And Östberg had, in fact, radically improved 'Malardrott' on many points. The jury thought that the design, more than any other, exploited artistically the unique position of the planned building site. They described the design in its entirety as organic, purposeful and stately'. The exterior, they said, was monumental and yet simple, the interior was praised for its many splendid compositions and the impressive central hall.

'If this project is carried out on this location, Stockholm and Sweden will be enriched by a modern building in which the nation can justly take pride.' The chief criticism concerned the 'granite façades and the covered courtyard which might raise the costs too much', but the jury did not think these were insuperable difficulties.

THE WAY IN WHICH THE JURY judged the entries met with almost universal approval in architectural circles, as was clearly seen in articles from the influential journal *Architektur* whose editors had intially been highly sceptical about the competition. In the July/August number of 1904, the journal had voiced the opinion of many architects: the briefing was an impossible one. The Steam Mill site required a striking silhouette, preferably with a tower, yet there was no reason to provide a court of justice with a tower or upper structure, certainly not if one of the most important requirements was to keep costs as low as possible. The journal expected the quality of the entries to be mediocre and awaited the outcome with little confidence.

However in the September/October number, even chief editor Torben Grut had changed his mind. He noted with satisfaction that the competition committee had respected the demands of the location: 'The participants who adhered strictly to the programme, sacrificing the exterior to it, failed and were therefore excluded.' Grut thought that Westman's 'Hörne' stood the best chance. He wrote: 'This design is superior to the others because of two strokes of genius: firstly the shifting of the building towards the direction of the lake, whereby an attractive square is created by the bridge: secondly by locating prisoners' cells in the tower, so that this tower, demanded by the location, is also organically and artistically justified.'

He was much less positive about 'Malardrott'; he found it 'full of poorly lit rooms and dark, narrow courtyards'. And he also balked at the tower which was a mere frivolity: 'imposing but empty and without purpose.'

However, when the jury announced its decision in January 1905 even Grut agreed wholeheartedly with it. He wrote that there had rarely been a more interesting architectural competition in Sweden and that 'no better entry had been submitted than the one which had now been awarded first prize'. He now described his previous favourite 'Hörne' as 'not entirely in good taste'. He still considered the shift on the site ingenious, but the 'definitive plan does not seem to be finished. A footbridge intrudes in the covered courtyard (...) and the simplicity of the façades has been carried through to such an extent that one wonders whether this was caused by lack of time or by deliberate architectural nihilism'.

Östberg had won the competition, but the commission to build the court of justice was not yet his. Over the following years came a series of bizarre complications which eventually led to a new town hall.

To begin with, the city council did not want to commission Östberg to start building. Many were worried by the high building costs, so the council decided to organize a closed competition between Westman and Östberg: each would have to revise their projects in the light of costs. The reason for asking Westman rather than Tengbom and Torulf was probably because his design, more than that of the second prizewinners, bore resemblances to 'Malardrott'. Moreover, 'Hörne', with its estimated building costs of 2.9 million crowns, was by far the cheapest, while 'Lilleputt', at 3.5 million, was not far behind 'Malardrott's' 4 million. In this closed competition, Östberg replaced his granite façades with brick, thus reducing his estimated costs to 3.3 million. His design would now still be 0.5 million more expensive than Westman's. This had been planned in brick from the outset, but Westman now costed his design slightly higher than the first time,

Lindholm's second design is very different from his first, on p.85. Entrances and corners of the building are now more pronounced and there is a massive central tower. The jury was still not happy: 'This is a derivative design: let us hope that the talented architect will be more original next time.'

The front façade of Lindholm's second plan shows clearly what the jury appreciated in his design. 'It is executed with meticulous skill. It has the nature of a historic monument, admirably combining details from Swedish Baroque and Renaissance styles.'

estimating it at just under 3 million. The city council studied the new estimates and in June 1906 finally commissioned Östberg to build the court of justice. But when in July 1907 he presented his design ready for building, he turned out to have made further drastic alterations including shifting the building in the direction Westman had indicated in 'Hörne'. Rumour has it that Östberg struggled for a long time with this decision and finally wrote to Westman asking for his approval. This modification was one of the many that gave the design more style. So much so that Östberg unwittingly caused himself difficulties. The plans looked so attractive that more and more people felt that a building on that site should be not a court of justice, but the town hall. On 10 June 1907 the city council revoked its earlier building commission to Östberg and decided to choose another site for the court of justice. The town hall would be built on the Steam Mill site. As a commentor of the period put it: 'The city council felt that the psychological moment had come for the foundation of a town hall that would be more than just an administrative building (...) that would be a symbol of the greatness of the city.' A confused situation developed, and it took the politicians until May 1908 to find a solution. No architect would have produced this: Östberg was commissioned to build the new town hall at the Steam Mill site; but he should retain - as much as possible - the exterior of his design for a court of justice. So Östberg had to clothe something completely new with an old design: a difficult task which took him until the autumn of 1909 to achieve. The estimated building costs meanwhile rose to six million, but thanks to private donations the design was made feasible. On 27 March 1911 Östberg received the commission to build the new town hall.

EXACTLY TEN YEARS had passed since Östberg had made his first plans for a town hall, years in which he continued to alter his design, trying to free it more and more from the ballast of the plans for the court of justice. It entailed constant shifting of the ground plan, and a search for optimum use of space. Naturally, this had consequences for the exterior, but the changes occurred so gradually that the sponsor, in this case the city council, was always - albeit sometimes hesitatingly - persuaded of their necessity.

There was only one occasion when both the council and the public rebelled. That was in 1917 when Östberg changed his tower. Instead of the earlier shape, which closely resembled the original design for a granite tower, he chose a slim tower more suitable for building in brick. The city council was highly sceptical, called in expert advice, and organized a public discussion.

It was Carl Westman who defended Östberg on behalf of the Swedish Society of Architects: 'Do people think that buildings can be successfully created amid the shouting of spectators?' he asked, and continued: 'We understand those who are now angry that the old plan was scrapped. They had been given a clear picture of a tower for the town hall, they approved it and loved it. It was a dream they hoped would become real. But they did not notice that while they dreamt, the architect acted. The architect has in the course of the years completely identified himself with his task, he has experimented, weighed the pros and cons, and made a choice. The Town Hall has grown as a living creature grows. It expresses not only the architect's ideas at the beginning of construction, but also his development during construction. It will be an imaginative creation; it will be a home for both the work and the festivities that take place in it. It will reflect the spirit of Stockholm with its water and its light. A building whose towers, pinnacles and galleries reveal individual qualities, both echoing stone

No longer the dark dramatic effect of his first design, p.88/89; this is Bergsten's second plan, which the jury liked very much: 'The minaret, the domes, the imposing site, the restrained lines - all breathes both the spirit of Byzantium and the modern Viennese School.'

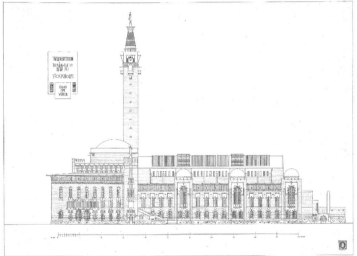

There was only praise for Bergsten's second design which was also commended for its elegant drawing. This time, however, the ground plan was unsatisfactory: 'The inner courtyard is too small and it is not suitable.'

monuments from the past as well as being part of our frenetic age.

'And would the person who created all this not be able to determine the shape of the tower, the focal point? Would he be capable of going so far and no further? Must the public now intervene, lest the town hall be destroyed? Must the civic guard be drummed up to defend the city? Perhaps there will be a debate and the city council will vote. Why not toss a coin!' And speaking on behalf of the entire Society of Architects he concluded: Östberg can manage the town hall tower on his own.'

WESTMAN PROVED CONVINCING, Östberg was allowed to carry on, and the design for the tower became reality. There were long, tedious years of building, and shortages during World War I added to the difficulties. But the town hall was opened in 1923 on a public holiday: 23 June, the Swedish Midsummer Eve.

Östberg's 1905 design for which he reduced the estimated costs from 4 million to 3.3 million crowns. To do so he made the tower smaller, scrapped the plan for woodcarving and brass decorations and reduced the size of rooms. He also substituted brick for the granite of his original plan.

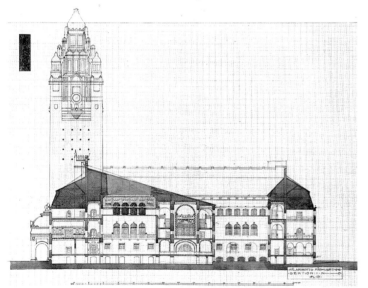

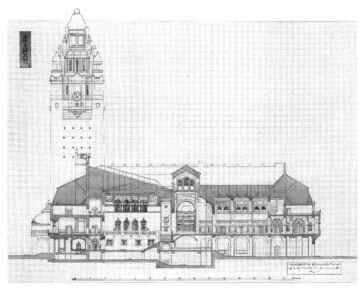

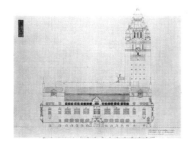

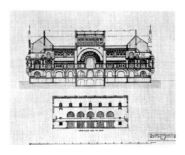

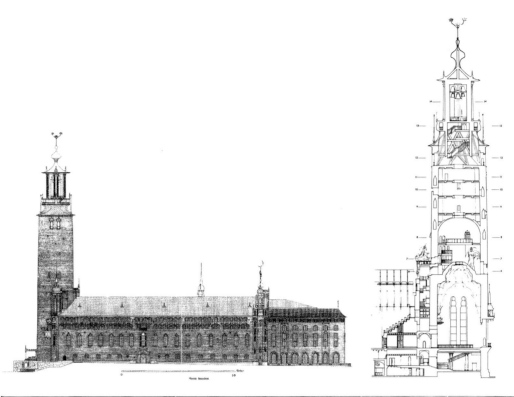

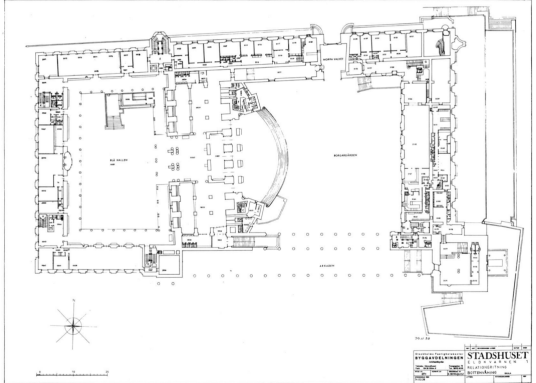

The definitive plan for Stockholm Town Hall is a far cry from the first design. What was first intended as a Court of Law became a civic centre; where granite walls had been planned, brick ones arose, and the original tower altered shape entirely. The position of the tower was also changed - Östberg gradually placed it more to the edge of the building - perhaps, many suggested, influenced by Westman, in whose first design, on p.84, the tower occupies this striking position.

HELSINKI STATION

NATIONAL ARCHITECTURAL COMPETITION FOR A NEW STATION IN HELSINKI, FINLAND.

ANNOUNCED: 15 December 1903; result published: 27 April 1904; number of participants: 21.

JURY: Three architects; Sebastian Gripenberg, director of the National Building Council; Gustav Nyström and Hugo Lindberg; August Granfelt and Colonel Dratschevski, respectively general director and track director of Finnish Railways.

WINNERS: 1. Eliel Saarinen; 2. Onni Törnqvist; 3. Hjalmar Aberg; Usko Nyström (shared third prize); 4. Paavo Uotila; 5. Lindahl and Thomé.

CONSTRUCTION: 1904-1914 (Gesellius, Lindgren, Saarinen; Saarinen).

FINLAND IS A LAND OF CLIMATIC EXTREMES. A country of brief, hot summers and long, cold winters. It is a land of a thousand lakes and vast uplands that breathe an atmosphere of limitless freedom. The freedom is deceptive: the people of Finland have a long history of oppression. Anyone wishing to understand

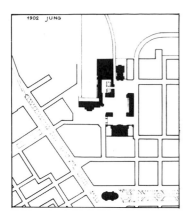

The Finnish Architects Association announced an ideas competition in 1902 to design Helsinki station square. Left: Bartel Jung's entry; he, like the five other entrants, wanted to reduce the size of the square and alter the alignment of the station buildings.
Right: 1903 plan of Finnish Rail, used as basis for the 1903 station competition. In spite of protests from many architects, the old alignments were retained.

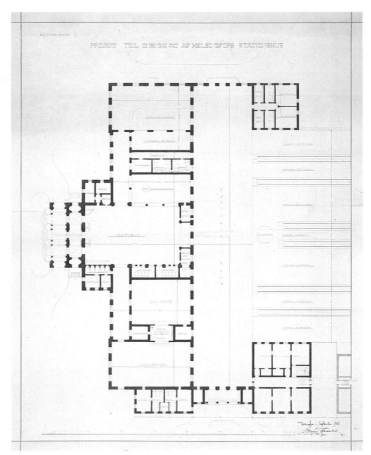

what was taking place in Finnish architecture at the turn of this century, should know a little about the political situation in the country at the time. Finland was only in name an autonomous principality, in fact it was controlled by the Russian Czar, who, in 1809, had taken Finland from Sweden, which had ruled it since the twelfth century.

The relative autonomy enjoyed in the nineteenth century stimulated Finnish national consciousness. The Finnish language, which had only with great difficulty survived centuries of foreign rule, began to gain in popularity.

A catalyst in this process was the *Kalevala*, a mythological Finnish-language epic, published in 1835 by a country doctor called Elias Lonnröt. The story was based on sagas and legends that Lonnröt had collected from people; it was immediately welcomed by thousands as the supreme embodiment of Finnish culture.

National consciousness was also a growing force in other forms of art. The influential painter, Akseli Gallen-Kalella, for instance, devoted his life to a revaluation of Finnish culture and drew virtually all his themes from the *Kalevala*. A similar

Törnquist, second prizewinner, was a major supporter of a specifically Finnish, National Romantic style of architecture. His design for a station, below, is very similar to his National Theatre for the station square, built in 1901, see p. 96.

development could be observed among architects; they searched for archetypal themes in Finnish tradition.

In 1893 one of the first written pleas appeared for specifically Finnish architecture. This would have to be contemporary and rational, but it should also be linked to tradition. In the 1890s many architects tried to determine what were the main features of that tradition. They examined medieval buildings which they regarded as examples of national architecture with typical northern features. They paid great attention to the materials and methods used. Timber was regarded as a characteristic Finnish material, but so was granite, which was in fact regarded as a symbol of the Finns' determined national character.

There came a change in the political situation in Finland towards the end of the nineteenth century. The new Russian Czar, Nicholas II, suddenly deprived the principality of certain rights it had hitherto enjoyed, suspended the constitution and appointed Russians to all important posts.

This also affected architecture: the Russian governor ordered several massive government buildings to be erected, almost all of them designed in Neo-Classicist style by the German architect, Carl Ludwig Engel. This served to fuel the fiery enthusiasm with which Finnish architects were searching for a style of their own. The quest for national architecture became more determined than ever.

The National Theatre in Helsinki was widely regarded as the first large public building in the new National Romantic style.

Its architect was Onni Törnqvist, who later adopted the Finnish form, Tarjanne, for his name. In 1899, before he was allowed to implement his design, an architectural competition for the façades was announced. People were not altogether satisfied with Tarjanne's design and others were asked to produce better ones. The only result of this, however, was that three prizes were awarded for designs that were no more satisfactory than the original one. Tarjanne, in collaboration with Yrjö Sadenius, finally succeeded in producing a design for the façade that accorded with the longing for a national architecture. The building was completed in 1901 and its shapely granite façades and medieval-inspired features were for a short time of great influence on other architects.

THE 1904 COMPETITION for a new station in Helsinki should be seen in connection with these developments. The National Theatre served as an example. It stood near the large station square, at that time a muddy wasteland badly in need of improvement. Many architects felt that with the National Theatre for inspiration, the entire square could become a monument to national architecture. This was also the aim of the Finnish architects' society, Arkitektclubben, when in 1902 it announced an ideas competition for the station square. There were only six participants and they all came up with ideas in which the square — by moving the station forward and by placing large buildings along its edges — was considerably reduced in size. All the proposals harmonized

Winning design by Saarinen, strongly National Romantic, contained many medieval elements. Saarinen clearly wanted his work to blend with Törnquist's National Theatre, seen here on the right, half in the picture, and he even made a footbridge connecting theatre and station.

with the National Theatre and were National Romantic in character.

The Finnish Railways and the National Building Council, joint sponsors of the new station, initially paid little attention to what went on in architectural circles. They had been planning a new station since 1895. In 1898 they had approached C.D. Gleim, a German engineer who in that same year had won two international architectural prizes for stations in neighbouring Sweden.

In 1903 Gleim completed his outline for the new station which would, like the old one, be a terminus in the form of a U-shape enclosing the tracks. The existing alignments would be maintained, and the station square would remain unaltered. Outlines were then drawn of the entire complex which, apart from the station itself, would also include offices and a royal waiting room. The design was largely the work of Bruno Granholm, although overall responsibility rested with the National Building Council and with Finnish Rail. Granholm designed a Neo-Classicist façade, in the same style as Engel's buildings. Predictably, these plans aroused strong indignation among Finnish architects. Their plans had been ignored (the alignments were left unchanged) and furthermore the station was to have a detestable Neo-Classicist exterior. The affair was widely publicized and public opinion supported the architects. In the end the Arkitektenclubben succeeded in bringing so much pressure to bear on Finnish Rail that it was decided to hold a public architectural competition, with the State as official sponsor.

On 15 December 1903 the competition was announced, to the satisfaction of the architects, although it was clearly a compromise: Gleim's outline plan was to be preserved unconditionally and the alignments were to be maintained,

Halmar Aberg won third prize with his design 'Helsingfors', a solid construction with high sloping roofs. The jury described it as 'correct and restrained' though also 'a little boring'.

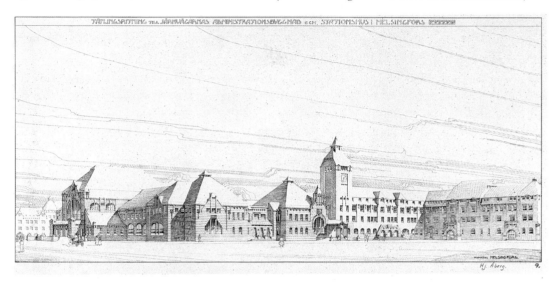

Fourth prize went to a design that was not National Romantic, by the young architect, Paavo Uotila. The style of drawing and the façade of the administration building on the right illustrate Uotila's interest in European Art Nouveau.

'unless the composition of the façade made alterations necessary'. In fact the competition dealt only with the exterior of the station. In one respect, however, the organisers complied with the architects' wishes: the façades would be largely executed in natural stone (read: granite). This was an implicit acknowledgment of the plans to make the station square truly Finnish..

THE PARTICIPANTS WERE GIVEN exactly four months; all entries had to be submitted by noon on 15 April 1904. The jury met for the first time on 16 April.

After a chairman (Gripenberg) and secretary (Lindberg) had been elected, the 21 sealed entries were opened and the mottos registered. A committee was then appointed, consisting of the three architects on the jury: Gripenberg, Nyström and Lindberg. Their task was to check the designs against the competition programme, and then make a comparison. On 27 April the jury met again, and the committee's report was publicized.

Two entries were excluded, motto 'H-fors-Europa' because the designers had 'in no way indicated the cladding of the façades', and motto 'Stephenson' because the 'required cross-sections, both of the station and of the office building and royal waiting room, were missing'. The committee had divided the remaining 19 entries into two groups: one for those that might be eligible for a prize and one for those that would definitely not qualify. Ten entrants ended up in the latter group; of the other nine, five were recommended for an award. Almost all the 21 entries were given detailed commentaries.

Clearly, the members of the committee thought highly of the National Romantic style. Not that this was explicitly stated, but almost all designs in other styles were rejected.

A characteristic comment was that which accompanied the rejection of Sigurd Fosterus' design, 'Eureka'. Its entire architectural concept was described as 'imported, eccentric and far from attractive'. And the station roof would 'not be a success in the Finnish climate'. Fosterus had indeed not based his design on Finnish traditions, but on what he had learnt in the preceding years from the Belgian architect, Henri van de Velde. His design was sensational and modern, though of all entries the least Finnish.

The designs that qualified for prizes were almost all in the National Romantic style. A design was recommended for the first prize that was not only an excellent example of this style but was also remarkable for the manner of its presentation: the drawings of perspectives and façades had all been produced with great detail and drawn completely free hand. Its motto was a drawing of a winged wheel on a globe, and it turned out to have come from the young architect, Eliel Saarinen. It was the only design that received the committee's wholehearted admiration. 'This entry is most interesting and is beautifully executed. The façades are exceedingly attractive. The two main sections of the complex have been harmonized with skill and competence and the stone is used efficiently and expertly, in such a way that the stucco blends in with it admirably. The whole project bears the mark of monumental

Fifth prize went to the design by Lindahl and Thomé. The jury thought the tower 'exceptionally pleasing with an attractive top' and said the whole design gave an impression of calm, clear security. But the doorways were too small and the royal entrance was not pleasing.

serenity and good modern design, and its overall effect is one of nobility. This entry, which is conceived with a delicate sense of form and is inspired by excellent artistic taste, is marked by both appealing charm and strong individuality.'

Another National Romantic design was awarded second prize under motto 'P': it came from Tarjanne, the designer of the National Theatre. This time the jury's comments were cool and curt, stating that the overall design was 'monumental and harmonious in character', though at the same time it was marked by 'a certain dull rigidity'. Such phrases were also used to describe the other prizewinning entries. The design that was jointly awarded third prize, motto 'Helsingfors' by Hjalmar Aberg, was termed 'correct, quiet', but 'somewhat dull'. For the fourth prize a design by Paavo Uotiloa was recommended; it was not exactly National Romantic but its main façade created 'an attractive impression'. However, the committee added in a note that 'the small tower with its squat top is less than successful while the façade of the royal waiting room clashes with the rest of the design'.

The jury's decision on the design submitted under motto

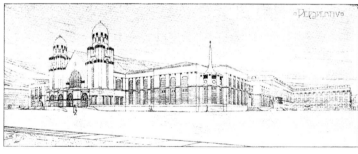

*'Semafor', was an exception. Unfortunately, this design has not been preserved, so that it is impossible to establish in how far it resembles Saarinen's design. Be that as it may, the committee immediately put on record that 'Semafor' breathed the same spirit as number 18 (winged wheel on globe, by Saarinen) and commented on it in greater detail than the other designs.

It was described as having 'great merit in many respects' although it was inferior in quality to number 18 and contained no novel ideas. It was also feared that 'Semafor' 'especially because of the height of the façade', would be more expensive to build than the other designs.

The committee recommended that the fourth prize should not be awarded to 'Semafor' if both designs were found to have been submitted by the same person, but to give the prize to motto 'Tunneliaukko' instead (which would otherwise receive the fifth prize). The fifth prize would in that case be awarded to the 'quiet, solid and clear' entry under motto 'La Gare' (Lindahl and Thomé), which was strongly reminiscent of Tarjanne's design.

THE PRIZES WERE AWARDED more or less in accordance with the committee's recommendations. Unfortunately, the committee had made an embarrassing mistake excluding motto 'Stephenson' from the competition. The missing cross-sections had in fact been sent in and during the exhibition following the publication of the result, they were found concealed by another drawing. The design was hurriedly given a belated shared third prize.

Sadly, 'Semafor' was denied the fourth prize for which it had been a candidate. The design proved to have come from the office of Gesellius, Saarinen and Lindgren, while the winning design had been prepared by Saarinen alone. The loss of this prize was not only a disappointment to Saarinen's closest collaborators, but it also precipitated a mutual crisis. It was the first time that Saarinen had taken part in a competition on his own, without Herman Gesellius and Armas Lindgren. Lindgren, his friends and housemates. They had studied together and, a year before completing their studies, had started a close and successful collaboration. By 1904 they had some fifty buildings to their joint names, whereby, within a few years, they had become known as fervent pursuers of a national style of building. In some of their designs the influence of the Scottish Arts and Crafts and the Viennese Sezession, with which they felt considerable affinity, were still recognizable. By the turn of the century, their designs — such

Finnish architects were generally well-informed about architectural trends elsewhere. The top design here, by Jung and Bomanson, shows the influence of the American, Richardson. Centre: Echoes of the Viennese, Otto Wagner, in this work by Gylden and Ullberg. Below: One of the most unusual designs, by Jarl Eklund: a mixture of English and *Scandinavian styles. None of the three designs received a prize.*

ATENEVMIN KESKIPORTAALTA KATSOTTUNA ··· SEDT FRÅN ATENEVMS MIDTELTRADDA ··· D = 5

This plan, under the motto 'Stephenson', was originally rejected by the jury because the entry contained no cross-sections. A painful mistake - at the exhibition following the competition, these cross-sections were found with another entry.

'Stephenson' was considered after all and won an award. But architects Usko Nyström and Alarik Tavaststjerna had to be content with the jury's brief comment: 'good elements, made an artistic impression, but insufficiently worked-out'.

Motto: Stephenson

10.

as that for the Finnish Pavilion at the Paris World Exhibition (1900) and the insurance building of Pohjola with its Kalevala-derived ornamentation (1902) were almost all in the National Romantic style.

The bond among the three young architects was so strong that in most of their designs the individual contribution of each could not be distinguished. In 1902 they even built a joint home-cum-workshop called Hvittrask. They were not only concerned with architecture; kindred spirits including the painter, Gallen Kalella, and the composer, Jean Sibelius, were regular guests.

WHEN SAARINEN SUBMITTED a plan of his own besides the joint design, this marked the beginning of an estrangement among the friends. Personal relationships were probably a factor; in the same year Gesellius married Saarinen's first wife, Mathilda Gylden, and Saarinen married Gesellius' sister, Loja. Armas Lindgren gradually separated from the other two and broke with them completely in 1905.

It seems probable that Saarinen was also searching for an individual voice in his architectural design. For no sooner had he secured the commission to build the new station, than he left for a long honeymoon trip in Europe where he made an extensive study of the latest developments in architecture. In Germany, England and Scotland he visited many stations in order to gather new ideas. He returned to Finland in the autumn of 1904, and in December he submitted a greatly altered design for the new station. This design had been stripped of many of its National Romantic features, while at the same time its kinship with the National Theatre had been weakened. This was the first of a long series of changes, all in the same direction, until in 1910 the definitive design was ready, this time in a highly individual, severe, modern style.

THIS WAS AN ABOUT-TURN for which no single explanation can be given. There are at least three possible reasons. First, Finland was becoming increasingly aware of architectural developments in other parts of Europe and in the United States. Each country, or culture-zone had its own forms of expression, but with certain features common to all. These included a departure from the imitation of old forms, a striving for candour, and the use of new materials. Possibly Saarinen became interested in these trends before his two friends did and this interest was undoubtedly further stimulated during his travels abroad.

A second reason may have been that Saarinen's design for Helsinki's station was not universally admired, even in Finland. Gustav Strengell and Sigurd Fosterus were the major prophets of the new age. In a lampoon, Strengell wrote that architecture should run parallel with technical, financial and cultural developments. He rejected the National Romantic style, and called an earlier design by Gesellius, Saarinen and Lindgren a 'contrived prehistoric monster'.

Fosterus also made an attack on Saarinen in which he propagated the ideas of his teacher, the Belgian Henry van de Velde. He advocated a rational architecture, in which form was determined by function. Fosterus wrote that modern architects should learn to 'see the beauty of those forms to which honesty leads them'. And he added: 'a station should symbolize the modern age, as the exponent of a new means of communication.'

Unfortunately, we do not have any writings in which Saarinen reacted to these attacks, but doubtless he was affected by the criticism. The radical changes he made to his design move unmistakably in the direction indicated by Strengell and especially Fosterus. The design that was put on the table in December 1904 has more in common superficially with

At the end of 1904 Saarinen presented an entirely new plan for the station, devoid of all National Romanticism elements. The design was modern and restrained. Even the playful bears at the entrance in the first design were replaced by tidy lamp-posts. Many factors contributed to this change in Saarinen: his exposure to modern movements abroad; growing estrangement from his friends, and criticism of his first design by such people as Sigurd Fosterus, see right.

Fosterus' design than with Saarinen's own prizewinning plan, delivered in January of that year.

THIRD REASON FOR Saarinen's abandoning his nationalistic ideas may have been that even in 1904 he sensed that National Romanticism would soon begin to lose support. The winter of 1904/1905 was an important period in this respect: Russia's grip on Finland weakened, partly because the Russian governor-general in Finland was assassinated, and partly because Russia was facing problems of its own.

The nationalistic feelings which had united the Finns in their opposition to Russian domination were no longer so intense. At the same time a deeply rooted conflict among the Finns themselves began to emerge. Parallel to the situation in Russia, there was violent opposition between the working and property-owning classes. In the years that followed, this conflict grew fiercer, and led to a bitter civil war, from which Finland was reborn as an independent republic.

It is scarcely surprising that during these years of political confusion the National Romantic style came to an end. Saarinen abandoned the style before many of his colleagues did. He developed an architectual language of his own, in harmony with current trends abroad. When the new station was finally completed in 1914, it was not a monument to National Romanticism; it was a building that later became the object of a new national pride and the first example of Finnish modern architecture.

Sigurd Fosterus' plan contained many Jugendstil elements which did not please the jury. However, he heralded a new age, which Saarinen soon recognized. After the competition, Fosterus published a seminal article, 'Architecture, a challenge', in which he put the case for 'dilettantism, internationalism and rationalism'. He wanted a style of 'brain and sinew' to replace that of 'heart and soul', by which he meant National Romantic which had held sway for so long in Finland. He said: 'Public opinion swings between these two extremes, they represent the contrast between left and right, between lack of prejudice, and dogmatism.' Fosterus' influence can be seen when we compare his design with Saarinen's final plan, left.

THE PEACE PALACE, THE HAGUE

INTERNATIONAL ARCHITECTURAL COMPETITION FOR A PEACE PALACE, SEAT OF THE PERMANENT COURT OF ARBITRATION, CONTAINING LIBRARY, THE HAGUE, NETHERLANDS.

PUBLISHED: August 1905; result: May 1906; number of participants: 221.

JURY: H.A. van Karnebeek, president of the Carnegie Foundation, and six architects: T.E. Collcutt (London): P.J.H. Cuypers (Netherlands); E. Ihne (Berlin); C. Konig (Vienna); M.H.P. Nenot (Paris); W.R. Ware (Mass., USA).

WINNERS:
1. L.M. Cordonnier (Lille, France)
2. A. Marcel (Paris)
3. F. Wendt (Charlottenburg, Germany)
4. Otto Wagner (Vienna)
5. H. Greenley & H.S. Olin (New York); F. Schwechten (Berlin)

CONSTRUCTED: 1907-1913 (design: L.M. Cordonnier and J.A.G. van der Steur)

IRONICALLY, JUST BEFORE THE OUTBREAK of the first world war, the Peace Palace was completed in the Dutch city of The Hague. Today it is one of the most famous institutions in the world. Both the International Court of Justice and the Permanent Court of Arbitration reside here. States from all over the world come to present their mutual disagreements before a council of the wise. Many international conflicts have found a peaceful solution here.

In 1913, when the building was opened, few people believed in the task of the new Peace Palace. Even the building itself was not generally regarded as a success. Several architectural journals called it an architectural failure, 'a blemish on the architecture of the twentieth century'. It could hardly have been otherwise; the building was the result of a string of compromises and the competition that preceded it was fraught with conflict. It seemed as though in those first decades of the twentieth century, the achievement of a Peace Palace was no more blessed with success than the achievement of world peace.

The idea of building a Peace Palace had a lengthy prehistory. For as long as people have waged war, voices have pleaded for peace. During the nineteenth century this plea began to penetrate the courts of the mighty. After the Franco-Prussian war the number of peace movements increased all over the world and the parliaments of countries such as the USA, Britain, Italy, Sweden, the Netherlands and Belgium pronounced themselves in favour of arbitration as a means of solving international conflicts. It was the Russian Czar Nicholas II (1868-1918) who took the initiative that led directly to establishing of a Peace Palace. He convoked an international conference that was held in The Hague in 1899, with the initial objective of reaching universal disarmament. When this proved unattainable, several motions were passed

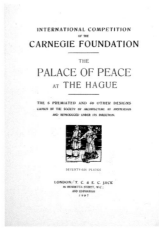

Andrew Carnegie, 1835-1919, who financed the Peace Palace, was the son of a Scottish weaver. In 1848 he went to America, where he built a fortune from the railways and the steel industry. He became a great social benefactor.

In 1907 the Carnegie Foundation issued a publication containing the jury report, illustrations of 46 of the competition entries, and a group photo of the jury members with Carnegie.

First prize went to the Frenchman, L.M. Cordonnier, who was greatly influenced by the Parisian Ecole des Beaux Arts, where ideas from neoclassical architecture predominated. Cordonnier's designs include Dunkirk Town Hall and the theatre in Rijssel. He took part in many competitions; his drawings are distinguished by their grace and beauty.

In 1884 he won the competition for the Exchange building in Amsterdam, but was accused of plagiarism: his design, it was said, bore remarkable similarities to the town hall in La Rochelle. Such conflict and recriminations ensued that Amsterdam city council decided in 1888 that no Exchange would be built. But in 1897 Dutchman H.P. Berlage, who had gained third place in the competition, was commissioned to build an Exchange. His building was completed in 1903 and has won international fame as one of the earliest examples of modern architecture.

to promote the peaceful solution of disputes.

It was also decided to set up a Permanent Court of Arbitration which could act as arbiter in disputes between states.

The Hague was chosen as its place of residence because of the neutrality of the Netherlands.

The actual possibility of establishing such a Court of Arbitration occured when the American steel tycoon, Andrew Carnegie (1835-1919), donated 1.5 million dollars for this purpose. Immediately, the Dutch ministry of foreign affairs set up a commission of prominent architects to prepare for the building of the Court. The commission started looking for a suitable site and also drew up the conditions for an international architectural competition to select the best design.

The birth of the Carnegie Foundation in 1904 ended the role of the commission; the Foundation took over its activities. This caused much future conflict as the commission's recommendations were largely set aside. Not only was a different site bought from the one suggested by the commission, but the competition was also entirelyre-organized.

The Carnegie Foundation preferred a closed competition in order to ensure the cooperation of the most competent architects. Although the Foundation finally bowed to the wishes
of Dutch architects by opening the competition to anyone, the grievance that not all participants were offered equal conditions, remained. The 20 architects who had been invited to take part received a fee of 2,000 Dutch guilders; all other participants had to meet their own costs.

This disadvantage was all the greater because considerable work was involved: the competition programme stipulated fully worked-out designs, including coloured three dimensional illustrations and detailed floor plans. All this had to be ready within eight months, which almost everyone found too soon. In several countries the architectural press warned that under such circumstances many prominent architects would refrain from taking part. Even so, 200 designs were submitted.

IN JUNE 1906 THE ENTRIES were made public. In a tightly packed display in the Royal Palace in The Hague, 216 designs were exhibited: a total of more than 3,000 drawings.

The architectural press reacted with reserve: mediocrity appeared trumps, and the majority of ideas were conventional. Certainly, few avant-gardists from the different countries had participated.

Almost all the French entrants belonged to the Academicians; innovators like Auguste Perret and Tony Garnier did not take part. Many of the Americans also showed evidence of their training at the Paris Academy; Frank Lloyd Wright was absent. In Germany, Peter Behrens was an architectural pioneer but his name was not on the list of entrants. Nor was that of the Belgian, Henry van de Velde, father of Art Nouveau and founder of the Bauhaus in Weimar. Otto Wagner from Austria, where the Sezession flourished in those years, was a competitor, but not Joseph Hoffmann, Adolf Loos nor Joseph Maria Olbrecht. Participants from the Netherlands included Berlage and Kromhout but not Michel de Klerk or K.P.C. de Bazel.

In the independent and critical Dutch architectural journal, 'De Opmerker', the architect, A.W. Weissmann, compared this competition with that for the Amsterdam Exchange in 1884. On that occasion he had called the drawings 'mostly very beautiful', though he had wondered if they did not strain after effect too much. Now he observed that draftmanship had reached true virtuosity, but was wasted on the most banal architectural commonplaces: 'The architectural trend triumphs everywhere, but never gets beyond the most appalling mediocrity.'

The matter-of-fact, Bouwkundig Weekblad, official organ of the Maatschappij ter bevordering van de Bouwkunst (Society for the Promotion of Architecture), the most important association of Dutch architects, was also unable to muster much enthusiasm for the outcome of the competition: 'Many designers were unable to detach themselves from their predilection for certain conventional forms . . . The revival of the classical temple, with the idea of suggesting peace among

Berlage's design for the Peace Palace; this did not gain a prize, unlike his design for the Amsterdam Exchange. See also note to illustration on p. 106.

the nations, was as predictable as the appearance of fantastic creations that tried, by means of overpowering boldness, massiveness and a not immediately comprehensible symbolism, to present an image of invincible peace on earth. Hence the collection includes designs of pyramids, temples, churches, casinos, stations, town-halls, palaces and even country mansions. It displays the labours of participants who do not seem to be aware that their ingenuity and talent were bound to be inadequate.'

THIS SAME *BOUWKUNDIG WEEKBLAD* analyzes the reasons for the lack of spectacular results. Partly, the fault lay in the choice of site; the chosen terrain was so restricted that it 'did not permit a truly grand design'. The briefing was also a difficult one — to design two buildings, each with a different purpose: a Court of Arbitration and a Library.
'But the greatest difficulty lay in the aesthetic problem.
The assignment was to design a building with a purpose such as there had never been before; a building that would have to symbolize in its outward form an ideal that had only recently come into existence — world peace — about the realization of which many of the participants were bound to have doubts. Although the task seemed capable of inspiring the artists to a high degree, their creations have not come up to expectation. On consideration, the outcome could not have been otherwise. To interpret a new idea, and embody a new ideology, is more than can be done by one artist, in a period of eight months.'

THE JURY, WHICH, BESIDE THE CHAIRMAN of the Carnegie Foundation, consisted of architects from six different countries, judged the more than 3,000 drawings within six days. First, each member of the jury examined all the designs separately, and each design that was regarded by at least one jury member to be worthy of further consideration was shortlisted. Out of the 44 designs that remained, 16 were selected, from which the winners were finally chosen.
First prize of 12,000 guilders went to the Frenchman L.M. Cordonnier, who, 20 years earlier, had also won the competition for the Exchange building in Amsterdam, the Dutch capital. That had been a Pyrrhic victory which made him exclaim 'Tout est perdu, hors l'honneur' (All is lost, except for honour.). Once again, he had submitted a strikingly flamboyant and exuberant design, even though composed of conventional elements. It must have been chiefly the radiance of the drawings that won the jury over to Cordonnier.
The second prize also went to a Frenchman, A. Marcel, from Paris, who had submitted his own version of the Petit Palais.

The Germans, Wendt and Schwechten (respectively third and shared fifth prizes), and the Americans, H. Greeney and H.S. Olin (shared fifth prize), had made comparable designs: domes and Classicist pillars. The only slightly adventurous decision was the award of the fourth prize to the Austrian, Otto Wagner. He was the only prizewinner representing the avant-garde, with his light and graceful Sezession building. The jury report did not really find favour anywhere except in France. Not just because of the choices made; Cordonnier's design was generally regarded as at least deserving, but there was criticism of the extremely succinct motivation behind this choice. Although all 44 designs from the first round were shown in the jury report, only the six prizewinning ones were given a few lines of commentary. And these few lines were remarkable chiefly for their obscure and inelegant use of language.
All that was said of Cordonnier's design was: 'This design displays a beautiful general order; its creator wished to give expression to the idea that, since The Hague had been chosen as the seat of the Court of Arbitration, the architecture of the Peace Palace must be inspired by Dutch sixteenth century architecture. This consideration was of chief importance in this design. The floor plan meets the requirements of the programme and separates, as was stipulated, the Library from the Palace. However, in pursuing this separation, the architect has not succeeded in achieving the ever-desirable concept of architectural unity.'
Of Marcel's design little more was said than 'It was only the general arrangement that drew the attention of the jury; the grouping is very good . . . and the arrangement of the rear building excellent. It is regrettable that excessive pomposity, both as indicated in the floor plan and in the drawing of the elevations, is not in accordance with the stately simplicity suitable for the architectural image of a Peace Palace. Besides, there is no evidence of any originality'.
Finally, Wagner was given this comment: 'The designer points out that, to express the peculiar needs of a Peace Palace, he has deemed it necessary to employ new means and new aesthetics. The jury considered this artistic expression to be important; it led to the creation of a monument to which a certain measure of originality cannot be denied.'
Some of the critics took offence at these remarks. 'Why, for instance give an award to a design that is inspired by Dutch architecture of the seventeenth century? Because that was the time when the Eighty Years War was fought?' Or why give second prize to a design devoid of any originality? they asked. Most of the criticism, however, was more fundamental:

Architects from many countries took part in the competition for the Peace Palace. The nationality of an architect could often be deduced from the design, as for example here left, top to bottom: 'Beaux Arts' design of Frenchman A. Marcel; 'Sezession' design by Viennese Otto Wagner; warmly coloured, somewhat oriental design by Hungarian Emil Töry. Right: Two designs heavy with symbolism: a tomb by G. Mancini of Rome, and a pyramid by Félix Debat of Paris.

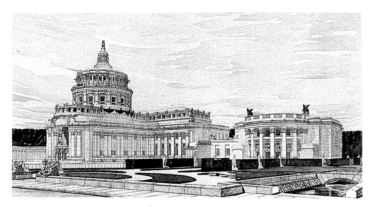

*Above: Design by Johannes Zimmerman from Zwickau.
Below: Design by Jan F. Groll, a Dutchman who worked for many years in England and seems to have been inspired by English Neo-Gothic.*

'One looks in vain for a principle that has guided the jurors,' was a general comment. Incomprehension was greatest in view of the fact that precisely those designs were selected which did not adhere to the programme. It was clear in the case of almost all the winning designs that they could never be built for the stipulated sum of 1.6 million guilders. Nor would any of them fit the relatively small site. Moreover, applicants had been asked to execute only the perspectives in colour, the rest had to be submitted in the form of line-drawings. In fact, the more exuberant and colourful the work, the greater proved the chance of an award.

As if all this was not bad enough, the jury declared it had not considered it its duty to choose a design that could actually be built. On the contrary: the eventual choice of a design to be constructed was handed over to the Carnegie Foundation, which now awarded six prizewinning entries that could form the basis for a definitive design.

THAT SUCH A LARGE JURY found it difficult to make a choice that met with universal approval was understandable.

That there were no true innovators among the prizewinners was perhaps scarcely surprising when one considers that the average age of jury members was sixty plus. But what really angered the architectural world in Britain, Germany, the United States and the Netherlands was the fact that an immense amount of work had been carried out which would book no concrete results at all. To produce a hodge-podge from six designs was seen as an absurdity. Whatever one might think of Cordonnier's design, everyone was agreed on one point: since he had won, his design must be carried out. The Dutch, in particular, feared a repetition of the Amsterdam Exchange affair, leading to loss of face in international circles.

FORTUNATELY, THE SECOND PEACE CONFERENCE took place in The Hague in 1907, this time at the initiative of the American president, Theodore Roosevelt (1858-1919). Not only did this draw the attention once again to the urgent need for a Peace Palace but all participating states decided to financially support its construction. In view of the high costs incurred by the competition, this support was most welcome.

The Carnegie Foundation therefore came under pressure to start building as soon as possible. And despite the fact that the award-winning design exceeded the budget, Cordonnier was chosen as architect. He secured the cooperation of the Dutchman, J.A.G. van der Steur, who strongly asserted his influence on the final design.

When the definitive plan was made public, Cordonnier's

flamboyant design was seen to have been drastically pruned. The impressive towers at each corner were gone; only a small turret was left. The exuberant decorations had disappeared, much glamour and elegance had gone. What remained was a building still recognizable as a palace, which could now be built without much delay.

On 28 August 1913 the Peace Palace was officially opened, a year before the outbreak of World War I made the Court of Arbitration temporarily superfluous. In 1920, however, when the League of Nations was founded in Geneva, the Peace Palace in The Hague was not only rehabilitated but was even given an additional function. Apart from the Permanent Court of Arbitration, it also became the home of the Permanent Court of International Justice, the predecessor of the International Court of Justice. The League of Nations was officially dissolved in 1946, but the International Court of Justice is still there, now part of the United Nations.

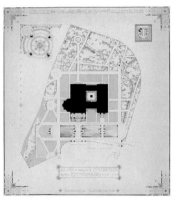

Willem Kromhout from the Netherlands was strongly opposed to architectural 'isms', and searched for new forms. His own styles were distinctive and different, with powerful shapes and imaginative decoration.

LIST OF INVITED ARCHITECTS:
Netherlands: J.L. Springer and E. Cuypers
United States: Peabody & Stearns, Boston; Carrere & Hastings, New York
France: A. Marcel, Paris; L.M. Cordonnier, Lille
Germany: F. Schwechten, Berlin; C. Hocheder, Munich
Austria: Otto Wagner, Vienna
Hungary: I. Alpar, Budapest
Switzerland: H. Auer, Berne
Belgium: E. Dieltjen, Antwerp
Rumania: I.D. Berindey, Bucharest
Italy: G. Calderini, Rome; E. Basile, Palermo
Spain: D.J. Urioste y Velada, Madrid
Portugal: J.L. Moneiro, Lisbon
Denmark: M. Nyrop, Copenhagen
Sweden: I.G. Clason, Stockholm
Russia: A. de Pomeranzeff, St. Petersburg; E. Saarinen, Helsinki (then under Russia)
Great Britain: H.T. Hare and J. Belcher, London

Eliel Saarinen was one of the architects specially invited by the Carnegie Foundation to take part in the competition. To the surprise and fury of many fellow architects, his design did not gain an award. Rumour had it that the reason for this was that the Russian Czar did not want a Finn to win. For more about Russo-Finnish tension see the chapter on Helsinki.

A great admirer of Saarinen's design was the Dutch architect, K.P.C. de Bazel, who, although he strongly supported the concept of world peace, had not taken part in this competition. From 1905 onwards he was engrossed in a design that conflicted with this competition: commissioned by Dr P.H. Eijkman and Paul Horrix, both fervent supporters of internationalism, De Bazel designed a World City just outside The Hague. But any hope that this plan would materialize was extinguished when the Carnegie Foundation decided to buy a site called Zorgvliet and build the Peace Palace there.

In 1906 De Bazel wrote a scathing article about the competition, slamming the entries and calling them 'a veritable mountain of dull pretension, lacking in any living inspiration'. But, he said, there was one exception: the design by Eliel Saarinen. 'This building stretches out horizontally with a slender necked dome in the middle.

The simplicity of this plan emanates a conscious and earnest conviction. Complete harmony is achieved in the main structure through a principle of balanced constrasts: repose and motion, the ground base of all building. This gives the building, despite its solemnity and solidity, a sense of life and movement, and this serious energy is underlined by the delicacy of the decoration.' De Bazel continued: 'It is most striking, though this design is worked out in considerable detail, how clearly we can distinguish the architect's indecision; should he produce something complete, deadly dull but acceptable — or something unfinished but throbbing with life? He chose the latter, but forgot that his work would come before a jury who would judge it; that they would be uncreative men of cramped spirit, and that they would fail to comprehend what he had made.'

In 1907 De Bazel made one last attempt to save his plan. Together with many other architects, including Berlage and Kromhout, who had taken part in the competition, he sent a letter to the Dutch Parliament, in which he demolished the report by the jury and clarified in detail the advantages of his proposal. Alas, in vain.

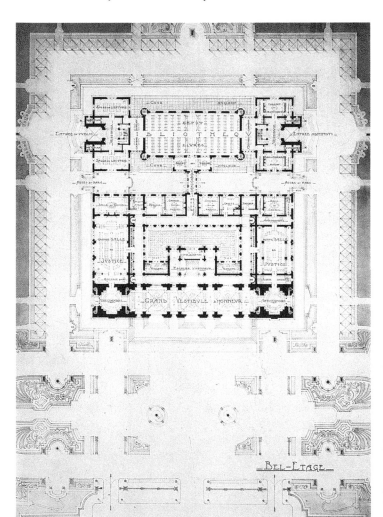

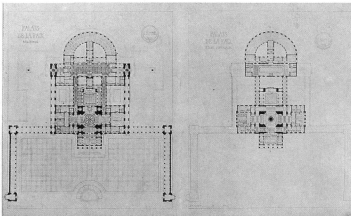

CHICAGO TRIBUNE TOWER

COMPETITION FOR AN OFFICE BUILDING FOR THE CHICAGO TRIBUNE.

PUBLISHED: 10 June 1922, closing date: 1 November 1922 (1 December for foreigners); result: 3 December 1922; number of participants: 204

JURY: Alfred Granger (architect), chairman; Colonel Robert R. McCormick; Captain Joseph M. Patterson; Edward S. Beck; Holmes Onderdonk.

WINNERS: 1. Raymond M. Hood and John Mead Howells 2. Eliel Saarinen 3. Holabird & Roche.

CONSTRUCTION: 1924/25 after the design of Holabird & Roche.

Chicago, that wonderful town: a view looking north from the Loop, with the Chicago river and the North Michigan Avenue Bridge in the foreground, and centre, the Chicago Tribune Building with its massive strainer arches, built in 1925. To its left, the first skyscraper on the site: the Wrigley Building, designed by Graham, Anderson, Probst and White, and built in 1921. The structure is typical of skyscrapers of the day; American architects, inspired by classical architecture abroad, embellished their huge edifices in sundry architectural styles. The tower of the building, for instance, missing in the picture, is modelled on the Giralda, a Moorish minaret with a Renaissance bell tower, in Seville, Spain.
The management of the Chicago Tribune must have been taken off guard by all the eclectic designs arriving daily for the competition for 'the most beautiful and striking building in the world'. The chosen design by Hood and Howells was reminiscent of the Tour de Beurre of Rouen Cathedral, and the tower of Mechlin Cathedral, Belgium. Right in the picture is the Equitable Building

(Skidmore, Owings and Merrill, 1965), evidence that the stark European architecture of the 1920s later gained a foothold in the United States.

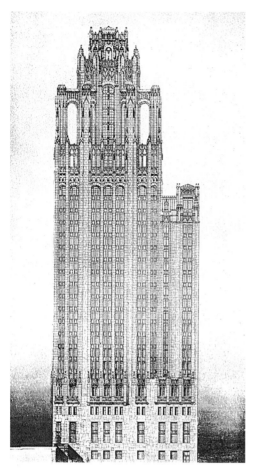
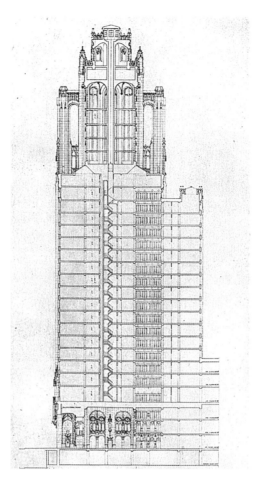

Raymond M. Hood, John Mead Howells

November 1, 1922, was the deadline for the competition, although entries arriving by boat from overseas were given a month's extra grace. Even so, the jury was impatient to begin, and on 13 November, with entries still arriving, an initial round was held and the design of Raymond M. Hood and John Mead Howells selected as firm favourite; a position it held throughout later ballots.
Few were convinced that the jury had reached the right decision when the building was finished in 1925. Yet opinion can change. In 1981, Paul Goldberger wrote in his book The Skyscraper: 'It is a building that has aged particularly well, and it is hard, looking back after 50 years at the designs that lost to it, to believe that the competition jury made a wrong choice. Their judgement was conservative but sound.'

'THERE IS NO PRECEDENT for this great contest, which has drawn upon the genius of the old world and the new. The competitive method is adopted in the case of public buildings with increasing frequency, but the new Tribune building will be the first privately owned edifice the design for which was awarded in a prize competition open to the world. There never has been such a contest and it is very doubtful there ever will be another.'

These are rather grandiloquent words written by the editor of the Chicago Tribune in a commentary of 3 December 1922. In that same edition, the Tribune published the results of a competition, organized earlier that year, for its own new office building.

On the day the competition had been announced, 10 June 1922, the Chicago Tribune was exactly 75 years old. In its own words, the newspaper was aiming to have,

'The most beautiful and distinctive office building in the world.'

As an incentive, the international competition offered no less than 100,000 dollars in prize money.

WHY ALL THE FUSS? Two years earlier, heavy traffic in the city centre had forced the Tribune to move its printing depot to North Michigan Avenue, north of the Chicago river, where the paper could be distributed more efficiently. Between the new printing works and the Avenue a site had been set aside for a future office building. It was not large, about 30 by 40 metres, and in view of the paper's ambitious plans, the building would have to be at least 55 metres high, according to the terms of the competition. Beyond that height the building was allowed to recede somewhat; local regulations prescribed that the maximum height for such buildings was 80 metres. Any tower added should be no higher than 120 metres.

The competition complied with the recommendations drawn up by the American Institute of Architects (AIA). The second winner would receive 20,000 dollars and the third winner, 10,000. dollars.

The remaining 10,000 dollars would be shared among the ten architects' firms who had been invited by the Chicago Tribune to participate in the competition: Bliss & Faville, San Francisco; Bertram G. Goodhue, James Gamble Roger, Benjamin Wistar Morris, Howells & Hood, New York City; and Holabird & Roche, Jarvis Hunt, Burnham & Co, Schmidt, Garden & Martin and Andrew Rebori, Chicago.

From this choice, American architects were able to gain some idea what kind of design the newspaper was looking for; the ten firms had a solid, rather traditional manner of building which met the prevailing taste of the time. Most of the foreign architects, none too familiar with the American scene, had to do without such clues.

To anyone who had not yet visited the United States, American architecture was difficult to follow. For instance, since 1890, Chicago had been erecting tall office buildings from weight-bearing steel structures, against which relatively sober, stone walls were placed. Between 1910 and 1920, architects increasingly reverted to the traditional forms of the

William Holabird, Martin Roche

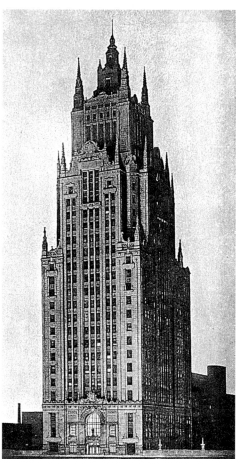

D.H. Burnham & Co

Far left: Right from the very beginning the design of William Holabird and Martin Roche was in the running for a prize: it eventually came third. Like the prizewinners, Hood and Howell, they were also invited by the newspaper, beforehand, to take part in the competition.

Left: D.H. Burnham and Co., a firm of architects from Chicago, also received a paid invitation from the Chicago Tribune to take part in the competition. From the architects invited, it was obvious that the newspaper wanted an office in the prevalent style of the day: imposing and eclectic. Burnham and Co. introduced late Renaissance touches: pinnacles at the corners, richly decorated cordons, and at points where the building narrows, volutes and curly adornments. The design received an honourable mention.

Right: Neo-Gothic entry from Jas. Gamble, New York, complete with ridge piece on a sloping roof. Its steeple is similar to the one on Antwerp Cathedral. The design was awarded an honourable mention.

Far right: The entry of Andrew Rebori, who was also invited by the newspaper, was well-received and won an honourable mention. It was sober in style and the adornments were borrowed from various building styles.

James Gamble Rogers

Andrew Rebori

*Right: This design won an
honourable mention for Arthur
Frederick Adams from Kansas City,
Mo. The competition regulations
specified the type of drawing to be
submitted: its size, its perspective and
its colour — in this case, none at all.
To give some idea of size, a human
figure on at least one of the studies
had to be drawn in proportion to the
structure. Far right: Giotto inspired
design from G.S. Bliss and William B.
Faville, San Francisco.*

Arthur Frederick Adams

G.S. Bliss, William B. Faville

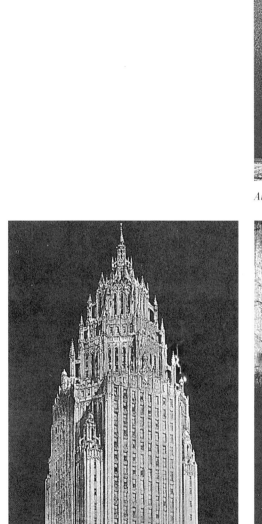

*Far left: Gothic style lent itself ideally
to huge vertical structures — a view
certainly shared by Frank J. Helmle
and Harvey Wiley Corbett.
Their design, however, failed to
capture the style's obvious elongated
form; it won no prizes.*

*Left: Schmidt, Garden and Martin,
a firm of architects from Chicago,
were also invited by the Chicago
Tribune, and their Gothic inspired
design received an honourable
mention.*

Frank J. Helmle, Harvey Wiley Corbett

Schmidt, Garden & Martin

Jarvis Hunt   *Benjamin Wistar Morris*

Parisian Ecole des Beaux Arts for the cladding; Gothicism, in particular, was extremely popular.

That the Chicago Tribune favoured traditional design was also evident from the choice of the jury. Its chairman was Alfred Granger, an architect who preferred buildings in the style of the Beaux Arts, while the other four members all contributed to the newspaper: Colonel Robert R. McCormick, Captain Joseph Medill Patterson, Edward S. Beck and Holmes Onderdonk. The jury was assisted by architectural adviser Howard Cheney, also from the more traditional camp.

Closing date for the entries was 1 November 1922, with a month's extra grace for submissions from abroad providing the jury was notified before 1 October. By 1 December, 204 designs had arrived with another 95 expected, although these were later excluded from taking part.

The designs were first submitted anonymously to Howard Cheney to see if they complied with the terms of the competition. 15 entries, including one from Jarvis Hunt in Chicago, were disqualified. From the remaining 189, 135 came from the United States and 54 from abroad. By 13 November the jury had already made a provisional choice, even though more entries were still expected.

First prize would go to design number 60; second prize to number 90; and third prize to number 104.

An advisory committee, comprising local councillors and town planners, also studied the designs and on 21 November drew up a shortlist of 12 designs including the three selected by the jury. On 27 November the jury took a second, secret vote.

Further foreign entries were arriving, but these in no way influenced the jury's choice, for the results of the second vote were identical to the first.

Among the recently arrived entries were a number of avant-garde designs which demonstrated that in Europe, at least, a new kind of building was emerging: more severe, with clean cut lines and with influences from De Stijl and Bauhaus schools. The jury members failed to recognize the modern elements in these designs. To them these austere entries were reminiscent of the stark buildings built in Chicago between 1880 and 1910, and were thus regarded as old-fashioned. Since more foreign entries were yet to come, the jury waited before announcing its definite verdict. On 29 November, two designs arrived from Finland that astonished the members of the jury. From then on, until the afternoon of 1 December, the jury was in almost continuous session deliberating what to do.

The jury finally decided to submit the three designs from the last ballot with design number 187 — the new arrival from Finland — for further detailed discussion.

Another ballot followed and the jury unanimously voted number 69 as winner. It was also unanimous about the second prize: number 187, the late arrival. Opinions differed about the third prize. Four jury members voted for number 90, while the chairman expressed a preference for number 104, submitted, as it turned out later, by A.F. Adams from Kansas City. In the minority, Alfred Granger withdrew his vote and the third prize was unanimously awarded to number 60.

In retrospect, it is clear that the jury did not act altogether

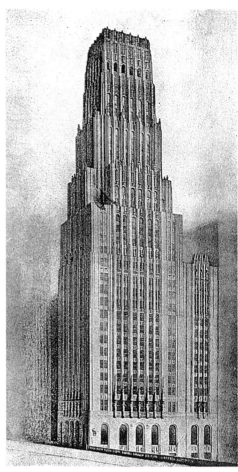

On the eve of the closing date for foreign entries, 29 November 1922, two Finnish designs arrived, one from Einar Sjostrom and Jarl Eklund, right, and the other from Eliel Saarinen. (left) The latter was particularly well-received by the jury, and they spent the rest of the day comparing and deliberating. The last minute entry was voted unanimously into second place.
Later, Saarinen's work was widely acclaimed, yet in 1981 Paul Goldberger wrote in his book The Skyscraper: 'Today the Saarinen design, while skilful, seems weaker than the winner — it has a quality of graciousness to it, but not the brilliance and genius ascribed to it.'

Eliel Saarinen

correctly. By taking preliminary votes when all the entries had not been received, an unequal situation arose. It can also be argued that the jury, whether consciously or not, exhibited nationalistic traits. Titles such as 'colonel' and 'captain' used by some jury members indicate, to some extent, certain patriotic attitudes. From the premature voting, too, it must be deduced that the jury subconsciously regarded the foreign entries as less important than the American ones.

These somewhat bold assumptions are reinforced by a sentence from the jury report: 'One of the gratifying results of the world competition was that it proved the superiority of the American designs . . .'

On 3 December 1922 the jury announced its decision.

First prize went to John Mead Howells and Raymond M. Hood, one of the firms invited by the Tribune. The sensational Finnish design was by Eliel Saarinen from Helsinki and the third prize went to Holabird and Roche, another firm that had been invited to take part in the competition.

The jury report concluded: 'When the winning design is executed we feel that the judgment of the Jury will be more than justified and the Tribune amply compensated for what it has done to elevate Commercial Architecture into the realm of the Fine Arts and create for its own administrative headquarters the most beautiful office building in the world to date, a fitting monument to the founders of the great middle west.'

When the office building was completed in 1925, few people saw it as the 'most beautiful and distinctive building in the world'. Today the building is mentioned in architectural books only as a typical skyscraper from the twenties, although there is usually some reference to the competition. A competition that produced superb contributions: a number of designs became almost more famous than the building itself.

Take the design of the unexpected (second prizewinner), Eliel Saarinen, made with the assistance of the Chicago architects, Dwight G. Wallace and Bertell Grenman. Soon after the competition, Louis H. Sullivan, the great architect reformer in the Chicago of the 1890s, wrote in the *Architectural Record* of February 1923: 'One glance of the trained eye, and instant judgment comes; that judgment comes, that judgment which flashes from inner experience, in recognition of a masterpiece. The verdict of the Jury of Award is at once reversed, and the second prize is placed first, where it belongs by virtue of its beautifully controlled and virile power.

The first prize is demoted to the level of those works of dying ideas, even as it sends forth a frantic cry to escape from the common bondage of those governed by ideas . . . The Finnish master-edifice is not a lonely cry in the wilderness, it is a voice, resonant and rich, ringing amidst the wealth and joy of life. In utterance sublime and melodious, it prophesies a time to come, and not so far away, when the wretched and the yearning, the sordid and the fierce, shall escape the bondage and the mania of fixed ideas.'

Further on Sullivan praises Saarinen on two counts. 'First that a Finlander who, in his prior experience, had no occasion to design a soaring office building, should as one to the manner

Einar Sjöstrom, Jarl Eklund

Nils Tvedt

Walter Burley Griffin

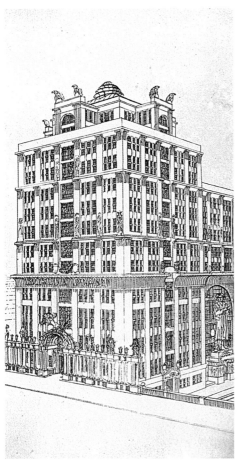

Wilhelm Hejda, Rudolf Tropsch

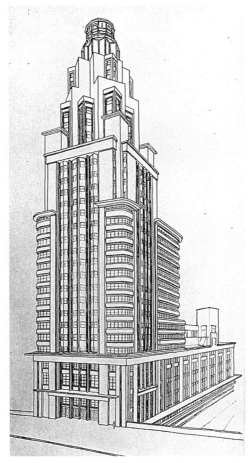

Thilo Schoder

Apart from the Gothic design of the Finns, Einar Sjostrom and Jarl Eklund, (above left,) the other foreign entrants were less influenced by neo-styles. The Norwegian, Nils Tvedt, a submitted a straightforward design in the classic style, above centre, which did not conform with the competition regulations.

Above right: Design submitted from Australia by Walter Burley Griffin.

Far left: Viennese architects Wilhelm Hejda and Rudolf Tropsch's design is reminiscent of the Sezession movement and the architectural style of turn-of-the-century Vienna. A remarkably large statue stands above the entrance of one of the side elevations.

Left: Contemporary vision from the German, Thilo Schoder, but he seemed to be at a loss on how to crown such a towering building.

Put all the entries together and they present a fascinating collage of a search to track down a true building style for a skyscraper. The Americans already had years of experience; initially they simply took the existing type of building and made it bigger. When this proved unsuccessful, they fell back on styles from the past, especially the decorative Gothic style of Ecole des Beaux-Arts. This meant the early rational approach to building, as witnessed in the first skyscrapers of Chicago, was more or less forgotten and regarded as 'old-fashioned'.

In Europe, however, architects were not inhibited by America's history, and after World War I young architects in particular were pre-occupied with 'tabula rasa': they wanted a complete break with the past. Their aim was a revolutionary new style of architecture: rational and simple of form.

The jury from the Chicago Tribune held out against these 'revolutionary' ideas, refusing to recognize the potential value to architecture of movements like De Stijl and Bauhaus. Only after the competition did the critics and experts begin to realize that, after all, these Europeans may have found just the answer to the 'right' design for a skyscraper.

born, have grasped the intricate problem of the lofty steel-framed structure, the significance of its origins, and held the solution unwaveringly in his mind, in such wise as no American architect has as yet shown the required depth of thought and steadfastness of purpose to achieve.'

Secondly, Sullivan was impressed 'that a foreigner should possess the insight required to penetrate to the depths of the sound, strong, kindly and aspiring idealism which lies at the core of the American people: one day to make them truly great sons of Earth; and that he should possess the poet's power to interpret and to proclaim in deep sympathy and understanding, incarnate in an edifice rising from Earth in response to this faith, an inspiring symbol to endure'.

The words are rather grandiloquent, but the intention is clear. And to those who might still fail to understand, Sullivan calls out almost in despair: 'Why did the men behind the Tribune throw this priceless pearl away? . . . These men made a solemn promise to the world. Why did they renege? Individually and jointly they made a triple promise as members of the Jury of Award. A design setting forth the most beautiful conception of a lofty building that has been evolved by the fertile mind of man, was presented squarely to them at the last moment. Were they frightened? Why did they welch?'

To Sullivan, the jury's choice was a brutish act, an act that deprived the world of a shining star, denied it a monument to beauty, faith, courage and hope. In conclusion, Sullivan sneeringly quoted that part of the Tribune's competition programme which repeatedly emphasized its intention to obtain the 'most beautiful building in the world'.

What does Saarinen's design have that prompted such admiring words? The design by Hood and Howells was typical for its time — a modern steel skeleton clad with a Gothic-style façade. The building has a clear understructure, a smooth and straight middle section and above this a recognizable culmination.

At first sight, Saarinen's design appears to be similar. It too gives a somewhat archaic, Gothic impression, but in its totality

the building has a more lyrical unity. Here, too, is a modest understructure, but this seems to blend into the straight vertical construction of the façade, which recedes almost imperceptibly. The culmination of the tower is not an afterthought but rises almost organically out of the design. The jury must take credit for immediately recognizing the remarkable design of Saarinen. It is understandable, however, that it clung to design number 69; the lines were familiar to the time, and the jury had already studied it for a month. Two days were hardly enough to fall for Saarinen's design, or to overcome a perhaps unconscious dislike of it because it was foreign.

The influence of Saarinen's design in the United States is undeniable, as can be seen in Raymond Hood's building for the New York *Daily News*, completed in 1930.

In 1923 Saarinen himself settled in the United States, and for him the competition was the beginning of a new era.

The competition, too, presented a varied picture of what was happening in architecture in 1922, which is why the Tribune

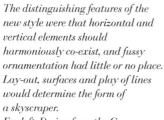

The distinguishing features of the new style were that horizontal and vertical elements should harmoniously co-exist, and fussy ornamentation had little or no place. Lay-out, surfaces and play of lines would determine the form of a skyscraper.
Far left: Design from the German team, Walter Gropius and Adolf Meyer.
Left: Design submitted by the German, Heribert Freiherr von Luttwitz.
Below left: Entry for the competition from B. Bijvoet and J. Duiker, a Dutch duo.
Centre: A German, Max Taut's, design.
Right: Study for the Chicago Tribune headquarters from Bruni Taut, in collaboration with Walter Gunther and Kurt Schutz.

Walter Gropius, Adolf Meyer

Heribert Freiherr von Luttwitz

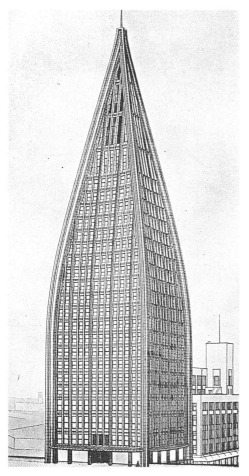

B. Bijvoet, J. Duiker

Max Taut

Bruno Taut, Walther Gunther, Kurt Schutz

123

K. Lønberg-Holm

organized a travelling exhibition of the submitted designs, which drew many visitors.

Judging from the European entries, the competition heralded a new concept in architecture, particularly evident in the designs submitted by Walter Gropius and Adolph Meyer, Bruno Taut, Bijvoet and Duiker, and Lonberg-Holm.

Their designs contained ideas about architecture that would strongly influence post-war building in the United States, but in 1922 America was not yet capable of recognizing these new forces; the shock of the new was too great.

The competition for an office building for the Chicago Tribune turned out to be unique. The men of the Tribune got theirs 'most beautiful building in the world'; a later generation got theirs by looking to the non-award-winning designs for inspiration. What the editor of the Chicago Tribune wrote in a leader of 3 December 1922 proved to be true. 'There never has been such a contest and it is very doubtful that there ever will be.'

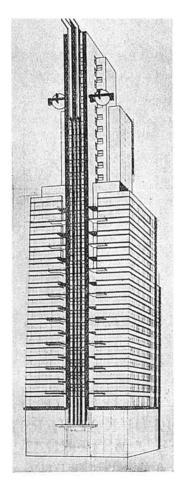

After the competition a book was published of most of the entries submitted. Among those that were omitted on request of the entrants was the design of K. Lønberg-Holm, although his work did not go unnoticed for long. According to the Dutch architect J.J.P. Oud, who published the design in November 1923, 'It was among the best the competition produced . . . Both the prizewinning and the runner-up design are pseudo-morphosis: modern requirements fossilised in time-worn, unartistic Gothicism . . . In comparison with these staid gentlemen, how fresh and vital, and far removed from all earlier traditional forms is the work of Lønberg-Holm.

It may not look 'properly' built but how much more modern it is, and how more realistically in keeping with what is required!'

The influence of this design can be seen in later American skyscrapers, such as the PSFS building in Philadelphia, from George Howe and William Lescaze (1929-1932).

Werkstatt für Massenform

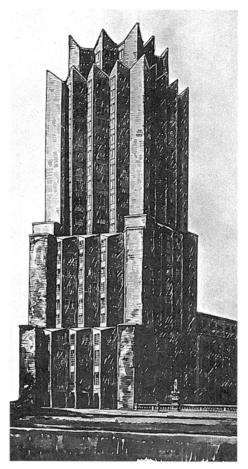

Gerhard Schröder

Above: Entry from the Viennese architect group, Werkstatt für Massenform.
Above right: Study from Gerhard Schroeder, Germany.

Right and far right: Designs by Fritz Sackermann, and Alb. H.W. Kruger and Hermann Zess (Germany).

Note: Turn to p.182 for an article by Dennis Sharp on the Chicago Tribune competition.

Fritz Sackermann

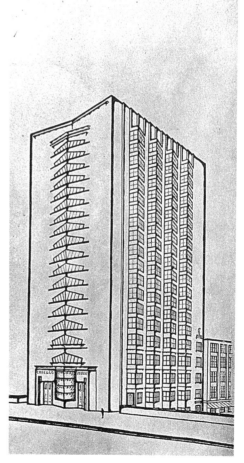

Alb. H.W. Kruger, Hermann Zess

Termini Station in Rome combines two designs. Its extensions were built in 1939 after a design by A. Mazzoni, who also planned an imposing colonnade for the main building, abandoned with the outbreak of World War II. The present main building dates from 1951 and is the outcome of an architectural competition organized in 1947. The winning team of six architects opted for a functional structure not entirely bereft of monumentality.

A modern Termini Station viewed from an ancient opening — an unusual illustration used for the cover of a publication on the new railway station published in 1951 by the Italian Union of Railway Engineers. The image is an appropriate one for the 'Eternal City', where new and old have been juxtaposed for more than 2,500 years.

TERMINI STATION IN ROME

NATIONAL ARCHITECTURAL COMPETITION FOR THE MAIN
BUILDING OF TERMINI STATION IN ROME.

ANNOUNCED: February 1947; result published; 31
October 1947; number of participants: 40

JURY: — five representatives of the Italian Railways:
G. di Raimondo, G.C. Pamieri, A. Gianelli,
E. Lo Cigno and R. Narducci; three representatives
from ministries: M. Visentini, R. Marino and
G. Nicolosi; a representative of the city of Rome:
A. Maccari; two representatives of the National
Society of Italian Engineers and Architects:
M. Urbinati and M. Paniconi; the secretary of the
study commission for the new station, R. Regnoni.

WINNERS: First prize: Leo Calini and Eugenio
Monuori; Massimo Castellazzi, Vasco Fadigati,
Achille Pintonello and Annibale Vitelozzi (runner
up); shared second prize: Vittorio Immirzi, Luigi
Cosenza, Francesco della Sala, Adriano Galli,
Guglielmo Ricciardi and Raffaello Salvatori; Saul
Greco; Claudio Longo Gerace shared third prize:
Casare Pascoletti; Bruno Ronca and Carlo Mutinelli;
Alfredo Scalpelli, Pietro Lombardi and Marco
Fagioli; Achille Petrignani, Constantino Forleo and
Nello Ena; Eugenio Rossi and Alberto Tonelli;
Mario Ridolfi, Ludovici Quaroni, Aldo Cardelli,
Mario Fiorentino, Giulio Ceradini and Enrico Caré;
Leonato Favini and Mariano Pallotini; Robaldo
Morozzo della Rocca and Carlo Domenico Rossi.

CONSTRUCTION: 1947-1951 (Leo Calini, Eugenio
Montuori, Massimo Castellazzi, Vasco Fadigati,
Achille Pintonello and Annibale Vitelozzi).

ROME IS NICKNAMED THE ETERNAL CITY, which seems fairly appropriate, given that it was founded more than 27 centuries ago. It has survived countless rulers and governments, enjoyed great prosperity and endured serious decline. The city centre bears many traces of its rich past. Remains of Imperial Rome stand side by side with monuments from the mighty days of the Popes; Renaissance masterworks alternate with ostentatious pomp from the Fascist period. The Romans themselves treat these relics of their past with respect, whilst to tourists they are among the greatest attractions Rome has to offer. There is scarcely any other city where the visitor is confronted to the same degree with the transience of worldly power.

ROME'S TERMINI STATION has a history all its own. This is no more than a 150 years old, but it is a typical Roman story. The station stands at the edge of the old city centre, and is surrounded by old buildings — such as the temple of Minerva, the Porta San Lorenzo and the Church of Santa Maria Maggiore. Moreover, placed obliquely against the front elevation, there is part of a wall dating from the fourth century BC, 80 metres long and up to nine metres high.
When, in the mid–nineteenth century, it was decided to build a station on this site, many thought it was an absurd choice: one of the highest points in Rome — 80 metres above sea level — and at that time still open country. However, a great many personal interests influenced the decision, not least the fact that the influential bishop, Saverio de Merode, owned large stretches of land in the area, which would rise considerably in value if the station were built there. It was characteristic of papal Rome in those days that the bishop got his way: influential people held posts in a number of secular and ecclesiastical administrative bodies. There was a constant interweaving of personal and professional interests; power lay

Architect Salvatore Bianchi's design was used for an earlier station built between 1864 and 1879. This quickly became too small to cope with Rome's growing status; in 1878 the city became the capital and more than ever a centre for trade and commerce. Above: Photograph of the former station taken shortly after completion. It was continually being improved and extended; a more drastic solution was needed.

in the hands of scheming manipulators.

In 1862 a temporary station was opened on this site, and in 1864 the building of a permanent station began. This station was designed by architect Salvatore Bianchi, and the story goes that the then Pope, Pius IX, exclaimed on seeing the drawings, 'Bravo, bravo, I see you want to build a station that befits the capital of Italy'.

These proved to be prophetic words. In 1870, a year before Bianchi's station started being used, the Pope lost his secular power. Rome did indeed become the capital of the young kingdom of Italy, proclaimed in 1860, and the Pope withdrew, as a nominal prisoner, to the Vatican.

Although Bianchi's station may have been a princely design for the residence of a Pope, as the main station for a capital it was soon inadequate. The railway network expanded fast in the years that followed, and before long Rome became what statesman Cavour had already predicted in 1846: 'The centre of the entire Mediterranean coast, which, situated on the road

from Orient to Occident, will attract streams of people from many countries.' As early as 1885 the station was totally inadequate and after 1905 it was constantly being adapted and expanded.

But only in 1937 was it decided to replace the station. Mussolini was then in power, and the design to which he gave his approval accorded exactly with his ideas. Il Duce favoured monumental architecture; he wanted the glory of the Roman Empire to be revived in modern Italy. This meant new buildings of a grandeur consonant with that of ancient Rome. However, they must also be modern, and for this to be achieved the most advanced building methods and materials would have to be used.

The designer of the new station was A. Mazzoni, chief architect of the Italian Railway Society. His grand gesture was a façade of 185 metres, consisting almost entirely of huge colonnades. The outer colonnade was 42 metres deep, the inner one 24 metres. These spacious areas were intended to be mere passageways: all amenities for passengers and railway offices were situated in two wings. Only the cellar of the main building was functionally planned: it would accommodate an *albergo diurno* — a kind of daytime hotel — a church and a cinema.

The main building would be sumptuously faced with marble, the pillars would be some 18 metres high, with spans of about 40 metres. The grandeur of the scheme would be reinforced still further by having the front elevation moved back 200 metres; this would proportionally enlarge the station precinct. This, too, was done at the expense of functionality: the already

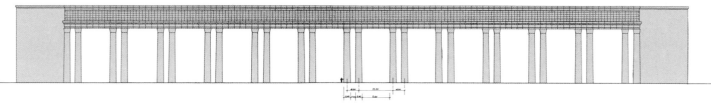

SEZIONE TRASVERSALE

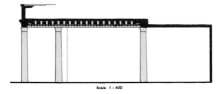

Scala 1 : 400

In 1938, the architect, A. Mazzoni, designed a monumental station to replace the 1879 building. Its most impressive feature was a giant double colonnade at the front, which had no apparent function other than to command respect from the travellers passing through it.
Left page: Mazzoni's study for the new Rome station.
Above: His cross-section and drawing of its façade, 1947. Entrants for the competition were requested to use the same measurements for the main

building as in Mazzoni's plan: a 185-metre-wide façade, with 18-metre-high columns, each spanning 40 metres.

short railway yard would become very cramped, and because of the steep incline at the other end it was impossible for it to be extended on that side. However, a publication of the time noted that, 'the design provides a unique, spacious colonnade, offering the public in the station square a view of the trains, whilst giving passengers the sensation of having arrived in the heart of the city, surrounded by the imposing relics of the Roman Empire'. In addition, 'this spacious precinct would, on the occasion of exhibitions, pilgrimages and other important events, be capable of coping swiftly with large numbers of people, who would receive a lasting impression of grandeur and power'.

In an official report, many deficiencies of the design were noted, and particular mention was made of the high costs expected, as well as constructional difficulties. But 'because traffic is constantly increasing and the conquest of Ethiopia (1936) had turned Italy into an Empire, and the World Exhibition of 1942 is approaching apace', there seemed little advantage in postponing the building of the new station. In

One of the joint winners of the 1947 competition was the design of Leo Calini and Eugenio Montuori. Its façade was severe, apart from a row of windows on its upper storey, and a 32-metre-wide relief. It was five metres shorter than Mazzoni's extensions, partly because the spacious central hall and restaurant were 'eased' forward, either side of the Aggere di Servio Tullio. The plan had

the motto 'Servio Tullio prende il treno' (Servius Tullius takes the train), to indicate the way in which the old wall of the station was incorporated into the new design.

Top: Design of Massimo Castellazzi, Vasco Fadigati, Achille Pintonello and Annibale Vitallozzi which won joint first prize. Like the other prizewinner, it had a restrained façade with the station's main public hall and restaurant projected each side of the Aggere. In an introduction to their design, the architects stated that they had deliberately avoided all architectonic rhetoric. They did, however, span an enormous arch over the main entrance.

Below: Final design for the station, made jointly by the prizewinners. The 1949 sketch is by Eugenio Montuori.

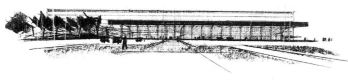

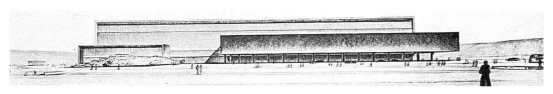

The runners-up also went for fairly austere designs. Claudio Longo Gerace's design, above, comprising three building blocks connected by passageways, was the most extreme. The jury's verdict was 'clear lay-out and use of space' but the details were 'insufficiently thought out'. Vittorio Immirzi's team plumped for a design (above it) that had an a-symmetric façade in which its separate components were distinguished in various building materials. The jury, while accepting the new trend away from being overtly concerned with exterior problems, thought many of the building's other solutions 'insufficiently practical'.

February 1938 demolition of the old station was begun and in 1939 the new building was started.

But before it was ready, power once again changed hands in Rome. The outbreak of World War II delayed construction, and when in 1943 Mussolini was deposed, only the two wings of the station had been completed.

That was the situation when shortly after the end of the war, in 1946, new plans were prepared. Mazzoni's design was now totally superseded; the dominant mood in Italy was one of wanting to wipe the slate clean. A study commission of 16 people — ten representatives of the Railways, two from ministries, and four from the city of Rome, set to work energetically. In July 1946 they met for the first time, in January 1947 they decided to hold a national architectural competition, and by the end of February the competition was published. It was clear from the programme sent on request to prospective participants that Mazzoni's ideas had been radically rejected.

The most important stipulations were a reduction in size of the station square and a lengthening of the railway yard by at least 50 metres. The main building would also have to be given a new function: it would have to house all passenger facilities. The upper stories of the main building also had to be used: all the district offices, then scattered throughout the city, were to be accommodated here.

No specific requirements were mentioned as to the design —

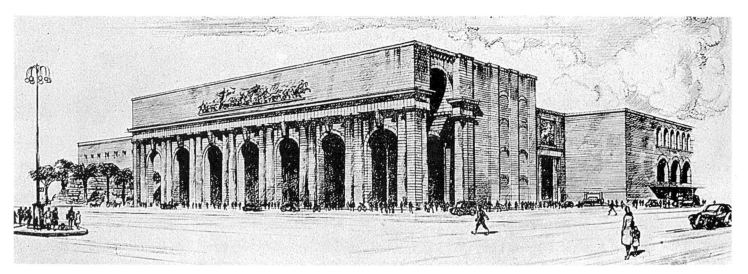

Many of the winners awarded third prize looked over their shoulders for inspiration. Above: The design from Ronca and Mutinelli is entirely in keeping with its Roman surroundings; a feature applauded by the judges, even if the building itself was described as 'exceedingly high'. Left: The building of Achille Petrignani is almost an exact replica of Mazzoni's design — strange if one considers that the search was actually for a more functional alternative. The architects wanted their building to be in 'perfect harmony with the existing extensions'. Their plan, unlike Mazzoni's, added several facilities to the main building.

monumentality was not demanded — although the old wall — the Aggere di Servio Tullio — should be conserved. The design of the new station had to be in harmony with it. More than that: the Aggere had to be exploited as a decorative element and must remain completely visible. It would also be a recommendation if the building materials already purchased and stored for Mazzoni's colonnades could be used.

DESIGNS HAD TO BE SUBMITTED by 30 June 1947; the jury took four months to judge the 40 entries. For a long time, opinions must have been divided — hardly surprising in view of the fact that it was a very large jury. Moreover, its members represented widely divergent interests which in the past had often conflicted. The eventual result was that the three available prizes were distributed among as many as 13 participants, while another six designs received honourable mention.

In its report the jury admitted that the issue had been chiefly settled by practical considerations: 'The functional element was paramount' and 'in making its judgment the commission had considered not only the structural possibilities but also the financial implications.' Even so, the architectural aspect 'weighed heavily'; it had led to the selection of those plans that 'have in an intelligent and modern way combined severity and decorum, not from a desire for the monumental but because of the special function of a building that should be in

harmony with its surroundings, of equal merit with them and not subordinate to them'.

Two projects were recommended for the first prize. They were the design submitted under the motto *Servio Tullio prende il treno* (Servius Tullius takes the train) by Calini and Montuori, because of its 'optimal planimetric solution and its clear architecture'; and the design submitted under the motto 'Y = 0.005 x 2' by Castellazzi, Fadigati, Pintonello and Vitellozzi, particularly because of its 'clear composition of spaces'. It was noted that 'both designs would be realizable within modest means and that, in spite of their boldness and elegance, no particular constructional difficulties could be foreseen'.

The second prize went to three projects that also aspired to modern design, but which, although possessing considerable merits, also displayed some fairly severe deficiencies. Gerace's design (*l'Uomo e l'edificio*, or, Man and his building) had not been worked out in sufficient detail; in Greco's design ('V 14') the aesthetic form was not in keeping with the function of a station, and in the design by Immirzi et al. *Rinascita*, or (Rebirth) insufficient regard had been paid to functionality. More remarkable, however, than the awards of the first and second prizes are the projects that were selected *ex aequo* for a third prize. In this category there was a wide variety of designs. In choosing them, the jury seemed somewhat to have lost sight of its initial ideas as to what kind of design it was looking for. Although the jury report stated that 'projects should

Designs that won third prize also displayed a penchant for colonnades in all shapes and sizes and were placed either behind, over, or next to the Aggere di Servio Tullio. In the designs from Favini, above, and Pascoletti, above right, the entire Aggere is outside the building. Favini placed a colonnade of modest proportions next to it, and added a stylised one along the length of the building behind. Pascoletti gave deliberate 'maximum, monumental expression' to his right hall in order to give the remaining parts of the building a neutral form.
Centre right: Robaldo Morozza della Rocca and Carlo Dominico Rossi submitted this design under the motto 'Independenza', or Independence. They allowed the Aggere to intrude right into the colonnade and into a courtyard, where a bar and restaurant was planned.

Mario Ridolfi also let the Aggere run into their design of the new station, with the intention of creating an unbroken line 'which would act as a natural barrier for the tracks, and bridge both extensions of the building'. They continued: 'The façade of the station may appear to be far too wide, but even so it hardly counterbalances the massive breadth of its immediate setting.' The jury described the design as 'a courageous and interesting attempt to express grandeur using modern, architectonic means'. Huge constructional problems were predicted, however, which would lead to a too big investment.

demonstrate the greatest possible detachment from a stylistically superseded and no longer contemporary architecture', some of the winning designs are all too clearly reminiscent of Mazzoni's plan. Seven of them have colonnades, though admittedly most of these are modern in form. *B3* especially, by Ronco and Mutinelli, clearly smacks of archaism and monumentality, and yet the jury speaks appreciatively of its classical form, calling it 'correctly interpreted'.
Probably many of the jury members still felt considerable affinity with 'stylistically superseded forms'. But this did not accord with the ideas of post-war reconstruction: a project of this kind had to be as businesslike as possible, and the demands of functionality and economy had to prevail.

THE WAY IN WHICH THE CONSTRUCTION of the new station was carried out is also characteristic of those post-war years. In order to prevent further loss of time, commission to build was given to both winning teams; together they would have to come up with a new design. This was done with equal speed: in November 1947 the official building contract was conferred, and in January 1948 building began on the new station. The final project was not a combination of the two winning designs: it was a new plan which strove even more strongly to exploit the features of the site. The architects had apparently

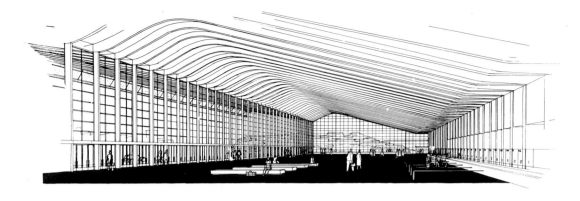

The station finally built is frequently admired for its large, airy booking hall with its 'wavy' roof; its feeling for space, and its unrestricted views of the platforms and station square. Yet the hall was not part of any of the winning designs — it was only developed after the two winning teams got down to work.

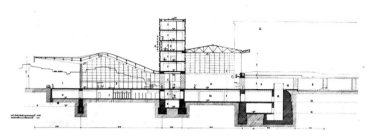

Below: 1949 maquette of the definite design for the station.
Left: Cross section at main entrance level with, from left, the awning; booking hall; five-storey office building; Galleria di Testa — an indoor passageway, between the Via Giolitti and the Via Marsala, built on both side of the station, with shops, banks and a hotel — and the roofed-in platforms. Left in the background, a fine line indicates the contours of the Aggere di Servio Tullio.

felt challenged and inspired by the vast empty space between the two wings of the station.

When in 1951 the new Termini Station was opened, the reactions of the architectural press were unanimously enthusiastic. They praised the beautiful texture of the front elevation, the magnificent ticket hall with its enormous expanses of glass and its vaulted roof, and the bold way in which the old wall had been integrated in the design, between ticket hall and restaurant. This praise of detail was invariably accompanied by some phrase implying that the station was more than a sum of its parts.

What appealed in particular to the critics was that these architects had, after all, made a grand gesture. A German journal called it 'Maniera Romana'. And rightly so: where else but in Rome could a building, conceived during the post-war reconstruction years marked by scarcity and haste, make such a bid for eternity? In order to win the competition, the architects had to show the functional superiority of their design. Once they had received the commission to build, another competition was added: they had to pit their wits against the demands of a setting soaked in history. They realized that there was no choice: the building would have to be both functional *and* monumental.

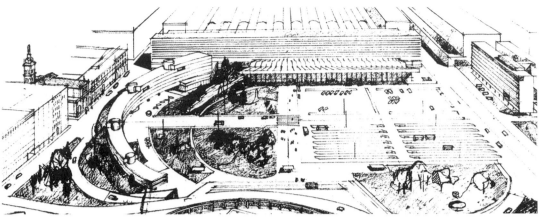

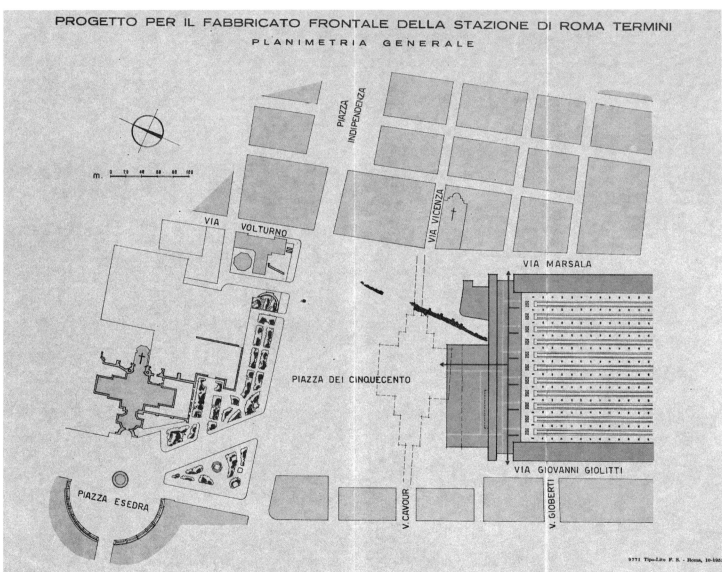

PROGETTO PER IL FABBRICATO FRONTALE DELLA STAZIONE DI ROMA TERMINI
PLANIMETRIA GENERALE

PIAZZA INDIPENDENZA

VIA VOLTURNO

VIA VICENZA

VIA MARSALA

PIAZZA DEI CINQUECENTO

VIA GIOVANNI GIOLITTI

V. CAVOUR

V. GIOBERTI

PIAZZA ESEDRA

9771 Tipo-Lito F. S. - Roma, 10-1951

Above left: Glass façade and entrance of Termini Station creates only a minimal barrier between the openness of the square and the spaciousness of the station hall.

The sheer size of Piazza dei Cinquecento, the station's square, had bothered many for a long time. In the site, above, made in 1951, can be seen how the designers of the new station tried to make the square smaller : its façade has been built right up to the Aggere di Servio Tullio, while its booking hall, directly under, and restaurant, above, have been built at the top of the square. Opposite the

station are the remains of the Baths of Diocletian. Since the 1960s an attempt has been made to relieve the enormous pressure of traffic on the Piazza dei Cinquecento, including a proposal, top of the page, developed in 1975, by Eugenio Montuori, together with son Franscesco and Studio Moretti, which has only partly been carried out.

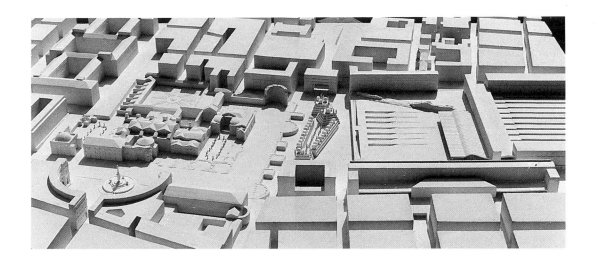

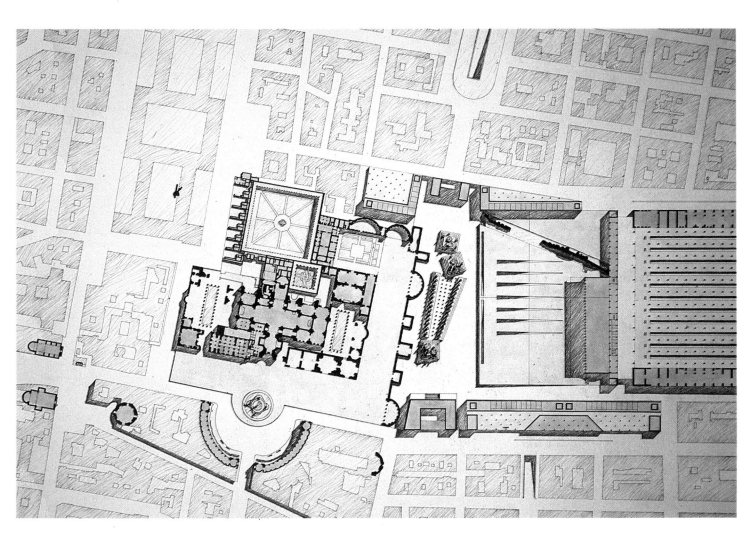

Above and below: Since the early 1980s, Franscesco Montuori, Anna di Notti and Guiseppe Milane have been working on a plan for the square which would drastically reduce its size. At the top of its incline, directly in front of the station, a car-free plateau, reached via seven steps, is planned. Underneath this, would be more parking facilities and other transport services. The scheme would also change the face of the square between the plateau and the Baths of Diocletian by adding more buildings, including pavilions.

SYDNEY OPERA HOUSE

INTERNATIONAL ARCHITECTURAL COMPETITION FOR AN
OPERA HOUSE IN SYDNEY, NEW SOUTH WALLES,
AUSTRALIA.

ANNOUNCED: May 1956; result published: 29 January
1957.

JURY: four architects: Eero Saarinen, USA;
J.L. Martin, England; Henry Ingham Ashworth,
Australia; Gobden Parkes, Australia; number of
participants: 233

WINNERS: 1. Jörn Utzon, Denmark; 2. J. Marzella,
L. Loschetter, W. Cunningham, W. Weisman,
N. Brecher, R. Geddes and G. Qualls, USA; 3.
Boissevain & Osmond, England.

CONSTRUCTION: 1957-1973 (Jörn Utzon, until 1963;
after that date Peter Hall, Lionel Todd and David
Littlemore).

THE OPERA HOUSE IN SYDNEY is one of the most controversial
buildings in the world. It is justly famous for its striking
appearance, with its gleaming white, shell-shaped roofs on a
spit of land called Bennelong Point. But at the same time it
has won notoriety because of its troubled genesis; building
seemed to go on interminably and the costs rocketed to seven
times the original estimate. Not to mention the drama that
took place between architect and sponsors, reaching its climax
when the architect, Jörn Utzon, resigned halfway through the
building process. This history is still well-known throughout
the architectural world as a horrifying example of how almost
everything can go wrong.

How did Sydney decide on an opera house? John Yeomans, a
journalist living in Sydney, was intrigued by this question and
found the following answer in 1967: 'Because a London
conductor of Belgian descent, determined to lodge the Sydney
Symphony Orchestra in a good permanent home, convinced a
Labour Party politician that Sydney needed a new cultural
and musical centre; the politician became so obsessed with the
idea that he pushed it through against all opposition from
within his own party or outside it.'

The people of Sydney themselves, wrote Yeomans, would never
ask for an opera house: they 'love the sun and the sea, excel in
outdoor sports and don't give a damn for either architecture or
opera.' But he hastened to add that he is 'in this case

everlastingly grateful to the manipulators who managed to
pilot the scheme past all obstacles'. He then goes on to praise
the opera house as 'an unforgettable palace built not for sports
but for the arts, a palace which, whether you like or dislike
this or that detail, gives off such an indestructible aura of
magnificence that it is hard not to think of it as another Taj
Mahal'.

Perhaps Yeomans exaggerates somewhat, but the fact remains
that few people in Sydney shared the desire for an opera
house. The spiritual father of the idea was Eugene Goossens,
from 1947 director of the city Music Conservatory and
conductor of Sydney's successful Symphony Orchestra. In the
early 1950s Goossens observed that in this increasingly
prosperous, fast-growing city there was no decent
accommodation for his orchestra. Alluding to the new opera
house in San Francisco he worked upon the feelings of
J.J. Cahill, Labour premier of the State of New South Wales,
who saw here an opportunity to improve the image of his
party. By acquiring a sensational music centre, Sydney would
be able to triumph over its rival city of Melbourne.

In November 1954 Cahill set up a small committee of
prominent city councillors and architects which was to advise
the government upon ways in which to realize his plans for an
opera house. The committee was assisted by the Royal
Australian Institute of Architects which appointed three

View from the east of the Sydney Opera House, which is actually three buildings, each with its own shell-shaped roof. The two largest, at the far end of Bennelong Point Pier, accommodate five theatres with seating for 5,500. In the smaller building behind are restaurants and a bar. Enclosing the buildings is a terrace and promenade — always well-visited because of the fine harbour views.

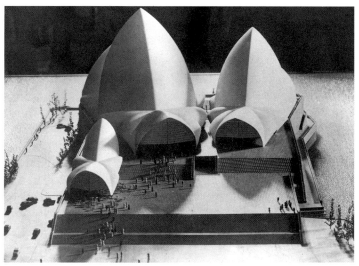

Above: Maquette of the winning design submitted by the Dane, Jörn Utzon, for the Sydney Opera House.
Left: Close encounters, from left to right, Utzon, Erik Andersson, his right-hand man, and Robert Quentin, general manager, Elizabethan Trust Opera Co.
Both pictures were taken in 1957.

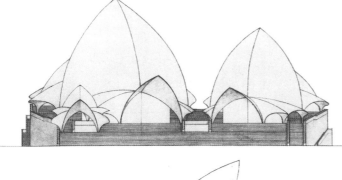

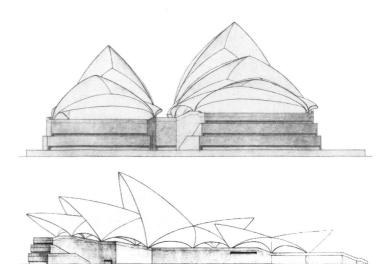

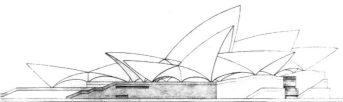

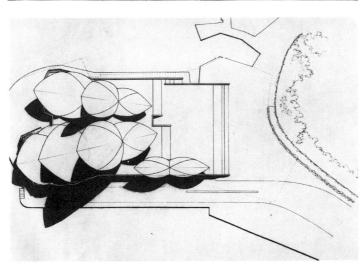

Utzon's opera house viewed from all angles. Top, south front with steps and entrances; top right, north front at the end of the pier; centre, east front (left) and west front; above, general plan.

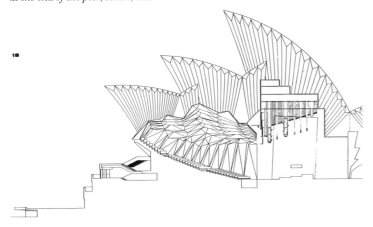

The shell-shaped roofs of the original winning design proved technically impossible to build, and it was only in 1962 that Utzon came up with a solution. He made the roof-components spherical instead of elliptic so that together they formed one huge globe — a step not without important consequences, but which, in fact, saved the design. Utzon presented his new vision in a so-called Yellow Book, from which this cross-section of the new roof is taken. The acoustic ceiling of the large auditorium and the stage tower in the main building can also be seen.

well-known architects to choose one out of thirty available sites. These three men, Henry Ingham Ashworth, Denis Winston and Walter Bunning, unanimously expressed their preference for Bennelong Point. They also agreed that there was only one way in which to obtain the best possible design: by holding an international competition.

In retrospect it is surprising that the competition was organized so quickley, before anyone was clear about how the project was to be financed. It is typical of the climate of growth and construction then prevalent not only in Sydney but throughout the young federation of Australia in those prosperous post-war years. If you wanted to get a thing done, you got up and did it. In May 1956 a 25-page booklet was published, setting out the conditions in detail of the competition. The main brief was a design for an opera house suitable for all kinds of dramatic art. Calling the building an opera house was in keeping with the grandeur of the gesture, but it was misleading from the start: the new building would in the first place be for the symphony orchestra. The programme required 'a large auditorium and a somewhat smaller one, as well as a restaurant and various other accommodations'. The large auditorium would have to be suitable for — in order of priority — symphony orchestras, large-scale operatic performances, ballet and dance, choirs, mass meetings and spectacles. It should hold between 3000 and 3500 people. The smaller auditorium, seating about 1200 people, would have to be suitable for stage performances, small opera, chamber music, concerts and recitals, and lectures.

It was a very complex briefing which nevertheless attracted a great deal of interest: 721 architects asked for the booklet, and paid the registration fee of 20 Australian dollars. After consideration, over two thirds of them decided not to participate, but at least it filled the purse with money for prizes.

The 233 participants who submitted their designs before the closing date in December 1957 came from all over the world. There were 61 from Australia, 53 from England, 26 from Germany, and 24 from the United States. The other entrants were from 27 other countries, ranging from Denmark, France and Switzerland to Japan, Egypt, Singapore and Ethiopia.

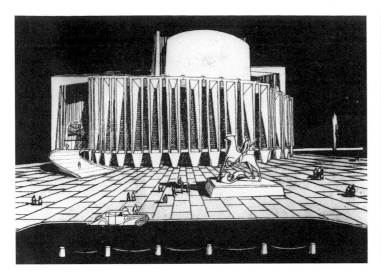

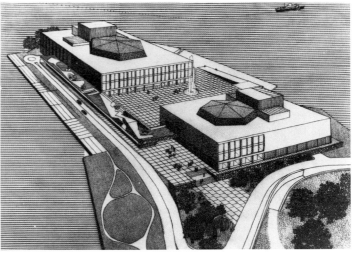

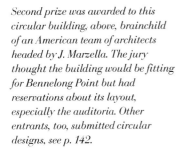

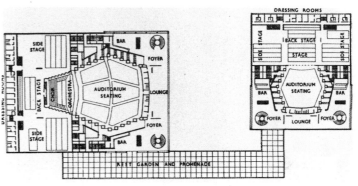

Second prize was awarded to this circular building, above, brainchild of an American team of architects headed by J. Marzella. The jury thought the building would be fitting for Bennelong Point but had reservations about its layout, especially the auditoria. Other entrants, too, submitted circular designs, see p. 142.

see p. 142.

Boissevain and Osmond gained third prize for designing the auditoria in two structures built around a square. The jury praised the plan but regarded the facilities for the auditoria as 'too ambitious': it meant having double the amenities, when these could all be combined under the roof of one single building.

This tremendous interest was not only due to the attractiveness of the briefing, but because the jury inspired confidence among architects: it consisted exclusively of colleagues. Apart from Ashworth there was Cobden Parkes, also from Australia, who was government architect, that is, director of public works in New South Wales. Then there were two foreign architects, both of international repute. One of these was an Englishman, J.L. Martin, designer of the London Festival Hall and professor of architecture at Cambridge University. The other was Eero Saarinen from the United States, who had worked together with his father Eliel until the latter's death in 1950, and who had in recent years caused a stir with sculptural architecture like the Kresge Auditorium in Cambridge, Massachusetts.

Another point in its favour was that the competition was organized according to the rules of the game: Ashworth had made sure that the conditions of both the International Institute of Architects and those of the British and American architects' organizations were complied with. Neither coloured perspective drawings, nor maquettes were permitted; only line drawings were allowed. Even so, an entry could be quite large: some participants submitted more than thirty sheets of detailed designs. No limit was placed on the number of drawings, and architecturally, entrants had great freedom. A design would be excluded from further consideration only if it did not offer the accommodation required. Furthermore, participants were given the opportunity to acquire more information. Questions were collected during several months and the replies were then sent simultaneously to all participants.

ON 29 JANUARY THE RESULT of the competition was announced by Premier Cahill. Only three prizes were awarded: a sum of 2,000 Australian dollars to the winners of the third prize, Boissevain and Osmond from London; 4,000 dollars to the large American partnership of J. Marzella, L. Loschetter, W. Cunningham, W. Weissman, N. Brecher, R. Geddes and G. Qualls, joint winners of the second prize; and 10,000 dollars together with the building assignment to the winner, Jörn Utzon, from Denmark.

The jury set out in detail the considerations that had influenced their decision. First they had examined how the design was located, in other words, whether the building would be shown to best advantage at the Bennelong Point site. Secondly they had studied the internal organization, paying special attention to the flow of traffic. The architectural interest of a design had been a constant consideration. The jury wrote: 'We have been impressed by the beauty and the exceptional possibilities of the site in relation to the harbour and we are convinced that the silhouette of any proposed building is of the greatest importance. We feel strongly that a large and massive building, however practical, would be entirely unsuitable on this particular site.'

The jury had been struck by the wide variety among the designs, though it was recognized that this was not surprising, since designers were 'free to produce conceptions which might vary very considerably'. But this freedom had also led to a general underestimation of the demands of traffic, whilst by contrast the stage requirements had been rather exaggerated. The jury: 'We feel convinced that the special requirements of the stage in Sydney could be met by an adequate but

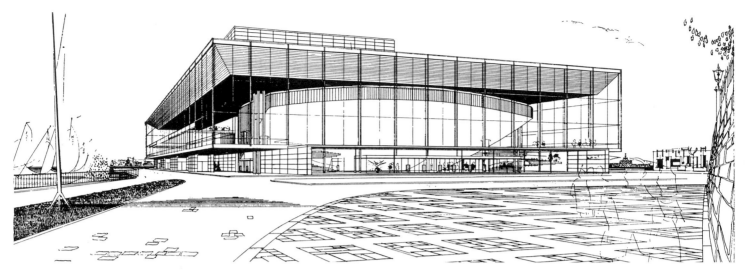

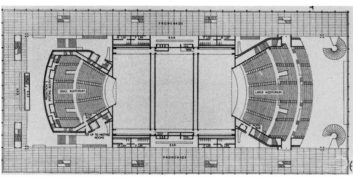

Top and left: The English team of
Dunster and Staughton placed the
stages of the two most important
auditoria facing one another, in

contrast to George Subiotto's plan,
below, which put maximum distance
between them.

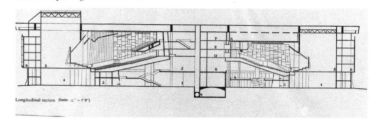

Longitudinal section Scale ½" = 1'0"

economical arrangement.'

About 20 designs received particularly favourable judgments
but as it had not been part of the jury's briefing to award the
prizes, only their names were mentioned. Each of the three
winning combinations was remarkable in its own way:
Marzella and Co. because of its robust building with
spiral-shaped ground plan which, according to the jury, 'would
form a total mass well suited to its position on Bennelong
Point... although the disadvantage of any spiral form of this
kind is a possibility of restriction and limitation of plan
arrangement.' Boissevain and Osmond had opted for two
separate buildings for the large and the small hall, and their
plan was praised for its 'simple arrangement of building
designed with a human scale and well placed around a
pedestrian promenade'. But the stage provisions were
considered 'too ambitious'.

Practical considerations of this kind were virtually absent
from the comments on Utzon's plan. Here the jury noted
saying that 'the drawings submitted for this scheme are simple
to the point of being diagrammatic'. Nevertheless, said the
report, 'we are convinced that they present a concept of an
opera house that is capable of becoming one of the great
buildings of the world. We consider this scheme to be the most
original and creative submission. Because of its very
originality, it is clearly a controversial design'.

The greatest merits of Utzon's design, according to the jury,
were its 'great simplicity of arrangement', 'the unity of its
structural expression', 'its striking architectural composition',
in which the 'white sail-like forms of the shell vaults relate as
naturally to the harbour as the sails of its yachts'.

Several reservations were made regarding the internal
arrangement of Utzon's design, and corrections would no
doubt prove necessary, but these objections were quickly
passed. Almost casually, it was added that the design would
probably also be one of the cheapest, at least according to the
rough estimates that had been made of all the prizewinning
designs as well as of several others.

NO SOONER HAD THE WINNER been announced than strange
rumours began to circulate. One of these, was that Eero
Saarinen, who was the last jury member to arrive and who
had left again a few days before the result was published, had
favoured Utzon. He was even said to have picked Utzon's
design out of a pile of rejected plans, with the remark:
'Gentleman, here is the winner.' This incident is mentioned by
authoritative architectural writers including Siegfried Giedion,
but both Parkes and Asworth, when asked, denied the story.
The only basis for it was probably the fact that Saarinen was
extremely taken with Utzon's design. He must have felt an
immediate attraction towards this expressive sculptural art,
which was akin to his own ideas. The form was here allowed to
be more than a reflection of the function, still a radical notion
in the architecture of the 1950s. But how much or how little
difficulty Saarinen had in persuading his fellow jurors is not
known.

Another rumour was that Utzon's design was far from being
completed. He was said to have submitted a number of
drawings more or less on the off-chance, without the slightest
expectation of success. This rumour was probably not only
prompted by the diagrammatic nature of Utzon's design —

which seems supported by the fact that the jury asked A.N. Baldwinson after the competition to make a coloured perspective drawing of the design for the exhibition — but also by Utzon's previous record. He had built very little, only one housing project of 63 low-budget homes. However, Utzon, at 38, was well-known in Scandinavia and elsewhere for his spectacular competition entries. He was a pupil of Alvar Aalto and Gunnar Asplund, was influenced by the town planner Steen Eiler Rasmussen and had in 1948 been introduced to Le Corbusier and the French sculptor, Henri Laurens, who had taught him to create shapes in space. He had also travelled extensively in the United States and Mexico, where he found inspiration in the work of Frank Lloyd Wright and in Aztec architecture. In brief, as an architect he might be a beginner, but he was a committed searcher, for whom architecture was certainly no frivolous pastime.

Utzon knew his limitations only too well. For 18 months after receiving the award he had only one concern: to find out exactly what the problems were and to surround himself with good advisers. Among these, the London construction bureau,

Ove Arup and Associates, played a crucial role. Others, including S. Malmquist for stage technique and V.L. Jordan for acoustics, were equally important.

In March 1958 Utzon had a provisional plan ready for his opera house, which he published in his Red Book. In this he listed a number of anticipated difficulties and put forward possible solutions. It was a tricky business, for instance, that the two largest halls were to be placed side by side on the headland, which would restrict the width of both. To overcome the problem of having too narrow a stage or podium, it was suggested that all scene shifts should take place vertically. An even greater problem was the construction of the roofs. Utzon had realized from the outset that it would not be easy to construct such huge shell-shaped roofs, certainly not on a spit of land in a windy harbour. In the Red Book no solution was offered, and Ove Arupe concluded his worried comments on this particular aspect with the observation that extensive experiments with models would have to be made.

It has often been said in retrospect that if only Utzon had been given more time, and if only the government had retained

The Austrian, Wilhelm Holzbauer, had only graduated a year earlier when he sent in this design for the Sydney Opera House. The jury were especially taken with the way Holzbauer exploited the site to maximum advantage; unsurprisingly, he was one of twenty who received a special mention in the jury report.

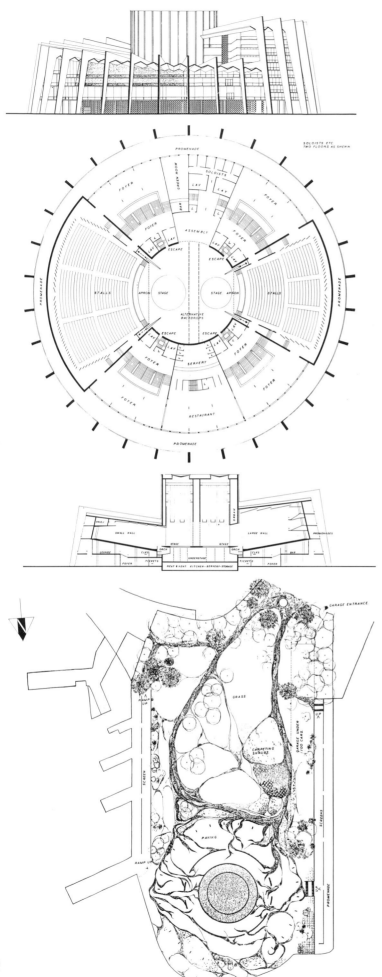

complete confidence in him, much trouble could have been avoided. It is true that even Cahill's well-disposed government was unwilling to postpone building until the structural problems had been solved. By the summer of 1958 a timetable had been drawn up, dividing the building work into three phases — understructure, roofs and interior — each of which would have to be completed within a specified period. In March 1959 a start was made: the foundations, stairs and podia were to be completed before anything could be said with certainty about the roofs.

WHEN UTZON FINALLY SOLVED THE PROBLEM of the roof, it was indeed a dramatic event. By then it was 1962, Ove Arup's bureau had spent more than a hundred thousand man-hours investigating shell roofs, but no satisfactory manner of construction had been found. Utzon himself then had the brilliant idea that the shells, instead of being elliptical, should be shaped in such a way that they formed, as it were, part of the same large sphere. They would then all have the same curvature, and could be built from prefabricated elements. Although this swept aside the results of years of study, Utzon managed to win over not only Arup but also his sponsors. Cahill's successor, Robert Heffron, was prepared to back Utzon, despite protests from the opposition. The objections were partly against the building costs which were now estimated at 25 million Australian dollars, while the jury had originally made an estimate of about seven million. But as the available funds continued to be supplemented by special lotteries, this was in itself no reason to withdraw support from Utzon. It is characteristic of Utzon that he did not move to Australia until 1963. In that year the building of the roofs was started.

THE GREATEST DRAMA IN CONNECTION with the Sydney Opera House was a political question. 1965 was election year in new South Wales, and in the preceding years the Labour government was increasingly criticized because of the Opera House affair. In 1964 it leaked out that the building costs would probably rise to 50 million, a rumour which could not be categorically denied. When in 1965 Labour lost the election, this marked, for Utzon, the end of a favourable climate.
Not only did the new government want the lotteries to be stopped, it also felt that the designer should be under stricter supervision. It was feared, not altogether without foundation, that when phase three was reached a similar problem would occur as had with phase two: there would be a building

Laurence Prynn designed a circular building similar to Marzella and his team (see p. 139), although he placed his opera house in a car-free park, with a garage underneath which took up the entire Bennelong Point. Marzella, on the other hand, envisaged the building on a square, accessible to all traffic. And whereas he chose a spiral-shaped lay-out, Prynn plumped for one composed of (see p. 139) *segments, with the auditoria facing one another; the stages back to back; and the main entrance on the second floor (see ground plan, third from the top). Between the entrance and the theatres, on either side, were two staircases separated from one another by a multi-purpose space.*

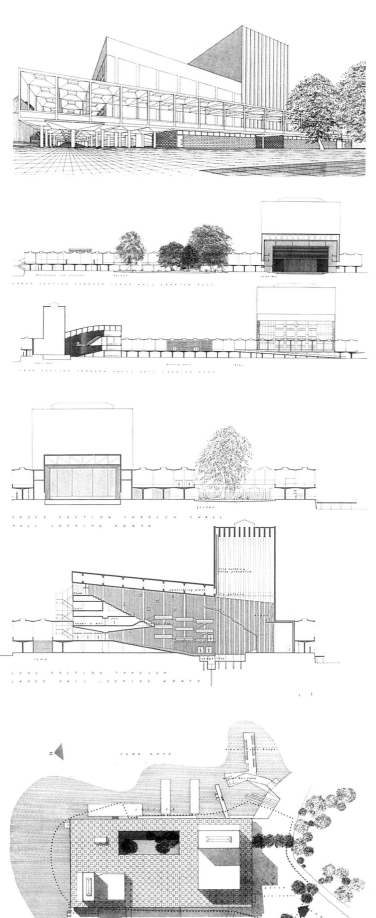

complete with roof, but the interior would have to wait for someone's inspiration. There was as yet nothing on paper with regard to the interior, except that further model studies were urgently needed.

The new government had no desire to let the affair drift on in this way. In an escalating series of complications, Utzon had to suffer the appointment of a supervisory state architect, while he himself was invited to stay on as 'design-architect', transferring his further duties to others. Utzon must have felt so threatened by this move that in February 1966 he tendered his resignation and to his probable astonishment this was only too gladly accepted.

Utzon's sudden departure drew protests from architects, other citizens of Sydney, and music lovers. However, neither protest marches nor petitions, nor the various attempts at reconciliation that were made, succeeded in tempting him back. In April 1966 Utzon left for Denmark and was never to see his opera house again, although in the following years he often let it be known that he would return at once if he were asked.

The building was completed by a team of architects, one of whom, Peter Hall, was appointed as design architect. In Spring 1966 Hall had still been a fervent supporter of Utzon, but when the tide had definitely turned, he did not shrink from radically altering Utzon's plans. The interior became totally unlike anything Utzon could ever have imagined.

It must have been a poor consolation for Utzon that after he left, the building progressed no faster than it had done when he was there. It was not until 1973 that the opera house was officially opened. The costs continued to mount, and finally exceeded 50 million Australian dollars.

Utzon must have felt bitter when he heard what happened to the opera house interior. He had racked his brains trying to find ways of fitting into the limited space 3000 seats as well as all the necessary stage facilities between the walls and roofs of the large hall. His successors simply disposed of the problem. Overnight it was decided to use the large hall exclusively for orchestral concerts, so that various facilities were no longer needed.

So it was that the Sydney Opera House lost not only its architect but also the basis for its proud claim. But the exterior of the building as designed by Utzon was completed, and that is what people see and admire and remember.

H.D. Krall's design incorporated all of Bennelong Point. On the ground floor would be a garage and park, and above this an indoor square, reached via an incline, and housing the two auditoria, a restaurant and the other amenities. From top to bottom: View of the opera house from the beginning of Bennelong Point; two transverse sections of the complex at the level of the garden, and small hall; two cross-sections at the level of the garden and large auditoria; and a bird's-eye view of the design.

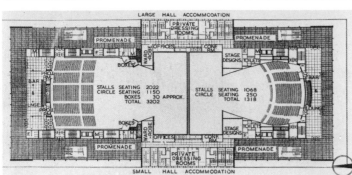

S.W. Milburn and partners, from Great Britain, designed a rectangular 'box' within which the halls faced one another. Much attention was given to its site; the rounded tip of the pier was sacrificed so that the extreme point of the building — with a sea-view terrace — would project above the water.

Bliss and Le Pelly located the two halls in two separate buildings connected by an indoor space accommodating the restaurants, foyers, meeting rooms etc. Their construction was interesting: the steel trusses of the auditoria jutted outwards like a ruffed collar and from these, at various levels, balconies were suspended.

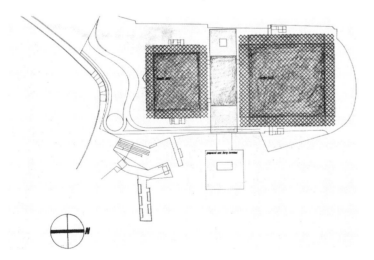

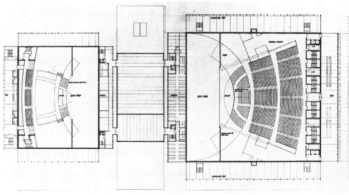

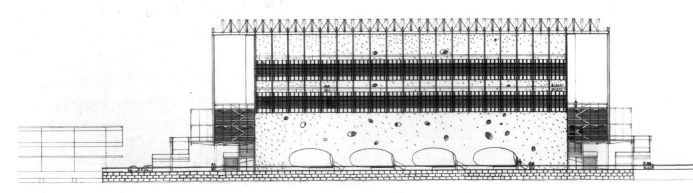

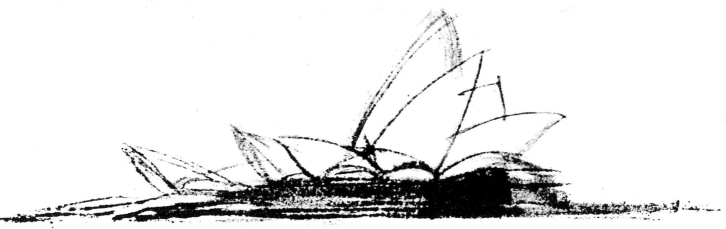

Above: Sketch of the opera house, made by Utzon in 1957, and published in the Red Book — which gave a first overview of the technical problems involved in realizing his design.

Top: The final result — the Sydney Opera House seen froom the south. The exterior, with its steps, is made entirely after Utzon's design; the interior is not — this was executed by others after Utzon's sudden departure in 1967. The large hall, left, deviates greatly from the original design, as does its function; it was no longer needed for operas but for symphony orchestras. This made it possible — by putting part of the seating accommodation on the stage — to realize the desired 3,000 seats, a problem which Utzon had been struggling with, to no avail, for some considerable time.

The Congress Building in Kyoto is huge, with a surface area of 33,500 square metres. Sachio Otani uses two basic shapes in his design: a trapezium for the congress halls, and an inverted one for services and office spaces, out of which he has made one coherent design.
Above: The building on the north bank of the river Takara-ga-ike.
Centre: Side perspective — in front, left, of the main study — has two

small congress halls and an exhibition space.
Below: Main congress hall, with a surface area of 3,500 square metres — hidden in the main study behind the greenery, right.

CONGRESS BUILDING, KYOTO, JAPAN

NATIONAL ARCHITECTURAL COMPETITION FOR AN INTERNATIONAL CONGRESS BUILDING IN KYOTO.

ANNOUNCED: December 1962; closing date: 1 July 1963; result: 29 July 1963.

JURY: — the mayor of Kyoto, Yoshizo Takayama; — three representatives from the business world: Chubei Ito, Koshiro Uemura and Soichiro Ohara; — an adviser from the Ministry of Foreign Affairs: Katsuzo Okumura; — six architects: Shigero Ito, Takeo Sato, Kennzo Tange, Kenzo Tohata, Kunio Mayekawa and Gumpei Matsuda.

WINNERS: 1st prize: Sachio Otani
shared 2nd prize: Yoshinuba Ashihara; Masato Otaka; Kiyonori Kikutake.
Building work executed: 1963-1966, extension 1969-1973 (Sachio Otani).

SHORTLY AFTER WORLD WAR II came the first plans to build an international congress building in Kyoto. In those years Japan was in an unenviable position: it had emerged from the war defeated. All its major cities except Kyoto had been severely damaged; stocks were exhausted, inflation was unacceptably high, and many survivors felt disillusioned and uprooted. Yet Japan was to recover within an amazingly short time. Economic revival began during the American occupation, which lasted until 1952. The financial injections came mainly from the United States, which at that time did not feel threatened since Japan was in a weak state, and was happy to profit from its strategic position. American influence was not, however, restricted to the economy: during the American presence a number of basic reforms were carried out. A new constitution was passed: women were given the vote, freedom of religion and of the press was granted, and the army and navy were abolished. Not surprisingly, the Japanese were greatly influenced by the US in those years, albeit with mixed feelings. Great value was placed on economic and cultural exchanges, and it is in this context that we can see the desire to create places for meetings, such as an international congress centre in Kyoto.

IN 1957 THE TIME APPEARED RIPE: the Japanese cabinet decided to build a congress centre in Kyoto. This would encourage holding important international conferences in Japan. It would aim to attract tourists as well as congress participants: so the architecture was very important.
Normally, such a building would be designed under the auspices of the Building Department of the Ministry of Construction. This was what happened with almost all important state buildings. But this time it was decided to hold an open architectural competition, which the Japanese architectural press took as a sign of welcome change in government departments. Here at last was a chance to produce a daring and original design for a public building. This chance was considered all the greater because out of a jury of eleven members, no fewer than six would be architects. Among these were leading innovators such as Kunio Mayekawa and Kenzo Tange, whose designs and ideas had won international acclaim.

THE COMPETITION TOOK SOME TIME to prepare; there was a great deal of argument about the site. Finally, in 1959, a definite

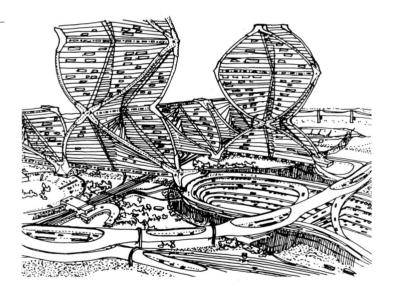

The helicoid project of Kisho Kurokawa, with its huge residential towers and futuristic traffic lanes, became world-famous in the early 1960s. The design was once a redevelopment scheme for Tokyo's Ginza district, but its influence spread much wider. It became the prototype of a group of young avant-garde architects, often students of Tange, who dreamed up mega- structures, in which every aspect of urban life would be played out, and together all these activities would form an 'organic whole'. See also pp. 153-154, and Kurokawa's design for Kyoto, p. 155.

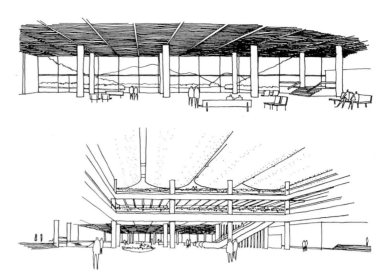

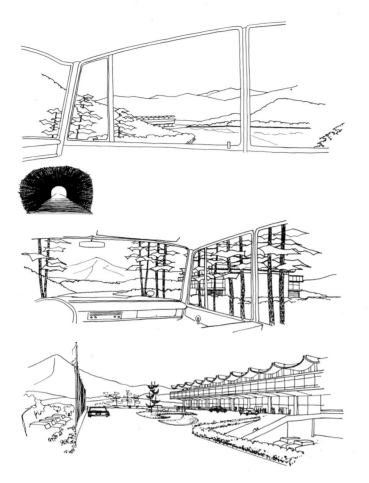

Junzo Yoshimura's design, a rectangular building, almost won a prize but was dropped in one of the final rounds. The jury praised the 'compactness' of the plan, but doubted whether a rectangular main hall would not impose limitations on its uses (see groundplan below). They also pronounced the shape of the roof 'not really showing taste or suitable'. Yoshimura was concerned, in his design, with creating the right views from the congress building (sketch right) and with the impression it made on the visitor. The three consecutive sketches, left, gave an idea of what the motorist could expect as he approached the complex.

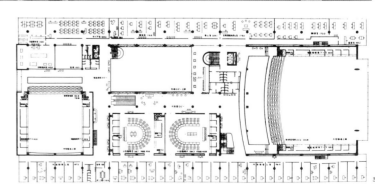

choice was made: Takara-ga-ike Park on the northern outskirts of Kyoto. The congress centre was to be built on the lake shore, in an attractive hilly, wooded area.

The organization of the competition programme was also beset with difficulties. Since little was known about the precise nature of the meetings to be held in the building, the architects were given a fairly free hand. There were certain stipulations, for instance, that the congress building should have its own entrance, as distinct from the entrance to the park; that different entrances were required for congress participants, visitors and staff; that the building should have a total surface area of 26,000 square metres, and that the estimated building costs should not exceed 3.2 milliard Japanese yen, that is to say 9 million US dollars; however, the relationship of elements of accommodation to one another was left for the architect to decide. Nothing was said about the design other than that the new building would have te have to be in keeping 'with the surroundings and with the atmosphere of Kyoto'. This thousand-years-old city was formerly an imperial centre and has a rich architectural tradition.

THE COMPETITION WAS OFFICIALLY ANNOUNCED at the end of December 1962, and prospective participants were given from 5 January until 11 February 1963 to register. There was overwhelming enthusiasm: 1124 architects registered, in spite of the fact that the competition was only open to 'first class architectural technicians', an official qualification normally required in Japan for any building of this scope and size. It proved to be an exceedingly difficult competition. The briefing was complicated and the amount of work required was considerable: apart from site drawings, perspectives, cross sections, elevations and ground plans, no fewer than seventeen kinds of explanatory notes were demanded, including an estimate of the building costs. The programme also produced many queries, something that had been anticipated by the organizers: from 1 February until 20 March questions could be submitted in writing. However, their numbers rose so alarmingly - to about 900 - that it took a month to reply to everyone. And although many participants were only then able to start on the actual work, by that time the closing date had almost passed. The designs had to be submitted by June, which left barely two months. In the end, only 1995 architects (or teams of architects) took part, that is, one out of every six that had initially registered.

'IT MUST HAVE BEEN an awesome task to choose a single winner', wrote the journal *Japan Architect* immediately after the result was published on 29 July 1963: 'With the exception of those who sat on the jury, virtually all the great names in architecture were there, as well as the design departments of all the important construction companies. Not surprisingly, it took the jury a month to judge the anonymous entries. There were six rounds, in each of which a different method of selection was used. At the end of each of these successive

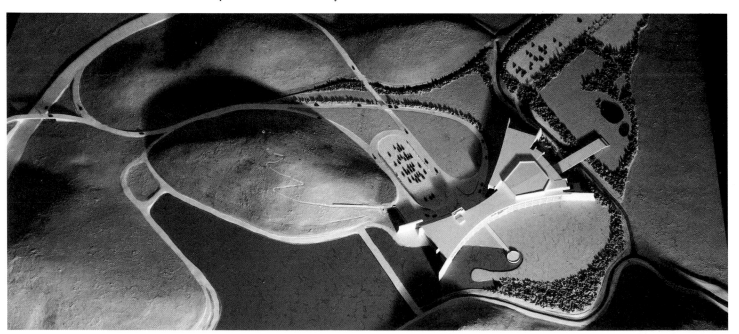

Yukio Sano used a diabolo shape for his building, which fanned out on one side towards the lake and on the other towards Mount Hiei. The jury pronounced it 'refreshing and interesting' but thought the entrance — located in the narrowest part of the building — too cramped.

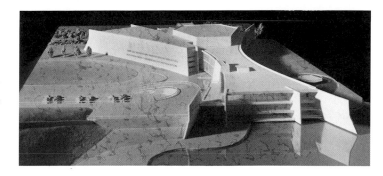

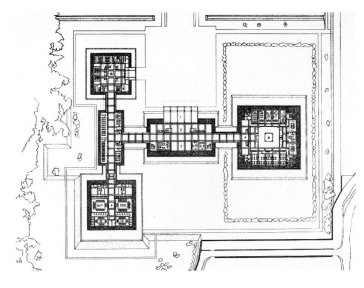

rounds, 67, then 30, 20, 12, 4 and finally one design remained. The final conclusion was unanimous: Sachio Otani's design was chosen.

The second prize was divided equally among the other three designers that had reached the penultimate round: Yoshinuba Ashihara, Asato Otaka and Kiyonori Kikutake. All the winners were relatively young, with an average age of around 35. Ashihara at just over forty was the oldest.

Japan Architect wrote: 'In general the winners represent the leaders of the younger generation who seem destined to succeed to the generation of Tange and Mayekawa. They are the people who a few years ago formed the lively 'Goki-kai', a group devoting itself to a fresh examination of subjects such as the organization of architectural design. Now that Tange and Mayekawa have become sufficiently venerable to sit on a jury, a younger generation is beginning to take their place as participants in competitions. It should be noted here that the winner of the first prize, Sachio Otani, was for a long time Kenzo Tange's closest collaborator, while Masato Otaka, who was awarded a second prize, held a similar position in Mayekawa's office. One feels one is witnessing a kind of apostolic succession.'

WE CAN UNDERSTAND why the journal spoke of an 'apostolic succession'. In those years, Mayekawa and especially Tange greatly influenced younger architects, and three out of the four prizewinners had been their pupils. In particular, their ideas about the relationship between architecture and public space,

taken from the West and then further developed, were very influential.

We should remember that contact between Japan and the Western world was a fairly recent phenomenon. Until 1867, the archipelago had lived isolated from the West, an isolation which, with the arrival of the Meji era, had been abruptly and radically terminated from above. The new government took extensive measures to strengthen relations with Europe, and this was reflected in architecture. European architects were brought to Japan, and Japanese master-builders had to be trained in Western techniques. Many buildings went up in pseudo-European styles.

The exchange of ideas increased still further in the early years of the 20th century. Leading Western architects such as Frank Lloyd Wright and Bruno Taut visited Japan, and their Japanese counterparts, such as Mayekawa, b.1905, and Sakakura, b.1904, worked in the West for many years. During the 1920s and 30s there were reactions against westernization, for instance from the Sezessionists who, around 1920, turned against the domination of European architectural styles, and from the traditionalists who, in the 1930s, advocated a return to traditional Japanese architecture. However, this does not alter the fact that the barriers against the West had been broken down for good, and that, after Japanese nationalism had finished in disaster at the end of World War II, contacts were fairly easily restored.

Both Mayekawa and Tange maintained intensive contacts with their Western colleagues. Before the war, Mayekawa, together with Sakakura, had worked for some time with Le Corbusier. He had also taken part in CIAM, international congresses of modern architecture, at which the principles of modern town planning had been formulated. After the war, Tange travelled to the West with Mayekawa; he too became personally acquainted with Le Corbusier, and began to take part in CIAM. However, at the CIAM of the 1950s, the principles of modern town planning were being revised and adapted, and there was much criticism against an allegedly over-rational approach to town planning. Instead, greater attention was given to the way in which space and buildings are experienced by people, and concepts such as 'human scale', 'meeting places' and 'transitional areas' were discussed. These were the ideas which Mayekawa and Tange introduced to many of their compatriots. In the 1950s, Japan went though a period of rapid reconstruction, in which anything was possible in architectural terms, but in which public space was treated

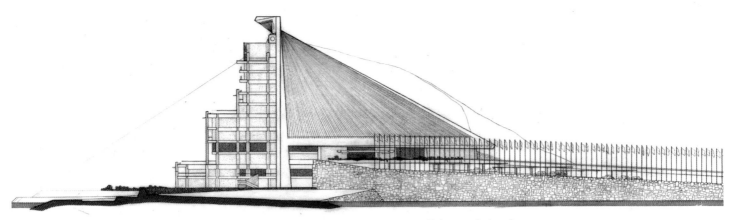

Kanashige Sakanaga designed a
building described by the jury as
'original and daring' (above).
The large conferencehall was situated
in a tent-like area on the hillside,
with it's platform in the western tipp.

In the cubic-shaped section of the
building, on the lake shore, were
smaller rooms to be used by
administration. The jury found the
design, however, 'too eccentric for
contemporary construction methods'.

Junzo Sakakura, 1901-1969, former
pupil of Le Corbusier's, was regarded
as one of the most important
architects of the early 60s. His
esthetically pleasing design, below
and p. 4, got no further than the
second round, and the jury offerecd
no explanation.

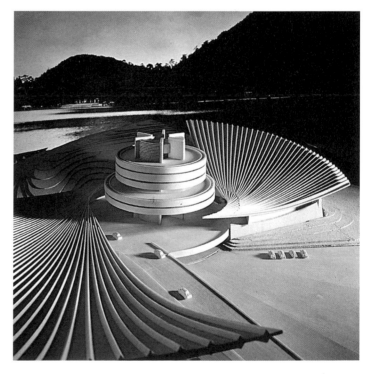

with great carelessness. Bluntly put: public space was not
designed, the entire urban area was simply filled up with
streets and buildings.

It was therefore not surprising that Mayekawa caused a great
stir. Some of his buildings, like those of Le Corbusier, were
partly raised on stilts, so as not to break up the urban space.
Other buildings by him, such as Tokyo's Metropolitan Festival
Hall and Kyoto's City Hall featured large inner courtyards,
like monumental public spaces.

Tange's influence lay partly in the same area, but his ideas
were wider in scope: he tried to find ways to structure entire
neighbourhoods and even cities. His first principle was that
the whole urban dynamic can be controlled, or at least, that
urban structures can be designed which encompass this entire
dynamic with all its growth and changes. Tange distanced
himself from a functionalism that took no account of the fact
that functions arise, change and disappear. On the contrary, he
tried to make room for flexibility. He wanted to design
neighbourhoods, or even better, cities, which would form a
'network of energy and communication', an 'urban tissue'
which would need to have a strong structure of its own. This
structure should not only be physically present but would also

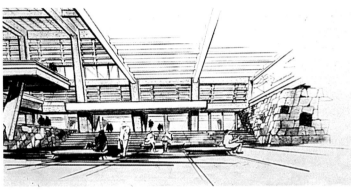

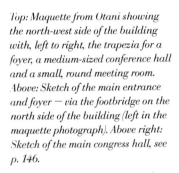

Top: Maquette from Otani showing the north-west side of the building with, left to right, the trapezia for a foyer, a medium-sized conference hall and a small, round meeting room. Above: Sketch of the main entrance and foyer — via the footbridge on the north side of the building (left in the maquette photograph). Above right: Sketch of the main congress hall, see p. 146.

Below: Hideo Yanagi's design exemplified clarity and simplicity. The two conference halls were in separate buildings linked to one another by a T-shape building containing other smaller meeting rooms and facilities. His watchword was 'mobility' both inside and outside the congress centre. The jury were not too sure about the communications lines and the triangular shape of the halls.

have to support a symbolic meaning, because people would otherwise be unable to understand it.

IN OTANI'S PRIZE-WINNING DESIGN for the congress building at Kyoto, it is Tange's influence in particular that can be seen. Otani had been Tange's closest associate for fourteen years, from 1946 until 1960, and collaborated on practically all Tange's important projects. In Otani's comments on his design for the congress building, he speaks of 'searching for a structure in which different, distinct functions are given a place.' He writes: 'My first objective was to find individual spatial forms that could serve different purposes, and my second objective was to develop a structural system that would create unity without destroying the individuality of the different spaces.' He finally opted for a structural system in which trapezoidal spaces (for the congress halls) and other spaces in the shape of upturned trapezoids (for the offices) were joined together, so as to form one spatial organization. Otani: 'This process (of organization) can be compared with the growth process of a small rural village which develops into a modern integrated city'.

The fact that Otani gave the basic elements of his design the

shape of a trapezoid — 'one of the oldest structural forms in Japanese architecture' — should not be regarded as traditionalism. Like his master Tange, he used this form chiefly because of its symbolic significance. Otani: 'The combination of an old form as a starting-point, and a growth process of urbanization, seems to me in keeping with the nature and the expression of this type of building.'

IN THE CASES OF THE WINNERS of the second prize, the relationship with Mayekawa and Tange was more complicated. The most they can be said to have in common is that, like Otani, Tange and Mayekawa, they were chiefly interested in structural aspects of architecture, and in the relationship between architecture and public space.

Yoshinura Ashihara was alone in not having studied with Tange, but he had become acquainted in his own way with Western architecture and Western use of space. In the 1950s he had worked in America, first completing his studies at Harvard University Graduate School, subsequently working for a year with Marcel Breuer in New York and finally visiting a number of European countries. In 1960 he published a study on the use of space in architectuure and town planning.

In his design, Ashihara explicitly sought ways of integrating interior and exterior so as to create an organic unity, and he devoted himself to a search for 'architectural spaces with human qualities'. All of this can be seen in his design for Kyoto: the congress hall and areas for visitors and press are all situated in a curved building which shapes itself almost naturally around a bay of lake Takara-ga-ike. The organization of the design is very clear; offices are in a separate tower, set apart from the areas for congress participants and visitors. The only criticism the jury had of this 'well-balanced, clear and simple design' was that it was probably not complex enough to

meet all the diverse demands of the ever-changing public that would use the congress building.'

Both of the other prize winners, Otaka and Kikutake, had been Tange's students. Both were members of a small group that had proclaimed itself as the 'Metabolists' in 1960. The name had been a rather opportunistic choice; the group had been given the task of preparing a World Design Conference in Tokyo, and decided, partly for publicity reasons, to link the occasion to the publication of a manifesto: the Metabolist Manifesto. However, the ideas and projects put forward by the Metabolists were a direct extension of Tange's ideas: they designed structures that were to embrace the entire urban dynamic, but the scale of their plans was larger, the forms much more utopian, than had been the case in any of Tange's designs. In this respect, the mega-structures designed by these Metabolists were characteristic of the 1960s: years that exuded an almost unlimited confidence in - partly futuristic - technical possibilities. These plans would provide alternatives to the unbridled expansion of cities, and would show how to manage space economically.

At first glance, little of the Metabolist ideas can be recognized in the designs submitted by Otaka and Kikutake for the Kyoto congress building. These designs are very different, which corresponds with the difference of the members of this group: individuals brought together for a specific occasion. If we look more closely, however, we see that in both designs a forceful structure was a first priority, sometimes at the expense of functionality. In both cases, the jury's opinion was that their main form was bold and original but that there were too many practical objections. Anyone studying all the competition designs some 25 years later, will be struck by their great diversity, by the wealth of forms and approaches represented by Japanese architects. Together, the designs provide an

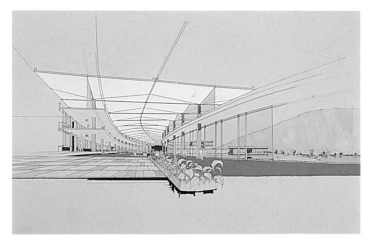

Yoshinura Ashihara won second prize with a design, according to the jury, that was 'symmetrical, clear and simple'.
Right: Maquette of the design — an oblong, curved foyer (above right) with the large conference hall at its far end (above left) and smaller meeting halls branching off.
Centre: Spacious office tower of the complex and, below, the round

pavilions, housing restaurants, bar. etc. The jury's final verdict was that it was perhaps too simple to meet the demands of a constantly changing public.

accurate picture of the Japanese architectural scene in those years, but the fact that such diversity was assembled is in this case mainly thanks to the scope of the competition. As *Japan Architect* wrote, the time allowed for submitting designs was so short that the main emphasis necessarily had to be placed on basic creativity rather than on architectural detail: 'The jury did not so much select a design as an architect'.

The journal's remark about 'apostolic succession' was vindicated in the sense that not only a design but an architectural opinion was rewarded. This was only to be expected with people like the influential Tange and Mayekawa on the jury. However, although all the winners were influential architects in their own right, none of them ever gained the following accorded to Mayekawa and especially Tange.

For no matter how intelligent and inspiring the ideas of the Metabolists and their supporters had been in the 60s, by 1970 these ideas began to lose ground. Perhaps many Metabolist plans were simply too utopian. It was only to be expected that, especially in Japan, people would one day realize that complicated processes such as urban dynamics cannot be contained in one all-embracing architectural structure.

Or perhaps it was because all over the world confidence in all-embracing structures was declining. It is probably for the same reason that over the past hundred years hardly any single architectural trend has remained dominant for more than a decade: architecture is too much in a state of flux and its field of action is too complex. When the first part of Otani's congress building was handed over in 1966, it could still be called avant-garde, but by the time the second part was completed in 1973, other architectural ideas were becoming dominant in Japan.

Time will show how Otani's congress building will be assessed: a memorial for an evanescent architectural idea, or a monument to eternal architectural values.

Kionore Kikutake shared second prize and the jury wrote that his plan raised more questions than any other of the entries submitted. Its funnel shape was reminiscent of the old wooden Buddhist temples and it had a well-organized interior: congress halls on the fourth floor; restaurants on the third, offices and tearooms on the second; and foyers on the first floor. The jury members deliberated long over the design; some were 'against using concrete as if it were wood', while others thought the shape lent itself 'admirably' for it. Finally they agreed on the design's originality and thought it 'interesting' to build such a structure. It didn't get very far. The jury had to admit that there were enormous practical problems — the large number of lifts, for instance, that would be needed because all the congress halls halls were on the fourth floor.

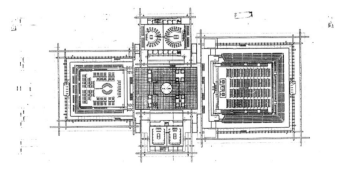

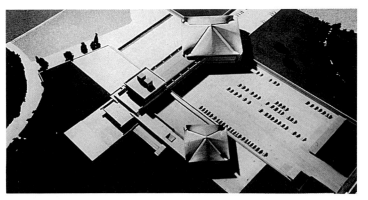

外観透視図
主連入路図 **13**

Masato Otaka could thank his clear design, above and right, for earning him second prize. It had an L-shape form — with separate entrances for delegates and visitors — with the main halls at the far points of the letter, offices in its right angle, and a restaurant located between this angle and a smaller conference hall. His design also featured free-standing, support pillars under the space connecting the entrance with the main hall. But the jury felt that practical matters were sometimes sacrificed to 'clarity of the design' — communication between the staff in the office building and visitors to the congress buildings, for instance, could well prove inadequate.

In the early 60s, Kisho Kurokawa, born in 1934, was one of the most vocal young architects, especially because of his contribution to Metabolism (see pp. 147 and 153-154). His design for Kyoto, left and below, also embraced Metabolist principles: an extensive building with the sum of its parts forming an organic whole. As Kurokawa explained, 'three-dimensional grids formed by perpendicular shafts and passageway beams are street spaces. The three-dimensional grid creates 'rooms', which include conference halls, meeting rooms and lobbies around it. The growth principle is also embodied in the three-dimensional grids' — in other words, scope to expand. But the jury was not convinced, and the design was dropped in the second round.

AMSTERDAM TOWN HALL

INTERNATIONAL COMPETITION FOR A NEW TOWN HALL IN
AMSTERDAM, THE NETHERLANDS, CONSISTING OF AN
OPEN IDEAS COMPETITION FOLLOWED BY A CLOSED
COMPETITION.

PUBLISHED: 1967; closing date open competition: 30
November 1967; closing date closed competition: 7
October 1968; result: 22 November 1968; number of
participants: 804.

JURY: H.A. Maaskant (Netherlands, architect),
chairman; Prof. J. Schader (Switzerland, architect),
Sir Robert Matthew (Great Britain, architect),
F.J. van Gool (Netherlands, architect).

WINNERS: Wilhelm Holzbauer (first prize).
Bernardo Winkler, Friedrich Hahmann, Hannah
Hahmann (second prize); Group GIA (third prize).

CONSTRUCTION of town hall in combination with an
opera house: 1980-1987, after the design of Wilhelm
Holzbauer and Cees Dam (as representative of
architects B. Bijvoet and G.H.M. Holt).

AMSTERDAM IS A COMPLICATED CITY full of complicated people. This
statement, often made affectionately and even indulgently, has
become a commonplace remark in the Netherlands. This does
not alter the fact that in Amsterdan matters sometimes
develop into long-drawn-out, increasingly complicated affairs
with mounting disagreements. One such matter was the
building of a new town hall which has only recently been
solved.
It began in November - yes - in 1645. Talks, discussions and
arguments about the building of a new, larger town hall went
on for six years. A thorough-going architect was engaged on
the task: Jacob van Campen (1595-1657). But many people had
a finger in the pie of his building and in the end the
Amsterdam City Fathers decided that they wanted no more of
all these alternative plans: 'We observe that various persons
busy themselves with making models of a new town hall, and
that with great uncertainty since no agreement has even been
reached regarding the site.'
The four burgomasters of the day intervened personally and
backed Van Campen's plan, which they wished to see executed

*Above: Engraving of the Dam made
circa 1750, with the town hall
designed by Jacob van Campen, left,
the Gothic Nieuwe Kerk, centre, and
the Weigh House, far right, which was
later pulled down by Lodewijk
Napoleon, the French King of the
Netherlands, because it restricted his
view.*

Top: Silkscreen print made by the prizewinner, Wilhelm Holzbauer, of the Amsterdam Town Hall and Muziektheater when completed in 1986.

Above: General view of the Amsterdam Muziektheater, completed in 1986, with the town hall, left, still under construction, and the river Amstel in the foreground.

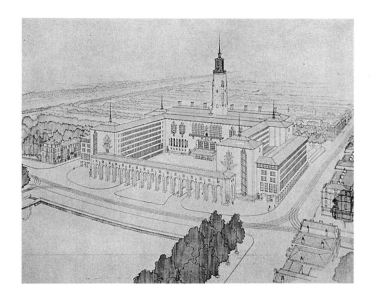

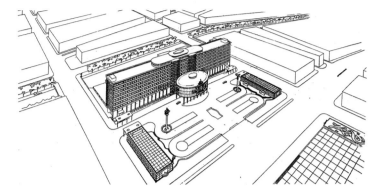

Left: Design submitted by H.T. Zwiers
for the open competition of 1937
under the motto 13659 — the number
indicating how many piles were
driven into the ground for the old

Below: Design by Mr Staal and son,
submitted under the motto 'Analkè',
for the 1937 open competition. The
site was the Frederiksplein.

on the site of previous town halls, in Dam Square between
Kalverstraat and New Church.

More pious city rulers wanted the church to be completed
first, with a bold tower, but the worthy merchants preferred a
new, grand town hall. A compromise was reached: the church
tower and the town hall would be built simultaneously.
Meanwhile another group forced through a decision that the
town hall would not have its façade opposite the church but
that the entrance and the longer side of the building would
face Dam Square. Furthermore, they ensured that the church
tower would not in fact be built.

At first, the building of the town hall draggedon. Van Campen
quarrelled with the city architect, Daniel Stalpaert, and the
work suffered from lack of funds. Only after the old town hall
burnt down in 1652, did construction start on the new
building. The local government moved temporarily to nearby
Prinsenhof.

In 1655 the town hall was inaugurated prematurely, although
building continued until 1705. When in 1806 the northern
Netherlands were annexed by France, Louis Napoleon was
proclaimed king. In 1808 he requisitioned the Amsterdam
Town Hall as his palace and the city council was given barely

a month and a half to find alternative accommodation: it
moved back to the Prinsenhof where it had also resided
temporarily between 1652 and 1655. This time, however, its
stay was to be considerably longer.

For although in 1813, after the departure of the French from
the Netherlands, the new Dutch King Willem I announced
that the town hall must be unconditionally returned to the
city of Amsterdam, nothing came of this. The king wanted a
new palace in Amsterdam, and as long as this was not ready
he was glad to have the use of 'a few rooms' in the town hall.
In view of the city's poor financial situation, the City Fathers
then offered him 'the provisional use of the palace ceded to
the city'. They would stay at the Prinsenhof for the time being.
Nothing ever came of the plans for a new royal palace in
Amsterdam. The king continued to use the town hall, though
not as a permanent residence. He only stayed there for a
number of days during the year. In about 1873 there was a
movement in Amsterdam to reclaim the town hall for the city,
and a 'Palace v. Town Hall' debate arose that smouldered for
more than sixty years. Not until 1935 did Amsterdam city
council decide to renounce all claims to the palace, against
payment by the state of ten million guilders for the building of

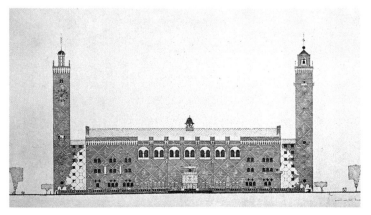

Following the 1937 competition, a
closed competition was organized and
four teams were invited to submit
designs.
Above and right: Designs for the

forefront and the Burgerzaal (Civic
hall) of the town hall, submitted by
Berghoef and Vegter under the motto
'Belfort'.

a new town hall. There was some vociferous opposition, but the decision stood.

Amsterdam now needed a town hall. As a possible location, Frederiksplein was considered. This was a site on the southern edge of the central canals, where the Palace of National Industry, burnt down in 1929, had stood. This was a spectacular building dating from 1859-1864, and inspired by London's Crystal Palace. In 1936 an international architectural competition was organized for the new town hall. At the inauguration of the jury on 21 October, the burgomaster, Mr W. de Vlugt, said: 'An appeal is about to be made to our Dutch architects to demonstrate their knowledge and ability to design. They will be asked to enrich our city with a town hall that may serve as an example of what our twentieth century architecture can achieve, a town hall that for years to come will bear witness to the vigorous life of the capital and its firm confidence in the future.'

The burgomaster himself was chairman of the jury, among whom were the alderman for Public Works, the director of Public Works, the city architect, A.R. Hulshof, and five other architects: M.J. Granpé Molière, H. van der Kloot Meijburg, S. van Ravesteyn, A. van der Steur and P. Vorkink. All of them were more or less traditional architects, albeit each had an idiosyncratic style. The jury was thus by no means homogeneous, and this would later become more apparent.

Until 10 March 1937, prospective participants had the opportunity of asking about the programme. The answers to these questions were printed in *Bouwkundig Weekblad* (Architectural Weekly). In total 273 questions were answered. By the time the competition was closed – 10 August 1937 – 225 entries had been received. The jury took a little over four months to reach its decision. It was unable to agree unanimously on a winning design, so it was proposed to invite the makers of four designs to take part in a closed competition.

These four entries were by H.T. Zwiers, M. Duintjer and Auke Komter, J.F. Staal and Arthur Staal, and J.F. Berghoef and J.J.M. Vegter. The prize money of 20,000 guilders, available for 'plans that could be regarded as valuable' was not awarded because, according to the jury, 'no such plans had presented themselves'. It is likely that the composition of the jury hindered a unanimous verdict, but the programme was partly to blame: it was so extensive and detailed that few candidates had the courage to create individual solutions. Nevertheless, commenting on the result, *Bouwkundig Weekblad* noted with satisfaction: 'When we vigorously urged for this competition to be set, one of our arguments was that, because such a small number of buildings had been made being during the depression, it was not possible to indicate the *primus inter pares* among architects who should clearly be given the

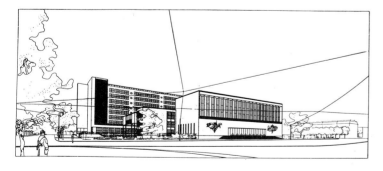

Above: Design for the 1937 open competition submitted by G.H. Holt and J.P. Kloos under the motto 'Arp', which received no recognition whatsoever from the jury.

Right: Design submitted by Van Duintjer and Komter for the double brief of 1940.

commission to design the Amsterdam town hall. Perhaps, outside the well-known, reputable architects, there would be younger architects of great skill, whose ability had remained unknown because they had done little independent work. The result of the recently terminated part of the competition has proved that our argument was correct. Beside two well-known architects, no fewer than five younger ones have come forward, not one of whom has so far been able to make his mark by carrying out important commissions.'

But even the closed competition did not produce the desired result. At the beginning of 1939 the jury announced its verdict: two designs, by Duintjer/Komter and by Berghoef/Vegter, appeared interesting, but not sufficiently so. 'The jury is convinced that from these designs, albeit after modification, the definitive draft design for the Amsterdam town hall can be obtained.' In brief, the jury proposed yet another closed competition.

Great was the discontent both among architects and outsiders. Many considered the competition had failed and some suggested holding a new competition for a town hall at a different location. On 7 May 1939 Mr P.J. Lugt wrote to the editor of a national newspaper suggesting that the town hall be placed 100 metres from Frederiksplein and built on the banks of the Amstel river. Some time later a maquette made by Lugt appeared in which this plan was worked out, with a town hall in the architectural style of the Amsterdam School, a style which was extremely popular in Amsterdam, especially in the early 1920s. Lugt: 'This architecture strikes a sensitive chord for the majority of Amsterdam people.'

Although architect W. van Tijen applauded Lugt's suggestion — 'he realized correctly that for a town hall the town-planning aspect, the situation, is of primary importance' — the plan was rejected. On 9 February 1940 the city council — after three days' discussion — agreed with the proposal by burgomaster and aldermen to have the two plans worked out under the same conditions as described in the competition programme, and then to make a choice from these.

The plans had to be submitted by 7 November 1941 and exactly two months later, the jury gave its verdict: the project called 'Belfort' by Berghoef and Vegter was chosen as the final winner of the competition.

But this was never to materialize. From May 1940, the Netherlands had been occupied by the Germans and building activity had virtually come to a standstill across the country. By the end of the World War II, ideas had changed. Amsterdam still wanted a town hall, but now on Waterlooplein. Once the heart of the Jewish quarter, this area was now largely deserted because so many Jews had been deported by the Germans and killed. It was a fine location: on the river and on the edge of the old inner city. The discussions that had taken place just before the war had shown many people that a town hall needs a spacious site, if possible by the water.

Not until 1954 was this idea definitively accepted by the city council and in 1957 burgomaster and aldermen commissioned Berghoef and Vegter to make a draft design for a town hall on Waterlooplein. The design was published in 1958 — and not approved. Criticism broke loose on all sides, but the architects were nevertheless asked to make a definitive design, although they had to take into account the reservations that had been made.

In 1961 the definitive, modified design appeared. A week before the city council was to take a decision about the plan, criticism erupted once more. Architect Aldo van Eyck triggered it off by speaking of a 'sickening plot' and later even of 'an inconceivably childish sample of provincial fascism'. Many architects took Van Eyck's side and in a request to the council they pleaded that Berghoef and Vegter should be advised by a committee of experts. The council agreed to this. On 30 October 1964 burgomaster and aldermen wrote to the council that the conditions had not been complied with. From then on, everything moved at top speed: after 10 days the council decided to withdraw the commission to Berghoef and Vegter and two weeks later they announced a new international competition for the Amsterdam town hall. This decision was taken after a debate lasting 10 hours during which fervent pleas were made to accommodate the administration once again in Van Campen's building, the present palace on Dam Square, which did not secure a majority. Amsterdam now prepared itself for a new chapter in its Town Hall affair; unavoidable after all the discussion. At least, after the debate few voices were heard against the proposal.

And what about Frederiksplein? At the same time that it was decided to establish the town hall on Waterlooplein, Frederiksplein was earmarked for the building of a *muziektheater* or opera house.

But Amsterdam remained a complicated city. In 1956 architect

Above and right: Sketches of the entrance to the town hall and the oval civic hall, submitted by Mr Staal and son for the 1938 competition. Their approach was to give a more modern interpretation to the classic Baroque style.

B. Bijvoet and his partner, G.H.M. Holt, were commissioned to make a preliminary design for an opera house but for a long time nothing materialised. In 1961 they received the commission for a definitive design, but by then much had changed. Frederiksplein was destined for the building of a new headoffice of the Nederlandse Bank, and it was thought that the opera should be built in the Pijp, a nineteenth century working class area south of the canal belt but this was never to be either.

The new competition for the town hall was organized in an exemplary fashion. After all the hassle of the past 30 years, the city council of Amsterdam did its best to make the competition successful in every respect. The council secured the advice of Chr. Nielsen, the city architect, who set to work with immense energy and drive.

Designing a large town hall is no sinecure. It demands a great deal of work and an intensive examination of the programme of requirements. This was why Nielsen suggested first holding an ideas competition from which a number of entrants would then be chosen who — in a closed competition — would produce more detailed designs.

In all other respects the competition was organized entirely according to the guidelines set down by the Union Internationale des Architectes. One of the most stringent requirements was the guarantee of anonymity, which was impeccably met.

Much thought was given to the composition of the jury. Members of the city administration were excluded from the jury. Only architects were to judge the designs and their choice would later be presented to the city council. Of course the question remained: which architects would sit on the jury?

Nielsen wrote later: 'From various sides names were suggested to me, usually prominent architects whom one would prefer to see among the participants. A competent architect and a good jury member are not synonymous, . . . The pursuit of great names was abandoned and a search was made for principles that could serve as a basis for the jury's choice.

The most important of these were the location and the fact that one would be 'building in an historic city'. This explains why we contacted the Bund Schweizer Architekten and the Danske Landforsbund fa Arkitekten. The response to this led to the designation of one member each by the Danish, Swiss and Dutch societies.'

The final jury consisted of the Dutchman, H.A. Maaskant (who was later elected as chairman), Sir Robert H. Matthew from Great Britain, the Swiss J. Schader and the Dutchmen P. Zandstra and F.J. van Gool. Deputy jury members included the Dane, N.O. Lund. A secretary and an assistant secretary were also added.

The programme was set up by Nielsen and was — in his words — 'an interpretation, made intelligible to architects, of much deliberation, and of a thousand and one desires'.

By 30 November 1967, when the designs had to be in, 804 entries had been received, of which one was disqualified because it arrived too late. Over a month later, the jury was officially inaugurated and immediately set to work. In carrying out its task, the jury followed the guidelines laid down by the Union Internationale des Architectes. For instance, article 8 of these guidelines prescribes that the members of a jury must first submit all the projects to a preliminary examination. The jury did so, very extensively in fact, in order to determine the assessment criteria for itself. The first few days were therefore

spent on examining 803 entries. The jury also visited the future building site in order to study the actual location. After mutual consultation, four assessment criteria were drawn up: the building must have easy access for traffic; all the stipulated areas had to be provided; the exterior of the building had to be acceptable in the city scene, and lastly — and perhaps the most important criterion — 'the building will have to be, both in its entirety and in its constituent parts, an inviting building, and reflect the character of a town hall in its role as citizens' meeting place.'

With these criteria in mind, all members of the jury examined the designs again, and each noted for himself which should be admitted to the second round and which should not. When everyone was ready, the lists were compared. Naturally, no design was admitted to the second round unless all jury members were in agreement. If only one jury member thought a particular design should move on to the next round, he was asked to reconsider his decision. If he stuck to his opinion, the design would indeed be admitted to the next round, but if not, it was dropped. If two jury members thought a design was good enough for the next round, while the other members had already rejected it, it would still go to the second round. If three or more jury members thought a design was good enough, it would automatically be admitted to the third round.

A ballot was taken on all designs that had reached the second round and the majority decided whether these should move on to the third round. In this way 67 designs reached the third round.

This already very correct procedure was further refined by the jury. Clearly, nothing was to be left to chance, and before starting on the third round, all the jury members separately examined all hitherto rejected designs once again. Thirteen designs were reconsidered, and another ballot was taken, but none of them obtained enough votes to reach the third round.

In the third round there were more extensive discussions and ballots on each of the 67 plans, and 20 designs moved to the fourth round. The jury then suspended its activities for about a month and during that time maquettes were made of the 20 remaining designs. Instructions were also given for detailed technical reports, to ascertain whether the designs complied with the architectural requirements of the programme. All 20 obtained a pass mark, so they all remained in the race.

In February 1968 the jury studied the reports and maquettes and after lengthy discussions there was a ballot: seven projects were selected for the next round. The jury also chose designs for the ten money prizes available, and again acted with meticulous care. It might have seemed the obvious thing to share out the money prizes among the entries that had reached the last round, but the jury genuinely wanted to award these prizes to those entrants who had incorporated interesting ideas in their projects. Three designs that had come to grief in the third round were thus considered for a reward. In each case, the idea was interesting, but the project as a whole could not stand up to all the criteria.

In February the jury announced its decision to adviser Nielsen that seven entrants were to be invited to take part in the closed competition. The anonymity of the entrants was maintained and the designers were notified at their correspondence addresses, which the jury did not know. The seven entrants were given until 7 October to work out their plans. In the meantime time a small incident occurred. A group of lovers of old Amsterdam published an advertisement in a foreign journal appealing to the seven entrants to make themselves known so that they might be sent a copy of an article stressing the historical importance of Amsterdam's old inner city. An apparently insignificant incident, all the more so because none of the entrants responded to it. But to the attentive observer it revealed that not everyone in Amsterdam had entire confidence in the competition.

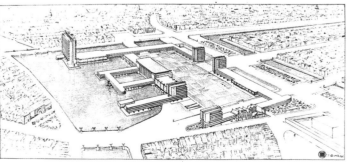

Berghoef and Vegter's winning design of 1940 was put on ice during the German occupation. In 1957 they were again invited to design a town hall, with a new site, the Waterlooplein. The result was so controversial that they were obliged to come up with a second design, above, which also caused such an outcry that other architects felt compelled to submit alternatives, *including the one, left, by 78-year-old H.Th. Wijdeveld. In 1964 Amsterdam city council gave up: an international competition was announced.*

Much interest was shown in the competition for a new town hall for Amsterdam, and international competitors were sent literature on the city — its history, local government, economy and climate — in Dutch, English or French. Initially the request was for only rough sketches, and from these a number of competitors was selected to submit more detailed studies.

Above: This design by José Rafael Moneo, from Madrid, got him through to the second 'closed' round of the competition. The jury at a later stage, however, thought the roof was 'weak'. Below and right: Two studies made by the Dane, Arne Jacobson, which got him as far as the fourth round and won him 3,000 guilders.

Below: Maquette submitted by S. Kondo, from Japan, which earned him the fourth round of the competition and 4,000 guilders.

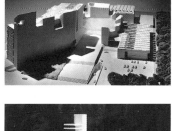

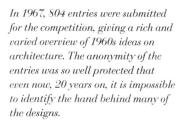

In 1967, 804 entries were submitted for the competition, giving a rich and varied overview of 1960s ideas on architecture. The anonymity of the entries was so well protected that even now, 20 years on, it is impossible to identify the hand behind many of the designs.

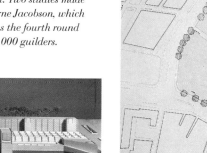

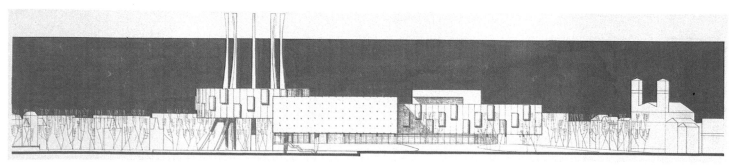

When in October the seven designs were submitted, the jury studied them intensively, on this occasion paying close attention to the financial aspects. In November 1968 the jury published the result: project number 769 received first prize; second prize went to number 245 and the third prize to number 286. The jury also proposed that number 154, 'because of its special qualities, be rewarded by purchase or otherwise with a sum equal to that of the third prize.' Shortly after the result was published, adviser Nielsen was able to announce the names of the winners. The first prize went to Wilhelm Holzbauer from Vienna. Second prizewinners were Bernardo Winkler and Friedrich and Hannah Hahmann from Starnberg in West Germany, and the third prize went to Group GIA consisting of Eva and Jan Karczewska from Paris, Andrzej Kozielevski from Warsaw and J.H. Maisonneuve from Paris. Motto number 154, which received a special mention, was by L.J. Heidenrijk from Amersfoort, the Netherlands. An almost perfectly organized competition was hereby concluded. Amsterdam seemed to have taken revenge for the rather sad happenings around the Town Hall affair, and further progress seemed straightforward. The jury would propose that the city council definitely commission Wilhelm Holzbauer to build a town hall on Waterlooplein. The end seemed in sight.

Seemed . . . but then, Amsterdam is a complicated place. The jury's verdict had hardly been published when a veritable tornado of protest burst loose. Holzbauer's design was said to be far too grand, not in keeping with the spirit of Amsterdam, too much a symbol of power and authority. A large-scale campaign was started to use the palace on Dam Square as a town hall after all, and posters appeared all over the city with the slogan: 'The town hall stands on the Dam.' No one seemed to have a good word for Holzbauer's design.

Why all the commotion? There are several possible explanations but the chief one is probably that between 1964, when the competition was opened, and 1969, Dutch society had changed radically. Amsterdam was the centre of the new Provo movement, comprised of youthful rebellious members determined that everything should be done differently. Student protest and the events in Paris in 1968 also left their mark. Society was ripe for renewal, and in that atmosphere of hope and change, people no longer believed in the old or the established order. Government should be decentralized, and brought closer to the people. There should be local government centres, and for representative functions there was always the Palace on the Dam, which — oh irony — was once the seat of the mighty and the wealthy.

Newspapers, professional journals, lampoons were all choked

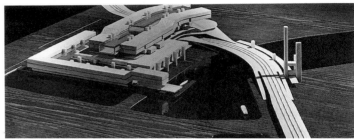

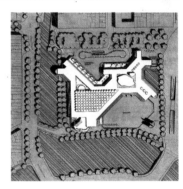

Top: Dutch entry from Jan Hoogstad, made in collaboration with M.C. Deudekom, W. Schulze and A.S. van Tilburg, which reached the third round and a prize of 4,000 guilders. Above: Design from Van den Broek and Bakema, a Dutch firm of architects.

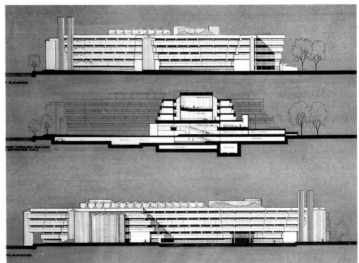

Above: Site, forefront and cross-section for the Amsterdam Town Hall which got the Canadian duo, Robert Fairfield and Macy DuBois, to the second 'closed' round. The jury's final verdict was that their plan was 'excessive of form, which weakened rather than strengthened the original design, and which made it more fitting for a new development scheme than for the old heart of Amsterdam,

where, despite a certain playfulness of style in individual buildings, there was an overall discipline in principle form and use of material'.

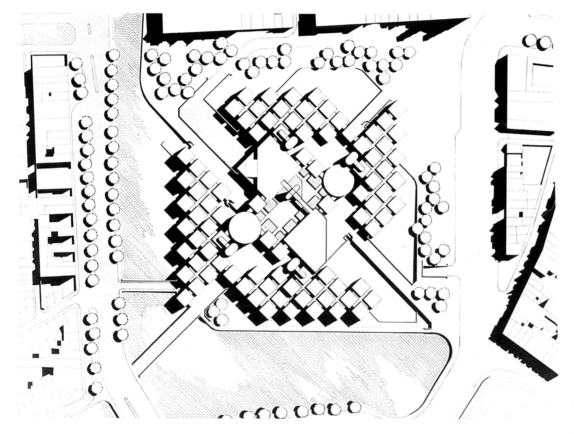

Entrants for the competition for Amsterdam's new town hall fell into two broad categories: those that wanted a 'grand' building befitting the local government, and those that considered the local council was for local people and their headquarters should simply blend in with other public buildings. The latter view was prevalent among the younger entrants, who after the social upheavals of the 1960s saw no place for authoritarian governing bodies. Their entries endorsed the views of Dutch architects Aldo van Eyck, Piet Blom and Herman Hertzberger, in the architectual journal Forum: small is beautiful. A structure split into units was more accommodating for the human scale. After the competition, these extreme viewpoints were more openly expressed: the winning design was regarded as a 'power' symbol by anti-authoritarians and was roundly denounced.

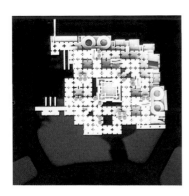

Dutchman L.J. Heijdenrijk reached the second closed round of the competition and was awarded 15,000 guilders. Above, his initial design for the open competition, and right, his entry for the closed round. His building comprised construction units grouped around several larger and smaller courtyards which the jury thought 'was an interesting visual interpretation of new thoughts on the relationship between a city council and its local community'.

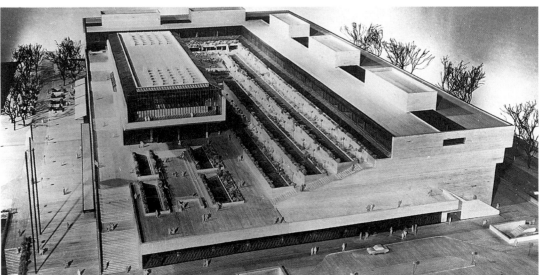

with protest against the coming town hall in those months. The city council kept a cool head and realized it was morally obliged to commission Holzbauer to make a definitive design. This was ready in 1970, and in June that year the council had to give its final decision. Once again protest burst out. In vain. The council agreed to the building of a town hall according to Holzbauer's design. Still no blessing seemed to rest on the project: national government thought the plan was too expensive, especially in view of the fact that for some time Amsterdam had been unable to balance its own municipal budget. Money would be made available only when Amsterdam managed to balance its own books. This could take some time, and meanwhile the town hall plans were put on ice. Architect Wilhelm Holzbauer, who had bought a house in Amsterdam for his big project, returned to Vienna in 1973. No large investments for the time being. This decision applied also to the building of a music centre in the working class district of the Pijp. By mid-1978 architects Bijvoet and Holt had prepared their design ready for specification, but the go-ahead did not come. The leftwing political parties wondered whether such a colossus of a temple of culture was really appropriate in a working-class neighbourhood. They wanted to look for a different location. Everything remained as it was: Waterlooplein without a town hall, the Pijp without an opera house.

Then, on 4 April 1979, Wilhelm Holzbauer launched an idea: combine the town hall and the opera house and build both on Waterlooplein. He had already put the idea down in a sketch and his arguments appealed to the city council: the combination was cheaper than the two buildings separately, it was more efficient because car parks and canteens, for instance, could be used jointly, and moreover it gave an extra fillip to the Waterlooplein area.

The architects of the opera were astounded. However, the 75-year old Holt and the 90-year-old Bijvoet realized that this would probably be the only way their *muziektheater* would ever be built. They accepted, but handed all further work over to Cees Dam, Holt's son-in-law.

Now the story threatens to become monotonous, for when Holzbauer and Dam presented their joint design in 1981,

The closed competition, in which seven teams took part, was finally won by the Viennese architect, Wilhelm Holzbauer. The jury praised his design, centre and left, for its 'exceptional symmetry', its 'extreme sensitivity', and its 'informal spatial quality'. The council chamber, running parallel with the river Amstel (left in the maquette), was in a 'highly unexpected manner integrated with the administration and other departments of the town hall'.

protest erupted once again. Artists, architects, publicists and others were agitated about the large-scale design, and architect Aldo van Eyck sneered that he could make such a design 'standing on his head'. An action group was formed with the name 'Stop the Opera', soon shortened to 'Stopera'. which became the nickname of the combination of town hall and opera.

Holzbauer and Dam modified their design slightly, but this did not silence the critics. Scorn and derision were heaped upon their work and many alternatives were submitted: the palace on Dam Square was mentioned yet again. But the local council remained cool. They were convinced that this was the last chance of seeing both the town hall and the *muziektheater* realized.

To make a very long story short: on 25 August 1982 the first pile was driven for the new building. After long years of discussion and dispute, after two competitions, Amsterdam would get its new town hall, and an opera house, *muziektheater,* (opened in September 1986). Reality can sometimes be utterly different from the shape of one's wildest dreams.

Holzbauer's winning design proved a controversial one and it was made impossible for him to carry out his commission. Ten years later, on the suggestion of Chr. Nielson, he proposed building a town hall and opera house combined.
The preparatory sketch which quickly won the approval of the city council. Maquette of the design, made in 1981, which had to be adapted to meet a new storm of protest from Amsterdammers.

CENTRE POMPIDOU IN PARIS

INTERNATIONAL COMPETITION FOR A CENTRE NATIONAL D'ART ET DE CULTURE IN PARIS, FRANCE.

ANNOUNCED: End December 1970; closing date: 1 June 1971; result: 15 July 1971; number of participants: 681.

JURY: Jean Prouvé (French architect and chairman); Gaétan Picon (former director-general of the Ministry of Arts and Letters, France); Sir Frank Francis (honorary director of the British Museum, Great Britain); Philip Johnson (architect, United States); Michel Laclotte (chief curator of the Musée du Louvre, France); Oscar Niemeyer (architect, Brazil); Willem Sandberg (ex-director of the Stedelijk Museum in Amsterdam, Netherlands); Herman Liebaers (director of the Royal Library, Belgium).
Reserve jury member: Henri-Pierre Maillard (architect, France).
The jury was assisted by a technical commission led by Robert Regard.

WINNERS: Renzo Piano (Italy) and Richard Rogers (Great Britain) with the collaboration of Gianfranco Franchini (Italy) and with advice from Ove Arup & Associates (Great Britain).

CONSTRUCTION: 1971/1977 after a design by Piano and Rogers.

Les Halles in 1854 with the church of St. Eustache, 1532-1637, in the background. In the foreground the huge stone reminders of the never completed Les Halles, designed by architects Baltard and Callet in 1845. In 1851 President Louis Napoleon laid the first foundation stone, but two years later, as emperor, abandoned the plan for buildings made from cast iron, seen under construction, left in the illustration, and also designed by the same architects.

A FRENCH HEAD OF STATE can sometimes behave like the chief mayor of Paris. Take Emperor Napoleon III. In 1853, when he saw the new buildings going up for the covered market in Paris' first arrondissement, he was so shocked by architect Victor Baltard's bulky design that he immediately ordered the work to stop, and independently organized a competition among architects for a new design. He wanted something similar to the metal roof of the new Gare de l'Est, and drawing some shapes on a sheet of paper, he said to Baron Hausmann, his recently appointed prefect of the Department of the Seine, 'I want vast roofs and nothing else'.

Hausmann, concerned with the sad lot that had befallen Baltard, kept the emperor's sketch, worked it out a bit, and asked his friend to come and see him. 'Here's your chance to take revenge,' he said to Baltard, pointing at the paper. 'Draw up a design based on this idea, and make everything from iron, iron and more iron.'

Baltard demurred. 'Iron!' he said scornfully, 'that's for engineers, not architects. Did Brunelleschi or Michelangelo ever build in iron?' Haussmann laughed. 'That's because they never had to build the central market halls.' Baltard swallowed his pride and was won over.

When the emperor later saw a maquette of Baltard's new Halls, in the town hall, he was so delighted with it that he turned to his aide, removed his medal, and spontaneously pinned the decoration on the architect's breast. Returning to his carriage, the emperor asked Haussmann what other buildings this wonderful architect had designed. 'The old Halls, sire.' came the reply. Amazed, Napoleon exclaimed, 'What! did you use the same architect?' To which Haussmann is said to have replied, 'Certainly, sire, but it was not the same prefect.'

Thanks to Haussmann's intervention the emperor's competition failed, and Paris got its 'Baltard's Halls' which were officially opened by Napoleon III in 1857.

Over a hundred years later, in the summer of 1964, little seemed to have changed. President Charles de Gaulle asked to see Paul Delouvrier, whom he had appointed as prefect of

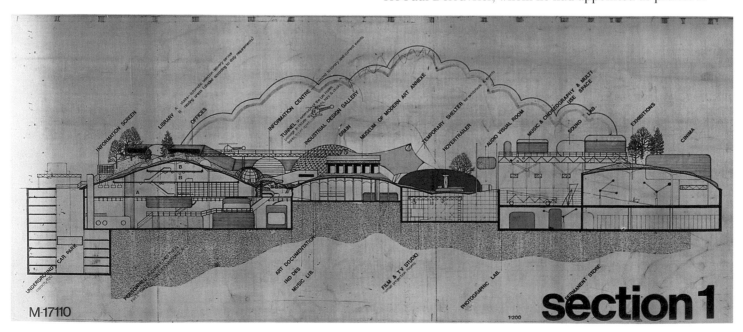

Paris in 1961, at the Elysée Palace, and instructed him to take charge of the city's building development. On this occasion, Delouvrier reminded the president of his predecessor, Haussmann, who had been lucky enough to work for 20 years under the same emperor. De Gaulle replied, 'We shan't remain in power for 20 years, but I shall support you unreservedly.' In the summer of 1964, Delouvrier showed De Gaulle his radical proposals for the city: new suburbs, new systems of public transport, new motorways, new building sites in Paris itself, as well as drastic forms of urban renewal. Delouvrier expected much opposition to these draconian plans, and told the general as much. With a grand sweep of his arm, De Gaulle assured Delouvrier, 'Tout cela se décidera ici' — 'It will all be decided here'.

De Gaulle was chief mayor of Paris, and one of the neighbourhoods to feel his influence was Les Halles. Although the French government had already decided to move the larger part of Les Halles to Rungis, it was now clear that the move was inevitable. The departure of the market would create a large gap in the heart of Paris which had to be filled. In January 1967 it was decided to hold a closed competition for a new development for the site. Since the area around Les Halles, especially towards the Marais quarter, had become run-down, this would also be included in the plans.

The 1967 competition concerned an area of 34 hectares, from the Bourse de Commerce to the Plateau Beaubourg, which in future would comprise a new commercial centre, a new Ministry of Finance, offices, hotels, dwellings, and — if any room was left — a national centre for modern art.

Initially, five architects were invited: Louis Arretche, Claude Charpentier, Jean Faugeron, Hoym de Marien and Michel Marot. At the insistence of the Minister of Culture, André Maurois, the Atelier d'Urbanisme et d'Architecture was also invited to take part.

The participants were asked to make maquettes, supplemented by drawings and function diagrams. The importance of the competition was further enhanced when in July 1967, in accordance with Delouvrier's grand plan, it was

Design number 0535 submitted under the name of the Englishman, Dennis Crompton, but in fact made by one of this third-year students, who used the name to gain access to the competition. He had reasonable success — his entry was one of thirty awarded 10,000 francs. The Plateau Beaubourg was created in a park, making it easily accessible for children. On ground level, park and exhibition halls met, and on the lower ground floor was a library, museum, storage space and garage. The jury praised the design because it could easily be adapted, over the years, for others purposes and interests.

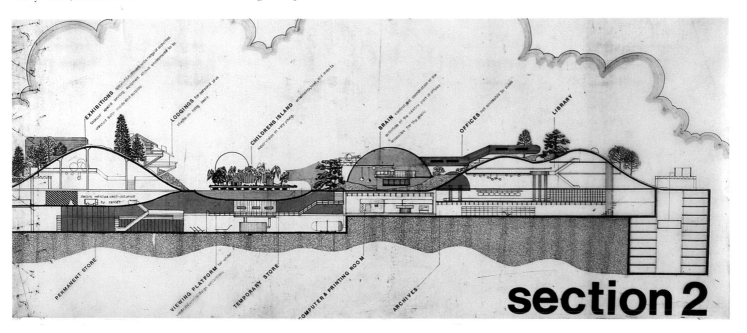

section 2

171

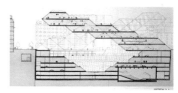

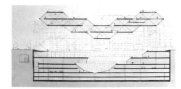

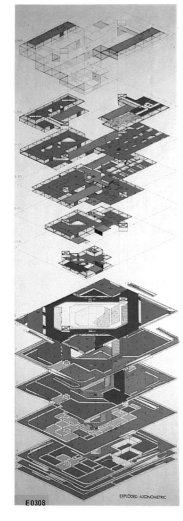

Above: Entry from the Israeli architect, Moshe Safdie, a crater-like shape with an overhanging structure which received 10,000 francs. Right: How the space would be used. Exhibition area is blue; general services, red; administration, yellow; and parking, green.

decided to build at Les Halles a super-fast metro for the new Réseau Express Régional (RER), which would link Paris with the new dormitory towns.

In March 1968 the maquettes were ready. First they were shown to President De Gaulle at the Elyséee, then to the city council, and finally Parisians could see them exhibited in the town hall.

The city council preferred the designs of Charpentier, Faugeron and De Marien. The public, however, were fiercely hostile to all six designs. At a meeting in March 1968, the chairman of the city council, René Capitant, expressed the feelings of Parisians in an inspired speech condemning the grandiose plans. Capitant urged for a city centre where Parisians and those from the suburbs could meet, and have access to diverse cultural manifestations — aspects he found lacking in the displayed maquettes.

The chairman's words were not without effect: the closed competition was a failure. The time was not ripe. Students were increasingly restless and there was a growing spirit for democratic reform. De Gaulle may have said to Delouvrier that the decision would be taken in the Elysée, but the Parisians thought differently. A commission was therefore set up, with Capitant as chairman, to prepare a second plan for Les Halles. Beside new buildings with underground facilities on the old site of Les Halles and the Plateau Beaubourg, much attention would this time be given to restoration. In this plan there was no room for a new Ministry of Finance.

In March 1969 most of Les Halles moved to Rungis and for a brief time it was quiet under Baltard's roofs, until Parisians triumphantly began taking over huge spaces for theatre, concerts, workshops, and a host of other activities. Parisians would have preferred to keep Les Halles for ever. Meanwhile

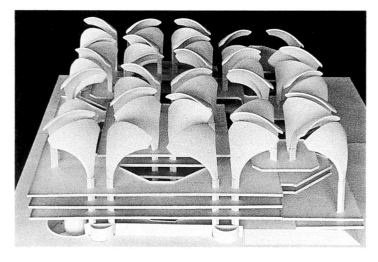

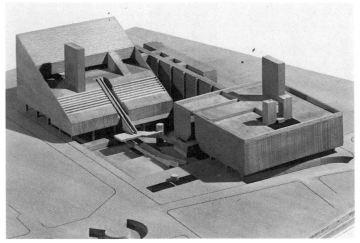

Top: Robert Stones, from Manchester, UK, and Wolfgang Pearlman's design of twelve-cornered, three-dimensional forms arranged haphazardly, posed questions for the jury. 'Could the public easily find their way around the complex? Was it technically viable?' Nevertheless, the design was financially rewarded.

Above: Giant 'flower petals' on massive 'stems' spanning a huge square, with underneath the exhibition halls. 'Aesthetically appealing', was the jury verdict, but again difficult to realize. Anyhow, worth 10,000 francs to Ahmet Gulgonen, Kemal Aran, Selhattin Onur and Matin Demiray from Turkey.

Above right: Dutchman Jan Hoogstad, who also submitted a study for the Amsterdam Town Hall, produced a design based on extreme mathematical precision.

the city of Paris was developing more modest plans.

Once again, though, it was to be shown that the real ruler of Paris was the French head of state. This was no longer General De Gaulle, who had resigned in April 1969, after the French people rejected some of his proposals for reform, but his successor, Georges Pompidou. He announced that a centre would be built at the Plateau Beaubourg entirely devoted to contemporary art.

The idea of a centre for modern art was not new. Minister André Malraux had launched this idea in 1959 and also had the site of Les Halles in mind. At the time, General De Gaulle had showed little enthusiasm for a modern building in the heart of Paris, and the project was moved to the new business quarter of La Défense. In 1965 Malraux commissioned Le Corbusier to design a museum for the twentieth century. Le Corbusier, although he was opposed to the location, accepted the commission. A few months later he died — his last signed architectural drawing, dated 29 June 1965, being a sketch for the museum.

President Pompidou, a connoisseur of modern art, attached great value to a national centre for contemporary art and culture. He justified his choice of the Plateau Beaubourg as a site, on the grounds that it was the only available spot in Paris where such a centre could be realized quickly. Once again, Paris was having its nose pushed under the facts by a head of state.

The Centre Beaubourg would be a building that 'crossed frontiers' and 'reflected current views of contemporary art'. To this end an international competition would be organized, which would break with the tradition of the Ministry of Culture co-opting its own architects.

For six months there were discussions, on what features the centre should have, between a government commission and its future users: the National Museum of Modern Art, the Bibliothèque des Halles, the Centre for Industrial Design and the Centre for Acoustic Research. Detailed function diagrams and flow charts were drawn up to be used as guidelines for future participants of the competition, if they so wished.

It was the first largescale, far-reaching competition ever set up in France, and was conducted in complete accordance with international guidelines. The names of the jury, made known in advance, indicated that the prize would not be awarded to any commonplace design. Chairman of the jury was the French architect, Jean Prouvé, known for his advanced technical designs, many of which could be manufactured industrially. True, other jury members were Gaétan Picon, former director-general of the Ministry of Art and Letters, Michel Lacotte, curator of the Louvre Museum, and Sir Frank Francis, honorary director of the British Museum in London, but from the modern art world there was Willem Sandberg, the former, strong-willed director of the Stedelijk Museum in Amsterdam. Under his leadership the Stedelijk had become one of the most important museums in the world for avant-garde art from the 1920s and 50s. There were also four other architects in the jury, Emile Aillaud from France, Philip Johnson from the United States, Oscar Niemeyer from Brazil and Jorn Utzon from Denmark — all renowned for their progressive views in architecture.

At the actual assessment, Utzon, winner of the competition for the opera house in Sydney, was unable to be present for health reasons. In order to retain the international character of the jury, Utzon was not replaced by Maillard, the original reserve jury member, but by the Belgian director of the Royal Library in Brussels, Herman Liebaers.

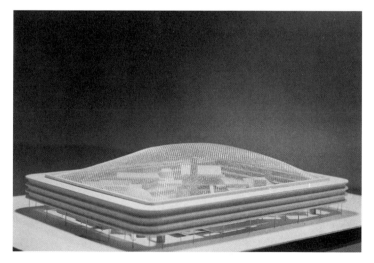

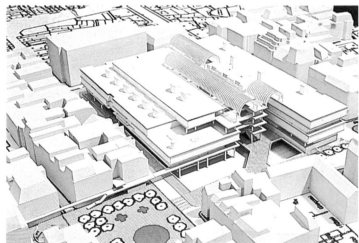

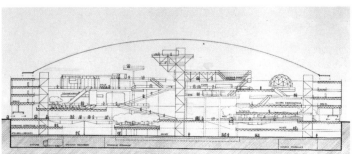

Above left and left: Manfred Schiedhelm, from West Berlin, kept the exterior of the complex surprisingly simple — an outsize transparent dome which would protect it from rain and pollution. Inside, however, a microclimate would be recreated. Interesting but too complicated, thought the jury; but it did win prize money.

Above: Dutchman J.L.C. Choisy's idea was to have the various spaces of the complex grouped around two covered-in, inner streets; a design which befitted its site, was the jury verdict, and awarded it 10,000 francs.

In December 1970, a year after President Pompidou had announced his proposal for a centre, the competition was officially opened. Few restraints were imposed on the architects regarding design and cost. The main objective, according to the programme, was to 'create a meeting place for the written word, plastic arts, architecture, music, film, and even for industrial design as an artistic genre. This meeting place for the various forms of art should enable the public at large to understand that despite the appearance of freedom surrounding the creation of a work of art . . . there exists a profound link between contemporary art and the relationships of production in society.'

In spite of the freedom given to architects, certain specific directives had to be complied with, such as the number of rooms required, but there were also more general ones, too. The centre had to be accessible. 'Everything is ultimately a question of the ease and the freedom with which the public can gain access to what is being offered and of the way in which the visitor is constantly being stimulated towards that which is being displayed.' And the rooms of the centre should be flexible: collections would be constantly renewed, which demanded a high degree of adaptability on the part of the architecture.

THE COMPETITION ATTRACTED much interest. By the end of May 1981, 681 entries had been received by the 'Délégation pour la réalization du Centre Beaubourg'. 186 of these came from France, the remaining 495 from 49 other countries.

On 5 July the jury met for the first time in the Grand Palais to familiarize themselves with all the entries anonymously on display. Some 100 designs were later selected and studied for their architectural suitability: the arrangement of spaces as stipulated in the programme; the internal communications; and the building's relationship to the world outside. The jury then made an initial selection.

Secondly, consideration was given to the result of an investigation made by the technical commission, under Robert Regard, into the technical aspects of the designs, including their 'permeability' and 'flexibility'. All the designs selected by the jury proved to meet these technical demands.

The technical commission was then invited to make separate assessments of some sixty designs already selected by the jury. After the jury had examined the future building site and its surroundings, the last selection took place, at which one design, number B 0493, was considered to be outstanding. Eight of the nine jurors favoured this design as the winner, and so the jury decided not to make any further awards.

This design by Kisho Kurokawa, from Japan, was, in the words of the jury, 'clear, thorough, consistent, and very flexible'. The focal point was an open-air square, which could be used for exhibitions, bordered by the various other complex spaces. These connected well, one with another, and because of their sloping planes fitted harmoniously into the immediate surroundings. In the plastic casings of the maquette, lifts were planned and an impressive moving staircase would transport visitors between the forecourt and the highest level of the complex.
Right-hand page: Preparatory study from Kurokawa, also financially rewarded by the jury.

However, 30 designs were deemed worthy of consolation prizes of 10,000 francs each for their 'esprit novateur', or spirit of renewal, and one design received a special mention for being of 'exceptional interest'.

On 15 July, after the names of the winning designers had been announced, number B 0493 was discovered to have been submitted by the architects, Renzo Piano and Richard Rogers, in cooperation with Gianfranco Franchini, and with the advice of the engineers' bureau, Arup and Associates. According to the jury, the design by Piano and Rogers was outstanding for a number of reasons. They were delighted that the building covered only half of the available site at the Plateau Beaubourg, and it was envisaged that the other half could be used as a square for a wide variety of lively activities. The building, although quite large and simple in shape, managed to avoid an impression of clumsiness and bulk by a transparent exterior which exposed the interior's lifts and elevators. The flexibility of the interior could be exploited to maximum effect because the internal spaces, measuring 50 by 150 metres, needed no weight-supporting columns. In short, technically and architecturally, this design met the expectations raised by the competition when it was first announced by President Pompidou in December 1969.

The public was less enthusiastic. After the jury's decision, a wave of protest broke which would continue for years. A group of prominent French architects, under the name 'Le Geste Architectural', tried six times via the courts to prevent the building of this 'Concord of Arts and Letters'. Even in the Assemblée Nationale, the French parliament, there were fierce debates about the desirability of Piano and Rogers' design. All criticism proved in vain. In 1972 Piano and Rogers, together with Ove Arup and Associates, worked out their design in further detail. Problems arose regarding fire regulations; the entire building had to be traversed with fire screens, and its height had to be adjusted to the length of the fire ladders used by the Paris Fire Brigade. The fire brigade also stipulated that the rear elevation at Rue Renard would have to be more or less walled up, which would lose the transparent quality of the building on that side. After one more thorough revision of the design, the construction at last started.

In a more general paper the jury wrote that the entries created the impression that 'we are currently entering a phase the effects of which will not be confined to France but which will make themselves felt throughout the world. This phase is undoubtedly characterized by the transition from a more

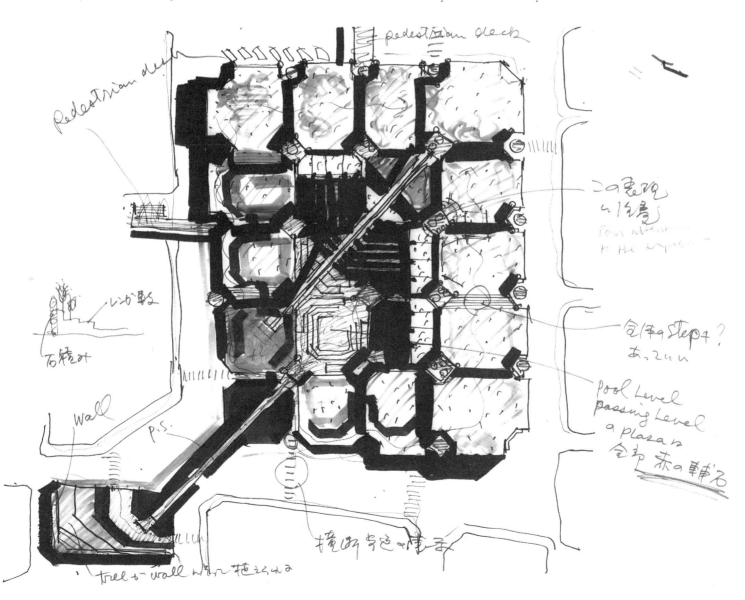

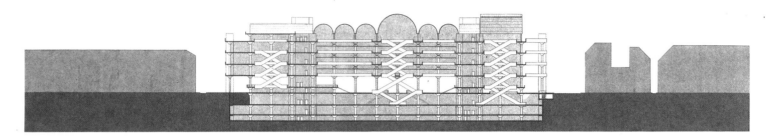

individual towards a more collective way of designing.' Even to outsiders, it is clear that the Centre Beaubourg marked a new phase in architecture. It is not too bold to state that the reactions of the prominent French architects were inspired by an uneasy feeling of insecurity. The competition had been deliberately used as a means to escape from the system of co-option which had hitherto been a feature of many important French architectural commissions. Moreover, the independent, international jury appears to have been fully alert to the latest developments in the world of architecture; developments with which many established architects were not yet in tune.

The design by Piano and Rogers arose directly from a number of more or less latent trends of the 1950s and 60s - from views on architecture that were so fanciful and free that they were rarely realized in practice. We can think here of Constant Nieuwenhuys' New Babylon, of works by Archigram, of the Fun Palace by Cedric Price and Joan Littlewood, to mention a few. Some writers even see a link with the equally imaginative — and equally unrealized — designs by the Russian constructivists.

The jury of the competition for the Plateau Beaubourg acknowledged these unorthodox ideas based on self-confident, radical techniques. This link with the avant-garde of the 1960s was later clearly appreciated and accepted by the public of the 1970s and 80s. The competition programme had asked for a building capable of accommodating 10,000 visitors a day, roughly 3 million per year. Within a few years of its opening,

seven to eight million people were visiting the centre a year; more than the total annual number of visitors to the Eiffel Tower and the Louvre combined.

It has been the strength of the architects Piano and Rogers that they were able to preserve the essence of their ideas in spite of pressure by many ill-disposed parties, sceptical fire experts and obstructionist politicians. The result is a building which, fifteen years after its conception, still inspires architects all over the world.

We must not forget, however, that the initiative for a building on this site came from President Georges Pompidou. He has often been reproached for not preventing the demolition of Baltard's Halles. This criticism is probably justified. But Pompidou understood very clearly that after the intervention of General De Gaulle, and his right hand, Paul Delouvrier, the time was ripe for a president to put his own idiosyncratic stamp on Paris and thereby on French culture. Pompidou wanted a building which emanated radiance.

It has been said that between 1945 and 1970 Paris produced only five buildings of international stature. Pompidou wanted to give Paris a building with charisma, and an international competition with an independent jury appeared to be the best means to stir up the sluggish architectural climate in France. Pompidou thus set the tone for the policy of later presidents. The fact that, in the 1980s, Paris regained something of her self-confident air of the Second Empire was largely the result of that strange building at the Plateau Beaubourg.

As contrast to the rather severe lines of his building, Charles Vandenhove, from Belgium, added a semi-circular transparent structure to its upper floor. This form was repeated in the portals on the ground floor.

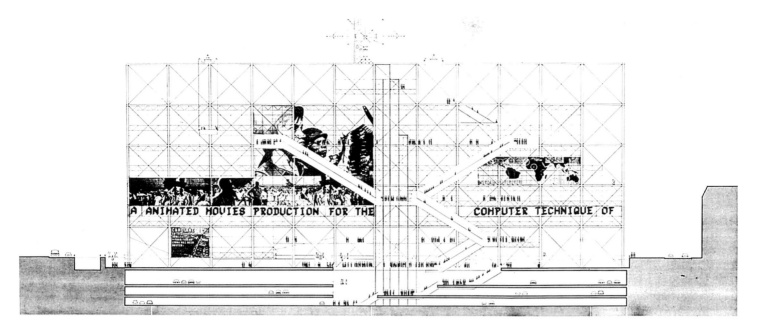

The winning entry, submitted by Piano and Rogers, was a transparent structure with a huge glass façade. Its floors were suspended on the building's three-dimensional steel framework, which eliminated the need for vertical constructions and provided outstanding freedom of movement. Communication — a keyword from the 1960s — was the intention behind the design. Life-size images, lighted text, and projection screens could all be hung on the steel structure. Even the roof of the complex had parabolic aerials.

GEORGES POMPIDOU DID NOT LIVE TO see the opening, in 1977, of the Centre for National Art and Culture. He died in 1974; but the building was named after him and is now known as the Centre Pompidou. Emperor Napoleon would have envied him.

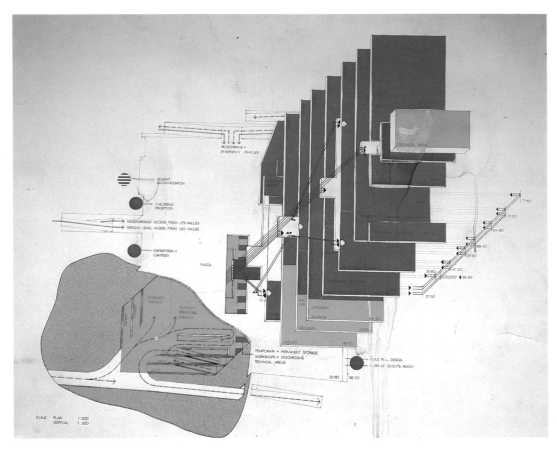

Left: Maquette of Piano and Rogers' design gives a good impression of the transparent quality of the building. The façade is hung with pictorial images and announcements of forthcoming attractions. After the results of the competition were made known, in 1971, Piano and Rogers made a second design to comply with local building regulations regarding height. Centre left: The lower structure with rounded corners won the full approval of President Pompidou, but it still was not right. Centre right: New designs were made; the curved corners disappeared and the escalator on the outside wall was rethought.

On 31 January 1977, the centre was officially opened, without the presence of President Pompidou, who died three years too soon. The building, however, was named after him: Centre Georges Pompidou.

Below: Due to fire regulations the rear of the building sacrificed its transparent quality for a massive structure of painted funnels and pipes.

ARCHITECTURAL COMPETITIONS: A WATERSHED BETWEEN OLD AND NEW

DENNIS SHARP

COMPETITIONS ARE BAROMETERS OF ARCHITECTURAL TASTE. They are often seen as useful gauges of contemporary architectural philosophies; a means whereby current trends, as well as new fashions, fads and fantasies can be explored. However, the composition of competition juries and the nature of competition briefs often militate against the successful outcome of this lively client-free genre. Indeed, it might be seriously argued that some juries and some briefs have so staunched creative originality and innovation that they have proved to be working against the values they appear to expound.

Some of the more spectacular competitions of the inter-war period were virtually nullified by disagreement amongst jury members, by idiosyncratic prejudices and acts, by chauvinism or even by downright chicanery. In the nineteenth century when the composition of juries and the nature of the brief often clearly indicated the predilections of the promoters for one architectural style or another — or even a mixture of architectural styles — the outcome was almost predictable. This century has seen fundamental conflicts between the ideological positions adopted by the traditionalists and the pre-occupation of so-called 'modern' architects and their promotion of the tenets and means of expression of the 'new' architecture.

While it would be an exaggeration to assume that all the major competitions of this century were distinguished by this dichotomy, it is worth exploring the history of some of them to illustrate the confusion caused by such strong irrational prejudices. It was never a simple trad-v-modernism argument but one fraught with 'in-between' judgements — often voiced by strong-minded jurists with international reputations at stake. Sometimes, as in the case of Le Corbusier and Jeanneret's submission for the League of Nations competition, Geneva, 1927, a competitor took up a David and Goliath stance in defending a scheme which it was felt far surpassed any other, by solving all the problems of the brief in a new and superior way.

In the following account of some of these important competitions of the first half of this century, I shall try to discuss, isolate and underline the ideological positions of the promoters, the juries and also the entrants. The competitions include the planning project for Canberra, the new political capital of Australia, won, despite the jury, by the hardly known Chicago architect, Walter Burley Griffin, in 1912; the new offices for the Chicago Tribune Tower, in 1922; and the highly unsuccessful competition for the League of Nations Building, for Geneva, in 1927. It is also an account of astounding stories of confused goals, misdirected aims, befuddled conclusions and ruined reputations. A sequence of international competitions, in fact, without any semblance of justice. Some of the most innovative schemes were condemned as impracticable and in most cases the promoters were forced, by compromise, to choose the most conservative schemes as alternative solutions.

THE NEW FEDERAL CAPITAL OF AUSTRALIA COMPETITION, 1911-1912
Some of the large-scale competitions of the early part of this century were neither clearly worked out, nor had adequate briefs. Even worse, sometimes jurors were not properly agreed upon or appointed.

The competition conditions for the erection of a New Federal Capital City of Australia on a virgin site at Canberra were notorious in this respect. The arrangements for the competition were considered so unsatisfactory, that many international architectural bodies declined to have anything at all to do with it. In this case, doubts arose over the

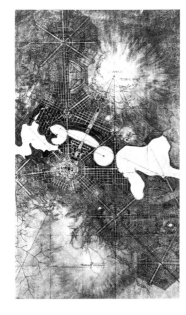

Left: Maquette of Piano and Rogers' design gives a good impression of the capital. Above left: Sketch from Griffin's design for Canberra. Right: Recent photograph of the city, seen from same aspect, north-east.

composition of a jury largely made up of local civil engineers — the brief, after all, was for an architecture and town planning scheme. The rightness of the site was also queried. When the secretary of the Royal Institute of British Architects in London questioned the make-up of the jury — mainly on behalf of his Australian architect members — he was brushed off by the Australian high commissioner and informed that: 'The nature of the competition must be kept in view. It is not for a building or a series of buildings. It is to submit a design for a new city ... '. Thus, the high commissioner seriously prevented the RIBA and its Australian membership from having more architectural representation on the jury, and created a stalemate. The institute and its affiliated architectural bodies all boycotted the competition, and it was left to independent outsiders to take advantage of the situation, which fortunately they did. The competition was eventually won by the remarkably talented American architect, Walter Burley Griffin, from Chicago, who had been one of Frank Lloyd Wright's most gifted early apprentices. The great Finnish architect and town planner, Eliel Saarinen, came second — a position that, ironically, he was again to achieve in the Chicago Tribune Tower competition, a decade later. Agache of Paris received the third premium.

Griffin's grandiose but extremely original entry was set out on 'civic design' lines which dramatically fleshed out in new form those principles of layout and massing that could be seen in l'Enfant's Washington DC, and somewhat paradoxically in Howard's diagram of the 'two magnets'. Similar proposals to these were set out in literary detail in Charles Mulford Robinson's book *Modern Civic Art: The city made beautiful*, a publication that advocated the practical basis of civic aesthetics. In his wonderfully evocative publication, Robinson extolled the virtues of a city composed from the hands of an artist who was a 'sort of social reformer' and who wanted the surroundings of man 'to be clean, wholesome and uplifting, as well as pleasant to see'. Griffin, in effect, produced a valley city (cp. P. Geddes) with an impressive new reflective waterfront controlled by two major axes: one, a land axis that lay between the moutains Ainslie and Bimberi and crossed a distance of some 30 miles; the other, an axis extending from the river to Black Mountain that required the development of the great ornamental waterway. These main axes and other minor ones focused on the proposed capital itself, which supported the major civic buildings. The lack of progress in implementing this geometrical design was later sharply criticized by Thomas Adams, one of the founding fathers of the British Garden City

movement. These fundamental criticisms, however, should not obscure the strength of the 'modern' designed buildings which owe something perhaps to Garnier, but are convincingly American.

CHICAGO TRIBUNE TOWER COMPETITION, 1922

It is now America's turn to play the lead in the drama of a major competition that focused attention on the modern idea of the skyscraper, a building which had fascinated American architects since the early part of this century. Many avant-garde designers in Europe found its 'modern' imagery compelling and in line with their views of the 'new' architecture. Publicity around the Chigaco Tribune Tower competition of 1922 claimed it was an opportunity to design the most advanced example of this new type of building on Michigan Boulevard. America was ready for it; Europe it appears was not far behind. The ensuing conflicting interests between those who had submitted designs and their external critics and supporters brought to a head the whole argument surrounding the future of the American skyscraper, long after the competition was over. However, although it was never explicitly stated, there is little doubt that the winners had to be seen to be American. The competition attracted worldwide interest: by the extended closing date for postal entries from abroad, 1 December 1923, 204 schemes had been received.

Competition entry by Eliel Saarinen won second prize.

59 more designs were received after the competition closed. Entries came from 23 countries.

Much of the foreign, European work was still in the classical style, although it was unpremiated designs like those submitted by Bruno Taut, and Gropius and Meyer that later received the approval of architectural critics and historians. Indeed, it could be argued that Gropius and Meyer's office block provided a framework for the idea of the modern office building, partly echoing the pioneering example of Frank Lloyd Wright for the Larking firm in Buffalo, NY, in 1904. If one uses something like a Richter scale, but then for avant-garde principles, Gropius and Meyer's scheme would undoubtedly score high; its effect was explosive. Yet, unfortunately, it was not received in time to be properly considered. This project was as 'modern', in terms of inventing a new acceptable technology and in its expressive 'functional' aesthetics, as it could be. But in competition terms perhaps, like other schemes by Bijvoet and Duiker, was its simplicity too forthright? Undoubtedly, the fact that the competition itself established a precedent for the use of monotone drawings, made the drawing of a repetitive and undecorated façade easier to assimilate. Interestingly enough, the competition conditions (Part 2-15-J) excluded the use of colour drawings, although it was later agreed in the 'Replies to Questions' that black ink washes could be used for the rendering of the black and white drawings themselves. This technique, one could argue, played right into the hands of the modernists, leaving the traditionalists with little opportunity of preparing the elaborate watercolour washes usually associated with their type of projects.

The competition conditions, however, left the question of any preferred style for the building wide open. The promotors merely required designs for: 'The most beautiful office building in the world.' In choosing the prizewinning scheme by Howells and Hood, it was an aim unfortunately not achieved. Although a remarkable design, carried out in the then much

Perspective drawing, looking at the city from the north-east, from Saarinen's first entry.

favoured Gothic Revival style, it did not achieve the 'built' quality or even the civic sense of the Woolworth Building, New York, nor, indeed, that sense of special significance shared by some of its more famous neighbouring structures in Chicago. It was a building that extolled 'the craving for beauty', a notion imbued with high romance, as Louis Sullivan observed. Whether 'high romance' is a strong enough motive to achieve a 'living symbol' for the headquarters of a national newspaper is a vexed question. In the 1920s one would have thought that a building that symbolised swift and efficient production of newspapers would have commanded the most respect, like Sir Owen Williams' buildings for the *Daily Express* newspaper in London, Manchester and Glasgow did a decade or so later in Great Britain.

Many people felt that the competition would lead to an early acceptance of the 'new' architecture. It didn't. But it did provide the opportunity — at least in theory — to erect the best design for a brand new type of skyscraper. The progressive city of Chicago, it was argued, could provide the site for such a stupendous challenge. Indeed, the widely admired entry by the Finnish architect, Eliel Saarinen, was, according to a preliminary announcement, to be the first prizewinner. But the judges went back on this decision and a safe Gothic and local scheme, the one by Howells and Hood, was pronounced the most appropriate for the newspaper's headquarters.

The decision provoked scorn in many quarters. Writing in the *Architectural Record* in February 1923, Louis Sullivan protested passionately against the decision. He began his article by reiterating the primary aim of the competition which, he states, was 'to secure the design for a structure distinctive and imposing — the most beautiful office building in the world'. The *Tribune*, he said, 'set its bow in the cloud' and the ideas of the promoters were imbued 'with romance; with that high romance which is the essence, vital impulse that inheres in all the great works of man . . . ' He went on: 'Viewed in this light, the second and the first prize stand before us side by side . . . The verdict of the jury of award is twice reversed, and the second prize is placed first where it belongs by virtue of its beautifully controlled and virile power. The first prize is devoted to the level of those works evolved of dying ideas . . . the Finnish master-edifice is not a lonely voice crying in the wilderness; it is a voice resonant and rich ringing against the tide and wilderness of life.' Sullivan went on to extol the virtues of the 'master of ideas' from Finland and in his effusive way claims that this foreigner possessed the insight to read the heart of the American people. So why did the jury throw this priceless pearl away? Firstly, Sullivan concludes, it is an imaginary structure, its formula was literary. Sullivan surmised that the Finn believed that he had a great idea but did not quite understand the nature of his design. The jury lost faith. They played safe.

In his book, *The Arch Lectures*, of 1942, Sullivan's friend and admirer, Claude Bragdon, cited Cass Gilbert's important influence on skyscraper design which culminated in the award-winning scheme by Howells and Hood. Bragdon described the winning project as pseudo-Gothic in style, a fine piece of stage scenery made to look as picturesquely medieval as possible but 'with an unresolved crown lantern'. He treated Saarinen's second premiated design in a more conciliatory tone, referring to it as the one in which 'the loser wins'. He spoke of it as 'simple, direct, unpretentious with a square tower that stopped, but with an indefinable felicity ...' He justified his remarks by referring to Louis Sullivan: 'Sullivan hailed this design as a return to and a carrying forward of those principles of which he had been an advocate and exemplar.' Indeed, much of the argument at the time was concerned with the swaying of opinion about these two main designs. Although there were many other examples of American pseudo-Gothic among the entries and some examples of what Hitchcock called 'the new tradition' among the foreign entries, most critics were prepared to save their discussions of the proposals for the virtues and defects of the Howells and Hood, and Saarinen projects. Even fellow competitors like Bernard Goodhue declared that Saarinen's design was 'in a class by itself and superior to all the others'. G.H. Edgel in his influential book *American Architecture of Today*, (New York, 1928) later spoke of Howells and Hood's scheme as 'the most successful design in one of the most sensational competitions of the last decade, and its selection was a triumph for conservation.' It was, he claimed: 'one of the most beautiful buildings in America.' Sheldon Cheney in his book *New World Architecture* called the competition 'the most dramatic event of the transitional years which occurred in Chicago, the original home of the skyscraper'.

The impact of Saarinen's design, though never built, was decisive and monumental. There is some kind of poetic justice in Bragdon's remark that Hood's unornamented and vertical Daily News Building in New York was 'entirely in the spirit of Saarinen's unsuccessful design (for the Tribune Tower) and as unlike the successful one as can be imagined'! There was in Hood's own work a new simplifying of architectural elements. More generally, Bragdon indicated that 'Saarinen's influence on skyscraper architecture has been pronounced, particularly in Chicago, where his formula has been followed in the Board of Trade and in the Palmolive Buildings'. Indeed, these buildings brought into focus 'certain tendencies which had already been making themselves felt and which reached their full flower in the Rockefeller Center group — simple rectilinear masses, soaring lines, no crowning cornices and a general absence of applied ornament'.

With George Howe's Philadelphia Saving Fund Society Bank and Office Tower of 1929 — projected as early as 1926 — a truly progressive style had emerged for the American skyscraper. The traditional values of architects like Raymond Hood and Ralph Adams Cram, who earlier had been totally opposed to the modernism of Europe, were challenged by this new design which gave credence to the sophisticated treatment of the exterior of the new skyscraper. 'In terms of previous American design, this project stands as a synthesis between Sullivan's concern between horizontal and vertical in a building, best seen in the Bayard and Guaranty Buildings, and the design, not so refined structurally but more concerned with a statement of power, produced by Frank Lloyd Wright for the San Francisco Call in 1912.' With this statement, Robert A.M. Stern in his book on George Howe underlines the Philadelphia Saving Fund Society connection with the Chicago Tribune Tower competition. 'In its external effects, it resembles most closely the scheme drawn up but never submitted by the Danish architect, Knud Lønberg-Holm, a project which was widely illustrated in European magazines. Although poorly worked out from a construction and functional point of view its elegant design of coloured facing materials 'compares with Howe's more direct, if less dazzling attempts at such expression'.

To return to Saarinen; his near success in the competition led eventually to his staying in the United States. He was appointed visiting professor at the University of Michigan in 1924, where one of his students was the son of the British publisher, George Booth, whose newspaper empire included the *Detroit News*. It was Booth who commissioned Saarinen to design a number of educational buildings including a museum and library, and a boys' school on the Booth estate at Bloomfield Hills, Michigan, called Cranbrook. Saarinen was appointed president of the Cranbrook Academy of Art, a post

P. 185 shows six designs for the Chicago Tribune Tower, 1922. Above, l. to r.: Winning design by Hood and Howell; design by second prizewinner Eliel Saarinen; design by Bertram G. Goodhue of New York. Below: Plans by Paul Gerhardt of Chicago; Adolf Loos of Vienna; Bijvoet and Duiker from the Netherlands.

Hood, Howells

Eliel Saarinen

Bertram G. Goodhue

Paul Gerhardt

Adolf Loos

Bijvoet, Duiker

he held from 1932 until his death in 1950. At Cranbrook, Saarinen, helped by the great Swedish sculptor, Carl Milles, built a craft-orientated emphasis into his postgraduate curriculum. He also practised as an architect, designing a number of churches and schools in various parts of the United States and later worked in collaboration with his son. Eero.

DEMANDS ACHIEVED?

The Chicago Tribune Tower competition was a confusion of aims. On the one hand it was promoted as a competition to produce a modern, sturdy efficient office building, but on the other demanded that the result would also produce the most 'beautiful office building' in the world. These commercial and aesthetic goals were utterly conflicting and underscored the gap between the American promoters, who saw their competition in the context of the new 'artistic' skyscraper ideals, and the architects of the Continental *Neue Bauen*, who were wedded to the idea of new style of glass architecture, light and simple of form. The Europeans were also concerned with the functional efficiency of planning, but very much against the applied ornamentation beloved of the immediate post-Sullivan generation of US architects. Indeed, decoration was anathema to the Europeans even, metaphorically speaking, a criminal offence. But this did not prevent Adolf Loos — whose own discussion of ornament as crime in 1908 became increasingly popular in Europe in the 1920s — from submitting a simple naked Doric column on a base for the new newspaper offices' design. He justified his 'outrageous' antique proposal by claiming that newspapers — Loos was a

journalist — were also set in columns and he wanted 'to erect something which, whether seen pictorially or in reality, should indelibly impress all beholders... a monument which intellectual people will instantly connect with the Chicago Tribune'. It was not a new idea; a similar but larger Doric column had been projected as the main feature for the nineteenth century bicentennial celebrations of the city of Detroit. Louis Sullivan, in one of his articles in the *Interstate Architect and Builder* of 1901-2, denounced it in characteristic fashion. Its design, he claimed, was a specific example of the 'lack of imagination' in architecture. Although he does not go so far as to reveal the designer's name, he pokes fun at Loos's claim that he had produced the 'largest column in the world' which will 'rank with the famous monuments of all time'. Rising to this bait, Sullivan added that it would probably be 'famous among the rank monuments of all time'! Somewhat paradoxically, Sullivan had earlier developed a tall buildings' vocabulary based on the parts of the classical column, with the moulded base of the column, for instance, 'typical of the lower stories of our building, the plain or fluted shaft suggesting the monotonous, uninterrupted series of office tiers'. Sullivan wrote a scornful criticism of the Chicago Tribune Tower competition in *The Architectural Record* of February, 1923, a year before his death. It applauded the appropriateness of Saarinen's reneged entry but offered no comment on Loos's column.

An extraordinary design — innovative and far reaching in its prophetic implications — was the one submitted by Bruno Taut. It has been termed a 'bell-shaped' skyscraper and there is little doubt that this pointed design was seen as an effective compromise between the American tradition of Gothicising the skyscraper and the utopian modernism of Scheerbart's transparent glass and concrete construction. Bijvoet and Duiker's design was in some ways even more extraordinary as it expanded to skyscraper scale the prairie house motifs of Frank Lloyd Wright and his followers, yet was itself a staccato-like symphony of horizontal and vertical concrete forms from the *De Stijl* vocabulary. H.R. Hitchcock in his *Modern Architecture* (1929) referred to the design as 'among the few projects which already represented in this competition a reaction from the New Tradition'.

INDECISION AND ROOTED CONSERVATISM

One of the more influential architectural competitions in Europe was staged in 1927 at Geneva for the new League of Nations Building. Victor Horta was the jury's president and other jury members included a number of modern

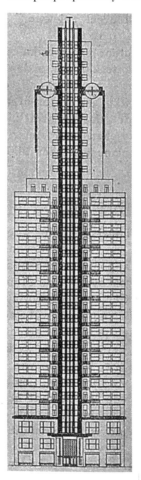
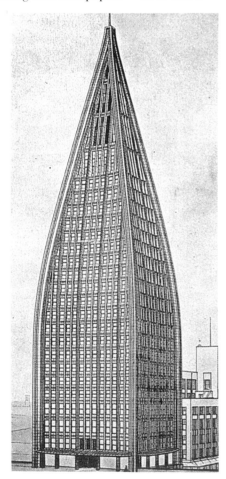

Right: Design for Tribune Tower by Bruno Taut, Walter Gunther and Kurt

Schutz; left: Design by Knud Lønberg-Holm from Denmark.

Three designs for the League of Nations Building in Geneva, 1927. Above left: Hakon Ahlberg from Sweden. Centre: Emil Fahrenkamp and Albert Deneke from Düsseldorf. Below: Plan by Parisian Louis H. Boileau, influenced by Auguste Perret.

architecture's elder statesmen: the Dutch master, H.P. Berlage, the Austrian, Josef Hoffmann, the Swiss architect (who, a year later, became the first president of the CIAM) Karl Moser and the Swedish architect, Ivan Tengbom. The remainder of the jury was made up of less well-known but eminently successful contemporary practising architects from various European countries, including Sir John Burnett (London), C. Gato (Madrid), C. Lemaresquier (Paris) and A. Muggia (Bologna). Such an eclectic mix of opinionated individualists ensured a wide range of premiated schemes from the outset. Looking back, it seems unlikely that such a mixed international group could ever agree on anything but a pragmatic solution and this was eventually confirmed after six weeks of deliberation about the 377 sets of drawings (estimated at the time to cover 14 kilometres, if laid end to end). Not one of these schemes was actually used: '. . . the jury unanimously decided that the results of the competition did not justify recommending any one of the plans for execution'. However, the jury did unanimously decide to distribute the sum of 165,000 Swiss francs that was placed at its disposal among 27 projects: 9 prizes at 12,000 francs; 9 prizes at 3,800 francs for Honourable Mentions, Class 1; and 9 prizes at 3,500 francs for Honourable Mentions, Class 2.

A few years later Le Corbusier was making similar noises

Palais de la Société
des Nations à Genève

about his rejected design for the Palace of Soviets competition in Moscow in 1931-33. But by this time the ideological paths we have been referring to earlier in this article had drastically diverged: traditional values were now to coincide more with the obscure tenets of a new 'social realism' than with a beaux-arts training. Modern architecture was accused of rejecting the class struggle. The compromise in this case was for the jury to advocate a synthesis of modern and classical ideas. Things had not changed.

Such indecisiveness as this, together with the catholicity of some members of the jury, was clearly shown in the 27 premiated designs. The level of competence and contemporary relevance of all the winning projects was never in doubt. Judging of this architectural competition was based on an 'anything goes' philosophy; a design only had to meet the jury's own disparate 'architectural and artistic qualities'. It was not surprising, therefore, to find monumental Schinkelesque schemes side by side with elaborate examples of the beaux-arts tradition. Also represented was the new architecture style, in mature works submitted by Le Corbusier and P. Jeanneret, and Hannes Meyer and Hans Witwer. They all appear to have justified being included on stylistic, rather than ideological grounds.

The published report of the jury gives some idea of the methods of assessment. Having 'proceeded to study the plans and examined their architectural and artistic qualities from the point of view of site, facilities for movement inside the building and traffic outside, arrangement and form of the building, construction and harmonious and logical architectural development' they discovered there was a 'wealth of ideas'. But, the jury concurred, few competitors adhered 'strictly enough to the material conditions required by the programme and rules. With regard to the carrying out of the programme, the fact that the designs show fundamental differences in their conception of the scheme is explained by the evolutionary phase through which contemporary architecture is now passing'.

This is a revealing statement, for it underlines the conviction the jury held that a kind of Darwinist evolutionary process was at work in the architectural world, and although it says little about its fate or purpose — one can infer that the new architecture was regarded as only a temporary climax of this trend. If this was the case, then one would have thought the entries which featured this new architectural direction would have been isolated from the rest. But this was not so and was also not borne out within the order of winning designs. In the first major prizewinning group, Le Corbusier and Pierre Jeanneret's design (No. 273) was the very antithesis to most other schemes. Only the nationalistic entry of Emil Fahrenkamp and A. Denike of Dusseldorf (332) played lip service to the new architecture and then with expressionistic overtones. Hannes Meyer and Hans Wittwer, fram Basle, in the Class 2 Honourable Mentions, sat uneasily between the overtly 'fantastical expressionism' of J.N. Luthman (The Hague), and the charming hint of Swedish nationalism present in the scheme of Hakon Ahlberg (Stockholm). In this group were three further examples of carefully worked out, middle-of-the-road modernism. H.T. Wijdeveld's scheme echoed the current and exciting store façade design style. This neat asymmetrical entry was exceptionally well worked out as regards free movement, and proposed a functional sub-division of planning uses, which became the symbolic elements of the project. The League's Council Chamber, for instance, with its huge curve represented a bold symbolic public statement on democratic procedures.

The scheme submitted by the Stuttgart Railway Station architects, Paul Bonatz and E.F. Scholar, Stuttgart (241) adopted a more robust Germanic approach to the problem in which a typical *Miethaus* façade contrasted with an open-entrance courtyard, placed asymmetrically, in which another huge semi-circular chamber sat.

Of all these projects, however, the one most closely associated with the New Architecture of Berlin was the design submitted by A. Fischer and R. Speidel (Essen), with its vast, flat-roofed square blocks, in a kind of Mendelsohnian style, and sequences of courtyards, diminishing in size.

None of these schemes could be described as 'traditional' nor positively stylistic in any Neo-Classical sense. That was left to masters of that grotesque academic civic style, like Broggi, Vaccaro and Franzi (Rome), Camille LeFèvre (Paris), and others whose designs were meant to impress the public and jury with grandeur. opulence and order. Putlitz, Klophaus and Schoch of Hamburg (298) saw the League's potentially symbolic purpose could be enshrined in a symmetric, rectangular, multi-columned Pantheon, monumental like Schinkel's Altes Museum. In such a heavy overcoat, this Neo-Classical design was meant to last for ever. What a contrast this was to the two major examples of the new architecture, with their freshness of architectural intent. They were expressions of light and harmony, incorporating the new constructional methods and inventions. Both the designs of Le Corbusier/Jeanneret, and

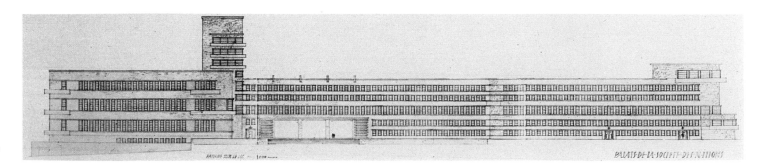

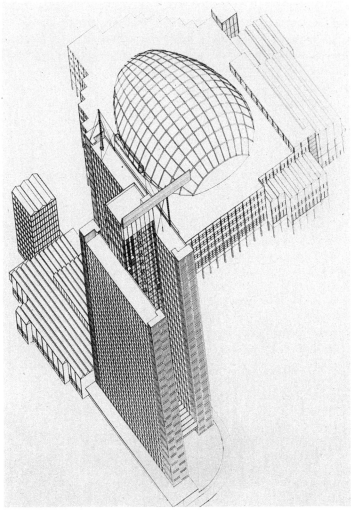

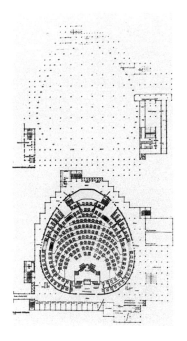

A 'peak in modern architecture' in the League of Nations competition was the design by Hannes Meyer and Hans Wittwer (ground plan and perspective, left). Together with eight other entries it received second-class honourable mention, as did the design by H.Th. Wijdeveld of Amsterdam — see below his drawing of perspective and façade.

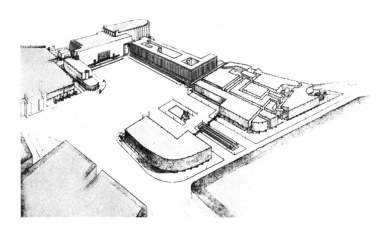

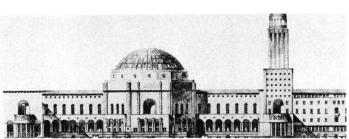

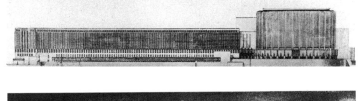

P. 188 shows the design for the League of Nations Building by A. Fischer-Essen and R. Speidel from Essen. Below: Design by Camille Lefèvre of Paris. Above: Giuseppe Vago of Rome, and Carlo Broggi. Right: Giuseppe Vaccaro and Luigi Franzi of Rome. Vago, Broggi and Lefèvre formed part of the team that finally designed the building.

Above: The Palais des Nations, or
League of Nations as it was known
until 1946; the building was officially
opened in 1937, after a definitive
design had been accepted in 1929.
This design was produced by a team
of five architects all of whom had
gained (first-class) honourable
mention in the competition.

Meyer/Witwer epitomized the cooperative and social democratic idea behind the optimistically created League. Whereas Walter Gropius's entry for the Chicago Tribune Tower competition of 1922 had taken into account the rectangular trabeated surface treatment of the new buildings with their formal abstract grids, cubic forms and recessive planes, Le Corbusier's and Meyer's schemes reached a new level of three dimensional sophistication and abstractionism.

The brief proved important for generating ideas both at the level of the plan as well as in façade treatment. In the Meyer/Wittwer scheme, the elegance and asymmetry of the plan suggested, by its columned supports, a profound abstract quality. The huge egg-shaped Council Chamber erupted out of a rectangular circulation block to articulate the plan by volume. In the Le Corbusier/Jeanneret project similar attitudes, but by no means identical, were at work. In both schemes features of symbolism and functionality merged; they were places in which to enjoy life and work. There is indeed a common line of architectural thought running through parts of the plans, which would lead one to believe that New Architecture had found a logical expression of its own, even though it had not yet become part of that evolutionary process, progressive and mythological, wished for by the jury. In the end they awarded the actual commission, as Le Corbusier later said 'to four academic architects' whose 'composite design was formally ratified and adopted' at a meeting of the League in 1929 in Madrid. Le Corbusier, understandably, was miffed. With Jeanneret he legally contested the acceptable design, claiming that it bore little resemblance to the original one submitted by the four architects. He wrote: 'It is incontestible that this joint design was directly inspired by the design of MM. Le Corbusier and Pierre Jeanneret which the assessors had premiated in 1927 and still more obviously by a second design the same architects submitted to them in April, 1929.' The plea was ignored.

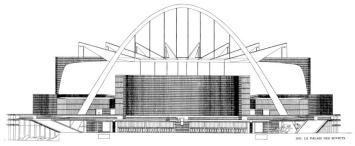

Above: Drawing from the design made by Le Corbusier — pseudonym for Charles Edouard Jeannerel — for the League of Nations Building, 1927. Below: Design by Le Corbusier for the Palace of the Soviets in Moscow, 1931-1933.

The former League of Nations
Building in Geneva is the result of
one of the most notorious
architectural competitions ever held:
it produced only losers. The palace
was finally designed by five architects
who had all received first-class
honourable mentions, sec p. 190.
Le Corbusier, who also received an
honourable mention but was not one
of the chosen five, objected that the
definitive design bore remarkable
resemblance to his competition entry.

Le Corbusier at Geneva: The Debacle of the Société des Nations 1926-1939

Kenneth Frampton

Monumental Purism

The three palatial public structures designed by Le Corbusier and Pierre Jeanneret between 1926 and 1931 are effectively the apotheosis of their Purist career, coming as they do at the end of a highly creative period during which they still subscribed to the manifest destiny of the machine age.

The three designs for the Société des Nations competition of 1927, the Centrosoyus, Moscow, of 1929, and the Palais des Soviets competition of 1931 are all uncompromisingly Functionalist proposals. And yet, while these works were all conceived as large 'mechanisms', they were nonetheless organized and inflected by monumental systems of axial order deriving directly from the French Rational Classical tradition. The dichotomy between the engineer's aesthetics and architecture — the dualistic theme of Le Corbusier's *Vers une architecture* of 1923 — was first formulated in overtly mechanical versus classical terms in Le Corbusier and Pierre Jeanneret's entry for the Société des Nations (SdN) competition, which they started in April 1926.

The programme of the SdN compelled Le Corbusier and Pierre Jeanneret to think out their Purist format on a new scale, and in so doing, they tackled for the first time the challenge of creating an appropriate modern architectural form for
a representative structure. Purism had yet to confront the problem of monumentality. The brief for the Société des Nations was challenging, not only because of the spectacular beauty of the lakefront site — the parkland bordering lake Geneva — but also because of the utopian and international scale of the programme. The basic accommodation required was for a 2,500-seat auditorium including foyers and ancillary suites for the general secretary, the press and for other communication purposes; six large meeting rooms; secretariat block for the 14 sections of the newly constituted SdN; a council chamber; six or seven extra committee rooms and a library. The complex had to be laid out on an awkwardly shaped site, bordered on the west by the Geneva-Lausanne road and on the east by Lake Geneva. On the site was an existing *Bureau International du Travail* which had to be incorporated into the new design.

While the general axial structure of Le Corbusier's SdN project is self-evident, the presence of certain specific iconographies is perhaps less obvious. However, the distinguished jury members — H.P. Berlage, John Burnet, Josef Hoffmann, Victor Horta, Charles Lemaresquier, Karl Moser and Ivar Tengbom — could hardly have missed the specific connotations embodied in the design.

Take the apparently casual caricature of two figures who appear under the peristyle/canopy in front of the Assembly Hall, for instance. The seated protagonist with his high-heeled boots and boater is patently August Perret, while the standing silhouette with homburg and walking stick is Le Corbusier himself. The ironic inference is clear enough; the old and the new representatives of Rational Classicism are for a moment placed side by side on the threshold of a new era. A reference, equally cryptic, and one which has come to light through the recent publication of archive material, is the sculpture above the general secretary's suite at the apex of the Assembly Hall, facing the lake. It comprises a lion on the left, a horse and a man standing in the center, and a crow on the right, and this strange iconography obviously requires some explanation. The central figures are apparently borrowed from the Dioscuri, which Behrens transposed into a symbol for the German State and used to crown his St Petersburg Embassy of 1912 and the Festhalle — erected for the Werkbund Exhibition — in 1914. It is interesting to note that the imperialist Dioscuri symbol would also appear in Carlo Broggi's entry for the SdN. Le Corbusier's free interpretation of this icon gave it new meaning; the horse instead of being restrained is now running free — a Dionysiac image — while the remaining male figure, instead of standing frontal and rigid, as in Behrens' version, adopts a graceful asymmetrical pose, evocative of Apollonian calm. The attendant creatures left and right elaborate on a more intimate level on the generic meaning of the pair: the lion seemingly refers to Jeanneret, while the crow, poised as if on the verge of flight, is clearly a metaphor for the personality of Le Corbusier himself. Le Corbusier's awareness of his own volatile creativity as opposed to the more controlled expertise of his partner and cousin, is confirmed by the somewhat bitter statement he made later in life: 'I am the sea and he is the mountain and as everyone knows these two can never meet.' Aside from these idiosyncratic, yet significant references, Rational Classicism is present in Le Corbusier's SdN Assembly Hall in more overt ways. First, in the Palladian structure of the auditorium about an ABABA rhythm, second in the provision of a consciously conceived peristyle entrance, and third, in a totally hierarchical conception of the entry sequence — visitors pass under the peristyle, up a *scala regia* and are then distributed under the belly of the auditorium, in a space labelled on the plans as *pas perdus*. A more direct allusion to the Baroque palace tradition than this would be hard to imagine. This hierarchical sequence continues around the auditorium as a *promenade architecturale* in a way comparable to the monumental corridor which appears in Albert Speer's Neoclassic New State Chancellery, built for the Third Reich in 1937. In this case, however, the long spatial sequence terminates at the grandeur of the general secretary's suite

Bird's-eye view of the design by Le Corbusier.

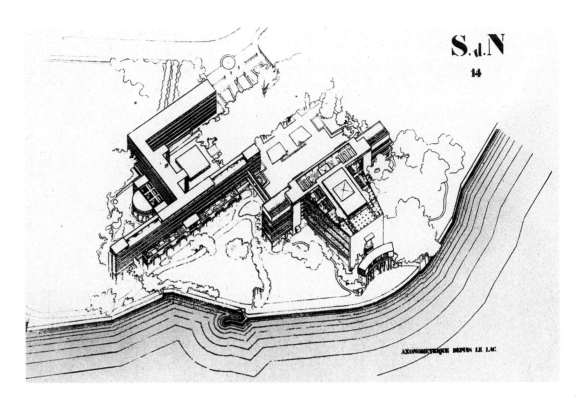

Details from Le Corbusier's design. Above: South façade of the Secretariat block, seen above left in the bird's-eye view. Below: Entrance to the Conference building.

Cross-section of the design by Le Corbusier, providing a good view of the steel framework and the extensive glazing in the large Assembly Hall.

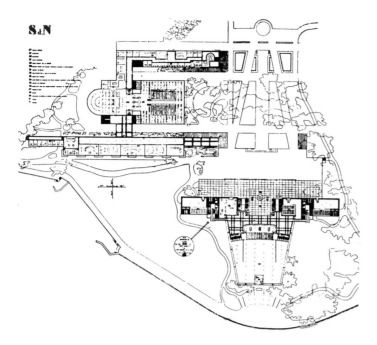

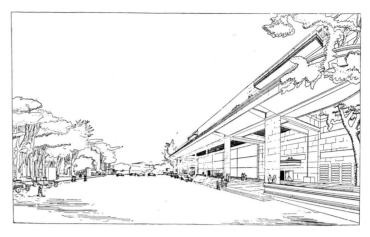

facing the lake.

Rational Classicism is evident again in the proposed cladding of the polished granite veneer; in the paving and intercolumnation of the main lobbies, also indebted perhaps to Perret's Theatre des Champs Elysées foyer of 1912; and even in the organization of the Secretariat library, which surely makes an explicit reference to Henri Labrouste's Bibliothèque Nationale of 1858, especially in the nine-square organization of the reading room and in the placement of the bookstack. Classicism is also evident in studies for the placement of sculpture like the low relief sculptures planned for the porte — cochère to the Assembly Hall. Apart from this, Julien Gaudet's classical 'elementarism' is used by Le Corbusier as a compositional method in the alternative layout which he appended to the main site plan with the caption: 'An alternative proposal employing the same compositional elements.'

This added elemental technique, equally evident in the project which was actually submitted, was precisely the same approach adopted in the Beaux Arts academic entries and the same method was used again in Le Corbusier's designs for the Palace of the Soviets.

TRANSCENDENTAL TECHNOLOGY

The celestial-mechanical symbolism of the Enlightenment can be seen in the dramatic proposals for illuminating the main auditorium. This large volume was to be lit by means of translucent glazed surfaces, through which light would enter irrespective of whether the source was natural or artificial. It is characteristic of Le Corbusier that he referred to this manner of illumination as though it were some kind of patent

invention comparable to the ducted air-conditioning which he adopted for the same space. Adjacent to his diagrams illustrating the system of *chauffage par le procédé d'aération ponctuelle*, he provided a parallel plate, demonstrating the precepts of *éclairage étincelant* or sparkling light, which showed how the Assembly Hall would be illuminated throughout the day by diffused light, coming through the top lanterns and the translucent double-glazed side walls. Aside from the Functionalist rationalization, this arrangement combined Enlightenment symbolism with modern technology. Thus, while permanently and evenly illuminated during the day, the hall would literally glow with light at night, thereby symbolically suggesting the wisdom and diligence with which the nocturnal deliberations of the SdN would maintain the security of the world. A notion of transcendental technology is also implicit in those plates which compare *les salles de formes favorables à l'acoustique* to more traditional circular or semi-circular shapes classified as *anti-acoustique*.

The ostensible care with which the acoustics of the hall were worked out, in consultation with Gustave Lyon, is evident in a caption which reads 'All the reflected sound waves are parallel to the walls, there are no secondary reflexions.'

The transcendence of modern technique is also evident in the steel framing to the Main Hall, where the two primary longitudinal trusses take their roller bearing support off two sets of twin reinforced-concrete pylons which are also used to brace the main elevator shafts. These primary girders are integrated with transverse trusses and in each case the trusses are treated like hinged frames, thereby producing a series of zero-bending hinges around the perimeter of the Assembly

Hall. This uses the same solution Peter Behrens adopted with the steel trusses of the AEG Turbine Factory in 1910.

How far his SdN design was regarded as an apotheosis for Le Corbusier may be judged not only from his attempts to re-combine the original elements of the project into a second version for a new site, but also from the way in which fragments of the design were to reappear in subsequent projects totally removed from the context of a monumental public building. Thus, the twin reinforced-concrete pylons of the SdN Assembly Hall reappear as the attached *piloti* supporting the Pavillon Suisse in 1932, thereby bestowing upon a fragmentary *redent* slab, drawn from the typology of La Ville Radieuse, the idea of it being a 'monumental' front, comparable to the one assumed for the SdN project. Transposition is also evident in the partial radial configuration of the foyer situated to the rear of the Pavillon Suisse. We are surely justified in seeing this irregular, shell-like element as the vestigial remains of the SdN auditorium.

The *machinism* which permeates Le Corbusier's SdN scheme is most manifest in the complex circulation system adopted for the Assembly Hall. That this was conceived as some kind of biological device is dramatically visible in the working of the interlocking staircases which were conceived as aorta-like forms, and were intended as a filtering device for the many types of visitors — from delegates to journalists — using the building.

Given the *machinism* inherent in his infamous slogan 'a house is a machine for living in', it is surprising that Le Corbusier should choose to treat the automobile in such a diffident manner, barely fulfilling the 100 parking spaces required by the competition conditions. This figure is dwarfed by the 500 parking places provided in Hannes Meyer's Constructivist and theoretically more egalitarian design. Unlike Le Corbusier, Meyer idealizes the automobile and literally inundates the site with vehicular movement. And unlike Le Corbusier's use of separated staircases as the main filtering device, automobile access itself is used by Meyer as a means of classifying the various groups of people using the building. Personnel, journalists, delegates and general visitors are separated before entering, by virtue of separate parking areas. Where Meyer uses the automobile for classification and distribution, Le Corbusier conducts his vehicular traffic to two main thresholds, the Secretariat/library foyer and the peristyle of the Assembly Building. Le Corbusier differentiates between classes of users by having them enter the building on foot through seven colour-coded points of entry. Thus, Meyer uses the machine, a car, as a classifying device, while Le Corbusier adopts a more static and time-honoured mode of approach.

Machinism of a more mechanical order is evident in the fenestration in the Secretariat, which is fitted throughout with sliding steel sashes or *fenêtre en longeur*, which Le Corbusier had described in his Five Points of a New Architecture of 1926 as the 'typical mechanical element of the house'. The fenestration of the Secretariat also has a sliding, lightweight tubular-steel cleaning cradle — the so-called *passerelle bicyclette* — which was designed to be suspended

One of the five final architects was Carlo Broggi of Rome. Here his design made for the competiton in 1927, together with fellow Romans Giuseppe Vaccaro and Luigi Franzi, see also p. 189.

from the reinforced-concrete cornice running around the top of the façade. This cornice was also envisaged as having roller shutters fitted to its underside, while a comparable inner slot provided a pelmet for curtains on the line of the internal sill below. While the external cornice offered a continuous horizontal track for the cleaning gear, it also doubled as a vestigial classical cornice. Through such complex metaphorical layerings, Le Corbusier was able to attain the Rational Classical ideal of synthesizing advanced technology with classical form (cp. Auguste Perret).

A HOUSE: A PALACE

In his account of what he saw as the SdN debacle, published in 1928 under the title *Une Maison — un palais*, Le Corbusier wrote, 'I have one master: it is the past', and elsewhere in the same text, opposite an axonometric of the Villa Garches which he regarded as a prototype for his Palais des Nations, he wrote: 'We are strengthened by the past because the past has proven to us that under conditions of clarity and lasting equilibrium, the house becomes typified, and that when the type is pure, it possesses an architectural potential ... it is able to elevate itself to the dignity of a palace.' Conversely, he referred to his Palais des Nations as 'the administration house of the nations; it is an organism, a mechanism of precise ends. It is a machine for living in'. In *Une Maison — un palais*, under the elevation of his SdN Secretariat block, he displayed a diagram of the garden façade at Garches, drawn to the same scale and accompanied by the caption: 'The disposition of the windows is the same as those of the Villa Garches.'

The transposition of a house into a palace and vice-versa is a key theme underlying Le Corbusier's pre-war output. The elaborate metaphorical substance of his oeuvre is incomprehensible if we do not perceive this fundamental intention of making a transposition between a given state and its apparent opposite. Thus in Le Corbusier's work every house is potentially a palace and every palace is potentially a house. The proposition that a palace may serve as a house recalls Charles Fourier's idea of the workers' colony as set forth in his writings of the 1820s. Fourier maintained that the collective form of the *phalanstère* would enable ordinary men to live like kings in palaces as commodious as Versailles. This utopian socialist vision seems to underline the entire body of Le Corbusier's work from his Purist villas to his Unité d'Habitation, realized in Marseilles in 1952. Its metaphorical appearance in his project for the Société des Nations meant combining the socially progressive form of this new international institution with the traditionally classical form of a Baroque palace, and it is significant that Le Corbusier always referred to his design as a 'Palais des Nations'. A similar conflation occurs in his book *Precisions*, published in 1930, in which he juxtaposes on one page a sequence of telling images — A.J. Gabriel's Palais de la Concorde, an ocean-going

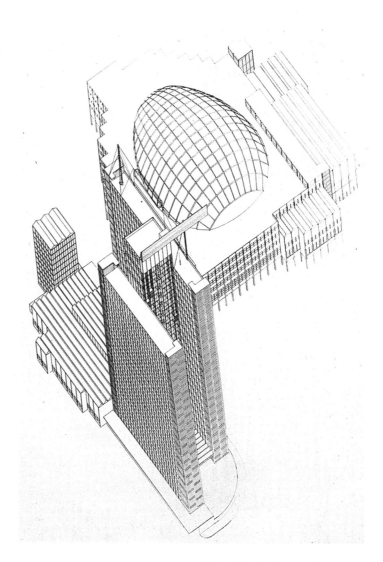

This striking design came from Hannes Meyer and Hans Wittwer of the Netherlands. It was an example of very modern architecture, paying great attention to traffic requirements. See also ground plan on p. 189.

Design for the League of Nations Building by Niels Einar Eriksson from Sweden.

A Boullée-like columnated block designed by Erich zu Pulitz, Rudolf Klophaus and August Schoch.

FAÇADE SUD LE LAC
ÉCHELLE
1 A 1:100

Architects from The Hague, J.H. Luthman and H. Wouda contributed this Neo-Wrightian design.

liner, the SdN Secretariat block, and his own version of an American skyscraper. Not only was the house now transposed into the palace, but the liner in its turn was to be read as the modern equivalent of a classical structure, thus permitting the SdN Secretariat to be seen as a transcendental integration of the two. Identifying a Baroque palace with a liner had its origins in the utopian socialist theories of Victor Considerant, as published in his *Considérations sociales sur l'architectonique* of 1834.

THE MACHINE IN THE GARDEN

Le Corbusier regarded his layout for the SdN as a *conception paysagiste*, a phrase evoking both the English picturesque tradition and French Baroque landscape. This hybrid intent seems to be confirmed by his use of both the *allée classique* and the *bosquet anglais*. However, the principles according to which the building would have integrated into its existing site went well beyond the scope of nineteenth-century eclecticism, for as Colin Rowe and Robert Slutzky have pointed out, Le Corbusier's SdN project introduces a series of parallel longitudinal planes and spatial slots running perpendicular to the main east-west axial approach. A visitor approaching via the *cour d'honneur* would have had to pass through a series of guillotine-like planes which, either built or planted, granite or green, would have had the effect of deflecting the eye to lateral views of the lake and foliage.

The central axis would alternately compress (frontally) and expand (diagonally) thereby playing tricks to the eye as to the actual size and scale of the space in front of the Assembly Hall.

Unlike Meyer, who proclaimed vehemently that the siting of his building depended solely on meeting the needs of traffic flow, Le Corbusier was highly knowledgeable about the topography of the site. Indeed, his horizontal complex was a deliberate attempt to layer the building into the topography so as to create a formal harmony with the horizontal lie of both the lake and the Alps. Nothing could have been further from Meyer's 24-storey Secretariat block which, had it been built, would have totally violated the harmony of the natural landscape. It was presumably out of a similar sensitivity to the site that Le Corbusier chose to forego the more functional version of his elemental *parti:* functional in the sense that a symmetrically laid out, H-plan Secretariat, set on an axis in front of the Assembly Hall, would have provided a better distribution of vehicles throughout the complex.

THE TRIUMPH OF THE NEW TRADITION.

It is hardly surprising, given the composition of the jury, that no official first prize was awarded for the Société des Nations competition, the results of which were finally announced in Geneva, on 5 May 1927. It is equally understandable that the prizewinning designs would seem to favour that which H.R. Hitchcock categorized two years later as the New Tradition: for the jury was largely composed of eclectic-Classicists, ranging from Charles Lemaresquier and Sir John Burnet, from France and England respectively, to Carlo

Pierre and Louis Giudetti of Paris were clearly influenced by the work of Auguste Perret, French architectural innovator, whose portrait Le Corbusier placed above the entrance to the League of Nations Building, see pp. 193 and 194.

Below: Design by Camille Lefèvre, who, like Vago — see right — was one of the final architects for the League of Nations Building.

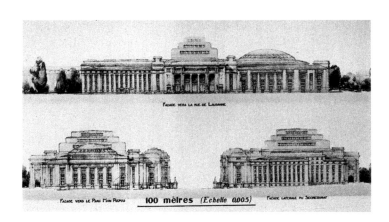

Henri Paul Nénot of Paris and Julien Flegenheimer of Geneva together entered this impressive design. They were both asked to take part in the final design team, probably because of their Franco-Swiss joint venture.

Gato from Madrid and Attilo Muggia from Bologna. Even if the 'progressive' members of the jury seemed to be the majority, the range of opinion represented by Victor Horta on the one hand and Ivar Tengbom on the other, could hardly be constituted the avant-garde. The fact that the project of Le Corbusier and Pierre Jeanneret was included among the nine schemes to be given an *ex aequo* prize of 12,000 francs was surely in no small part due to the presence of H.P. Berlage, Josef Hoffmann and Karl Moser. The same was surely the case with the other avant-gardist project to be honoured with a from Geneva by boat.

In his brief examination of the extant entries for the competition, Ritter gives a comprehensive summary of the spectrum of architectural ideology which was represented by the 160 works he was able to identify, from the Boullée-like solutions of Pulitz, Klophaus and Schoch and the Scandinavian Neo-Classicist, Christian Skagen, to the proto Art Deco, Neo-Gothic monumentality projected by Eliel Saarinen. Aside from the academic historicism which seems to have accounted for about a third of the entries that Ritter identified, the two prevalent other modes were a freely expressive organic style as evident in the entry of J. Klijnen from The Hague, and an international Constructivist line, most purely represented in the *hoogbouw* design submitted by Bernard Bijvoet and Johannes Duiker.

It is significant that just under a third of the 27 schemes awarded may be characterized in retrospect as Beaux Arts eclectic, while some five of the prizewinning designs displayed that form of atectonic abstraction typical of Scandinavian Neo-Classicism, which was derived in many respects from Tengbom himself. These two genres accounted for 13 of the prizewinning schemes. The predominantly classical approach and the stylistic nuances of the eight award-winning modernist projects, gives some idea of the ideological split dividing the European architectural establishment in the late 1920s. The modernist designs included not only the two avant-garde entries previously mentioned, but also two designs which were Expressionistic; a Mendelsohnian project by the German team of Fischer-Essen/Speidel and an Amsterdam School entry submitted by H.T. Wijdeveld.

The remainder of this group were modern in more 'retarditaire' ways; a Neo-Wrightian, ashlar faced, project by the Dutch team of Luthmann and Wouda and two Perret-influenced schemes — as opposed to the non-awarded entry submitted by Perret himself — by Louis Boileau and the Parisian firm of Pierre and Louis Guidetti. Last but not least within this group, we should consider a rather weak Neo-Constructivist scheme submitted by the Dutch architect, M.E. van Linge. It is curious to note in passing, the high value which Ritter attached to Van Linge's scheme. He was to write in 1964: 'The Assembly and Council block forms the climax of an approach axis; but the Secretariat on the right makes a continuous wall, instead of breaking back and forward again, as does Le Corbusier's. The Assembly front, at the end of this processional way, is a fine symmetrical composition of interpenetrating masses with generous glazing, some strip and corner windows and two short towers carrying the stairs and lifts to the upper roof level. With its hall planned for acoustics and general visibility this is among the best designs submitted.' The other award-winning designs displayed that form of crypto-classical monumentality which would soon become associated with fascist politics, as in the entries designed by Marcello Piacentini and Paul Bonatz, or in the monumental Boullée-like, columnated block projected by Zu Pulitz, Klophaus and Schoch. In the last analysis, if one excludes modernists and Beaux Arts classicists, over half of the schemes awarded can be considered as falling under the rubric of the New Tradition. A kind of Peter Behrens-influenced, brick pseudo-classical style can be considered as being as much a part of this genre as the then prevalent Scandinavian Neo-Classical mode. An excellent example of the former would be the design submitted by Farenkamp and Deneke. Style aside, these schemes also varied considerably in their spatial organization and in the everyday amenities offered through their detailed design. It is perhaps at this level, rather than in terms of their formal appearance, that the award-winning entries revealed their greatest ideological differences. What is most disturbing in retrospect is the formal rigidity of the planning adopted in almost every instance – the Durandesque mindlessness with which the accommodation was packed into the modular monumental masses. This approach is latent even in the Neo-Wrightian work of Luthman and Wouda. In general, however, the inflected delicacy of the planning displayed by the modern projects is in sharp contrast to the bureaucratic representational formality of the New Tradition or the planning methods of the Neo-Classical schemes.

The altogether more humane approach of the modern entries is evident at every turn from the asymmetrical low-rise, courtyard organization of the Secretariat block in the Fischer-Essen scheme to the Wrightian approach evident in the volumetric feeling to the Wijdeveld entry. An equivalent biological attitude towards spatial organization is evident in the schemes submitted by Le Corbusier and Hannes Meyer and in the remarkable Neo-Wrightian design produced by Rudolf Schindler and Richard Neutra. The latter was distinguished by its highly dramatic relationship to the water, with its Assembly Hall cantileering out over the lake and the architects' imagining the main honorific approach being made prize, the one submitted by Hannes Meyer and Hans Wittwer, who received second-class honourable mention, and one of the nine monetary prizes of 2,500 francs.

John Ritter has given us the clearest account of the way in which this decision was reached, after six weeks of deliberations on the part of the jury and the close scrutiny of some 377 entries. Apparently, four members of the jury were prepared to recommend Le Corbusier's design for the first prize after four weeks of discussion and debate, but this bold recommendation, presumably made by the modernists among the jury, was vetoed by the others on the grounds that Le Corbusier and Pierre Jeanneret had infringed the competition conditions by submitting dyeline prints rather than ink drawings. Out of this conflict arose the stalemate which led to the 'non-decision' of awarding 12 *ex-aequo* prizes, of various grades, and of appointing five non-architect diplomats to select the architects to implement the commission.

ACADEMIC NEUTRALITY
Once the responsibility for the appointment of the architect had been passed to them, the first thing the diplomatic team did was to increase the original budget by 30 per cent. They also moved the site to the adjacent and more spacious Parc d'Ariana. Due to a donation from John D. Rockefeller, they also added a 'world library' to the initial brief. Le Corbusier was justifiably outraged, not only by his arbitrary disqualification but also by this *ex post facto* modification of the original competition conditions. As far as Le Corbusier and a number of other competitors were concerned, these

changes warranted a totally new competition and their demands in this regard were met by the client, who allowed a certain number of competitors to re-submit for the new site and modified brief. Unfortunately, Le Corbusier had no more success on the Parc d'Ariana site than he had with his original scheme.

After this last round, the diplomats selected a team to prepare the final design; this scheme was put in hand on the Parc d'Ariana site in 1929 and finally completed and opened in 1937. The selection of the final Franco-Swiss-Italian team was certainly indicative of a compromise made in terms of diplomatic prestige and ruling taste. Julien Flegenheimer, from Geneva, and Henri Paul Nenot, from Paris, were no doubt selected as core members of the team because they had submitted a joint Franco-Swiss academic entry. Camille Lefèvre seems to have been included simply to reinforce the presence of the Parisian Beaux Arts, while the two Italians, Carlo Broggi and Giuseppe Vago, were no doubt chosen for their more rhetorical approach. Broggi for his almost imperialistic verve and Vago for his superior planning ability. It is possible to claim that the SdN as built, owes much to Vago's original plan, if not to his New Traditional mode of expression.

It would be difficult to imagine a more neutral academic work than the realized building with its somewhat modified accommodation and its austere, stripped classical syntax. If not exactly the New Tradition, this was certainly the European *ordre monumentale* as Franco Borsi has characterized it in a recent study. It typified that classical, Art Deco-cum-Rationalist manner which was to be found throughout Europe in the second half of the 1930s, from Piaccentini's *stile lictorale* to Speer's Schinkelesque monumentality. Nothing resembling the metaphorical and plastic poetics of Le Corbusier's initial design can be detected in the built work, and the circulation is nowhere near as compact or as efficient. Furthermore, the picturesqueness of the original site, so spatially enhanced by Le Corbusier's layered planting, seems to be totally two-dimensional here, and drained of all potential energy by the unduly formal parterres and the endlessly reiterated axes of the garden layout. Everywhere in fact, one senses a cultural form touched by both waning European imperialism and the latent prowess of the emerging Pax Americana. This latter is perhaps most evident in the Grande Salle du Conseil, seating

550 delegates, with murals created by the Spanish artist, José Maria Sert. Here, too, one detects the emerging power of the Rockefellers as international patrons, for a few years later Sert would create very similar murals for the lobby of the RCA Building in Rockefeller Center, New York.

It is ironic that this entire academic compromise was to be repeated again in 1947, when the centre of international power and conciliation was transfered to New York, and when the Rockefellers would again serve as the initial patrons of the undertaking. This irony is heightened by the fact that Le Corbusier's first sketch for the United Nations Building was apparently made while standing on the observation deck of the RCA Building in the Rockefeller Center. And while the United Nations Building was never made the subject of an open international competition, it was nonetheless to be the result of the intractable and demoralising process of design by committee. Twenty years had elapsed since the SdN competition, and the received ideas of a normative architecture had totally changed. Nevertheless, as the finally realized United Nations Building by Harrison and Abramovitz would indicate, Le Corbusier was to be thwarted once again; for while he was the prime originator of the compositional

principles ultimately adopted, the plastic poetry of his own design for the United Nations was lamentably absent.

The League of Nations Assembly Hall in use — a photo from the late 1930s.

Architectural competitions often gave rise to considerable differences of opinion and ill-feeling; so in the course of the 19th century the various architectural associations in different countries drew up lists of regulations. These were often aimed only at protecting the architect. The rules were frequently adapted and refined, so that they also served to protect those who organized competitions. The effect of these rules differs from country to country. In some places they are fairly strictly adhered to - for example Great Britain - while in other countries the competition regulations were not taken very seriously - take France, where local government in particular virtually ignored them. It is only in West Germany that the competition as such is officially supervised by the government.

The international architects' association UIA (Union Internationale des Architectes) has drawn up standard regulations for competitions dealing with architecture and town planning. These rules are printed here in one of the UIA languages. They are supported by UNESCO, and the UIA has also drawn up a separate list, that will be of use to competition jury members.

STANDARD REGULATIONS FOR INTERNATIONAL COMPETITIONS IN ARCHITECTURE AND TOWN PLANNING

INTRODUCTION

The purpose of these Standard Regulations is to state the principles upon which international competitions are based and by which promoters should be guided in organizing a competition. They have been drawn up in the interests of both promoters and competitors.

GENERAL PROVISIONS

ARTICLE 1

The designation *'international'* shall apply to any competition in which participation is open to architects, town planners or teams of specialists led by an architect or town planner who are of different nationalities and reside in different countries, as well as to members of other professions working in association with them. Competitions which are open to all architects, town planners and professionals working in association with them are termed *'open'*. These Regulations cover both open competitions and restricted competitions (where some form of restriction is imposed) and sometimes special competitions.

ARTICLE 2

International competitions may be classified into *'Project'* or *'Ideas'* competitions.

ARTICLE 3

International competitions may be organized in one or two stages.

ARTICLE 4

The regulations and conditions for an international competition shall be identical for all competitors.

ARTICLE 5

A copy of the regulations and full set of conditions for any competition shall be filed with the International Union of Architects, hereinafter referred to as the UIA, and sent free of charge at the same time to all the UIA National Sections concerned. The answers to competitors' questions shall also be sent to the UIA and to all UIA National Sections.

ARTICLE 6

Any set of conditions which is not published in one of the official languages of the International Union of Architects (English, French, Russian and Spanish) shall be accompanied by a translation into at least one of these languages. Such translations shall be issued at the same time as the original language version. Competitors shall not be required to submit material in more than one UIA language.

ARTICLE 7

All competitors' designs shall be submitted and judged anonymously.

ARTICLE 8

Notice of an international competition shall be issued by the promoter and/or the UIA Secretariat-General to all National Sections with a request for publication in technical journals or through other media at their disposal, as far as possible simultaneously, to enable those interested to apply for the regulations and full set of conditions in due time. This announcement shall state where and how copies of the conditions may be obtained and specify that the conditions have received UIA approval (see Article 15).

PROFESSIONAL ADVISER

ARTICLE 9

The promoter shall appoint a Professional Adviser, preferably an architect (but who could be a town planner in the case of a town-planning competition), to prepare the conditions and supervise the conduct of the competition.

DRAWING UP OF THE CONDITIONS

ARTICLE 10

The conditions for international competitions, whether single or two-stage, open or restricted, shall state clearly:
(a) the purpose of the competition and the intentions of the promoter;
(b) the nature of the problem to be solved;
(c) all the practical requirements to be met by competitions.

ARTICLE 11

A clear distinction shall be made in the conditions between mandatory requirements of an essential nature and those which permit the competitor freedom of interpretation, which should be as wide as possible. All competition entries shall be submitted in conformity with the regulations.

ARTICLE 12

The necessary background information supplied to competitors (social, economic, technical, geographical, topographical, etc.) must be specific and not open to misinterpretation. Supplementary information and instructions approved by the jury may be issued by the promoter to all competitors selected to proceed to the second stage of a two-stage competition.

ARTICLE 13

The regulations shall state the number, nature, scale and dimensions of the documents, plans or models required and the terms of acceptance of such documents, plans or models. Where an estimate of cost is required, this must be presented in standard form as set out in the regulations.

ARTICLE 14

As a general rule, the promoter of an international competition shall use the metric scale. Where this is not done the metric equivalent shall be annexed to the conditions.

UIA APPROVAL
ARTICLE 15
The promoter must obtain the UIA's written approval of the requirements for a competition - including the timetable, registration fee and membership of the jury - before announcing that it is being held under UIA auspices.

REGISTRATION OF COMPETITORS
ARTICLE 16
As soon as they have received details of the competition, competitors shall register with the promoter. Registration implies acceptance of the regulations for the competition.
ARTICLE 17
The promoter shall issue to competitors all the necessary documentation for preparing their designs. Where the furnishing of such documentation is conditional on payment of a deposit, unless otherwise stated this deposit shall be returned to competitors who submit a bona fide design.
ARTICLE 18
The names of those competitors selected to proceed to the second stage of a two-stage competition shall be made public only under exceptional conditions to be agreed on by the jury before the launching of the competition.

PRIZE-MONEY, COMPENSATION AND HONORARIA
ARTICLE 19
The regulations for any competition must state the number of prizes and the amount of prize-money. This must be related to the size of the project, the amount of work involved for competitors and the resulting expenses incurred by them.
ARTICLE 20
Town-planning competitions are, by their nature, ideas competitions, since the work is generally carried out by official bodies, frequently on a long-term basis. It is therefore particularly important for the promoter to allot adequate prize-money to recompense competitors for their ideas and the work they have done.
ARTICLE 21
The promoter undertakes to accept the decisions of the jury and to pay the prize-money within one month of the announcement of the competition results.
ARTICLE 22
Each participant in a competition by invitation shall receive an honorarium in addition to the prizes awarded.
ARTICLE 23
In two-stage competitions, a reasonable honorarium shall be paid to each of the competitors selected to take part in the second stage. This sum, which is intended to reimburse them for the additional work carried out in the second stage, shall be stated in the regulations for the competition and shall be in addition to the prizes awarded.

ARTICLE 24
The regulations shall state the exact use to which the promoter will put the winning design. Designs may not be put to any other use or altered in any way except by agreement with the author.
ARTICLE 25
In project competitions the award of first prize to a design places the promoter under the obligation to entrust the author of the design with the commission for the project. If the winner is unable to satisfy the jury of his ability to carry out the work, the jury may require him to collaborate with another architect or town planner of his choice approved by the jury and the promoter.
ARTICLE 26
In *project competitions* provision shall be made in the regulations for the competition for *a further sum* equal to the amount of the first prize if no contract for carrying out the project has been signed within twenty-four months of the announcement of the jury's award. In so compensating the first prize winner the promoter does not acquire the right to carry out the project except with the collaboration of its author.
ARTICLE 27
In *ideas competitions* the promoter, if he intends to make use of all or part of the winning or any other scheme, shall, wherever possible, consider some form of collaboration with its author. The terms of collaboration must be acceptable to the latter.

INSURANCE
ARTICLE 28
The *promoter shall insure* competitors' designs from the time when he assumes responsibility for them and for the duration of his responsibility. The amount of such insurance will be stated in the regulations.

COPYRIGHT AND RIGHT OF OWNERSHIP
ARTICLE 29
The *author* of any design shall retain the *copyright* of his work; no alterations may be made without his formal consent.
ARTICLE 30
The design awarded first prize can only be used by the promoter upon his commissioning the author to carry out the project. *No other design*, whether it has been awarded a prize or not, *may be used* wholly or in part by the promoter except by agreement with the author.
ARTICLE 31
As a general rule, the promoter's right of ownership on a design covers *one execution only*. However, the regulations for the competition may provide for repetitive work and specify the terms thereof.
ARTICLE 32
In all cases, unless otherwise stated in the regulations, the author of any design shall retain the *right of reproduction*.

THE JURY

ARTICLE 33

The jury shall be set up *before the opening* of the competition. The names of members and reserve members of the jury shall be listed in the regulations for the competition.

ARTICLE 34

As a general rule the members of the jury are appointed by the promoter after *approval by the* UIA. The UIA shall assist promoters in the selection of jury members.

ARTICLE 35

The jury shall be composed of the smallest reasonable number of persons of different nationalities, and in any event should be an odd number and should not exceed seven. The majority of them shall be independent architects, town planners or, in special circumstances, other professionals working in association with them.

ARTICLE 36

At least one member of the jury shall be appointed by the UIA and this should be stated in the regulations for the competition.

ARTICLE 37

It is essential that all full - i.e. voting - and reserve - i.e. non-voting - members of the jury be present throughout all meetings of the jury.

ARTICLE 38

If a voting jury member misses the first meeting, a non-voting member shall acquire his vote for the whole period of adjudication. If, for any reason, a voting jury member has to absent himself for a brief period of time, a non-voting member shall acquire his vote for that period and any decision taken shall be binding. If a voting jury member is absent for a prolonged period or leaves before the conclusion of the adjudication, his vote shall be acquired by a non-voting member for the remainder of the period of adjudication.

ARTICLE 39

Each member of the jury shall *approve* the regulations and conditions for the competition before they are made available to competitors.

ARTICLE 40

No member of the jury for a competition *shall take part*, either directly or indirectly, in that competition, or be entrusted either directly or indirectly with a commission connected with the carrying out of the object of the competition.

ARTICLE 41

No member of the promoting body, nor any associate or employee, nor any person who has been concerned with the preparation or organization of the competition, *shall be eligible to compete* or assist a competitor.

ARTICLE 42

The decisions of the jury shall be taken by a *majority vote*, with a separate vote on each design submitted. In the event of a tied vote, the chairman shall have the casting vote. The list of awards, as well as the *jury's report* to the promoter, shall be signed by all members of the jury before they disperse and one copy of this document shall be sent to the UIA.

ARTICLE 43

In two-stage competitions, the *same jury* should judge *both*

stages of the competition. In no case may a competition which has received UIA approval as a single-stage competition proceed to a second stage except with UIA approval of the conditions and the arrangements for payment of honoraria to the competitors involved, over and above the prize-money provided for in the original competition. In the event of such a secondary competition taking place, the jury appointed for the original competition must be reappointed by the promoter.

ARTICLE 44

Any drawings, photographs, models or other documents not required under the regulations shall be *excluded by the jury* before it examines a competitor's entry.

ARTICLE 45

The jury *shall disqualify* any design which does not conform to the mandatory requirements, instructions or regulations for the competition.

ARTICLE 46

The jury must make *awards*. The *awards* shall be final and shall be *made public* by a date agreed on with UIA and stated in the conditions. The jury, when distributing the awards, shall make full use of the amount set aside for prizes in the competition conditions. In an ideas competition, a first prize shall be awarded.

ARTICLE 47

The *fees* and travel and subsistence expenses of *jury* members shall be paid by the promoter.

EXHIBITION OF ENTRIES

ARTICLE 48

All designs, including those disqualified by the jury, shall be exhibited, as a general rule, for at least two weeks, together with a copy of the signed report of the jury. The exhibition shall be open to the public free of charge.

ARTICLE 49

The promoter shall notify registered competitors in good time of the date and place of the public exhibition and of the results of the competition, and send them a copy of the jury's report. He shall similarly inform the UIA and all National Sections. Photographs of the prize-winning designs shall be sent to the UIA with a view to possible publication.

ARTICLE 50

In two-stage competitions, designs submitted in the first stage shall be kept secret until the final results are announced.

RETURN OF DESIGNS

ARTICLE 51

All drawings and plans, other than those which have received prizes or been purchased and are retained by the promoter, *shall be destroyed* at the end of the public exhibition, unless provision is made to the contrary in the regulations for the competition. Where *models* are required, these will be returned to their author at the *expense of the promoter* within one month of the close of the public exhibition.

Bibliography

(Alphabetically per chapter; first books, then journals.)

COMPETITIONS, THE TREASURE HOUSES OF ARCHITECTURE

Chaslin, François: *Les Paris de François Mitterand — Histoire des grands projets architecturaux.* Gallimard, Paris, 1985. ISBN 2 07 032335 8

Oud, J.J.P.: 'Architectuur en prijsvragen', in: *Ter wille van een levende bouwkunst.* Nijgh & Van Ditmar, The Hague/Rotterdam, z.j.

RIGO: *Architectuurwedstrijden nader bekeken.* Stichting Bouwresearch/Kluwer/Ten Hagen, Deventer/The Hague, 1980. ISBN 90 201 1373 9

Spreiregen, Paul D.: *Design Competitons.* McGraw-Hill, New York N.Y., 1979. ISBN 0 07 060381 2

Strong, Judith: *Participating Architectural Competitions. A guide for competitors, promoters and assessors.* The Architectural Press, London, 1976. ISBN 0 85139 514 7

THE WHITE HOUSE IN WASHINGTON

Pearce, Mrs. John N. et al.: *The White House.* White House Historical Association, Washington D.C., 1964/66.

Ryan, William and Desmond Guinness: *The White House, an architectural History.* McGraw-Hill, New York, 1980. ISBN 0 07 054352 6

HOUSES OF PARLIAMENT, LONDON

Port, M.H. (ed.): *The Houses of Parliament.* Yale University Press, London, 1976. ISBN 0 300 02022 8

THE PARIS OPERA

Hitchcock, Henry-Russell: *Architecture: Nineteenth and Twentieth Centuries.* Penguin Books Ltd, Harmondsworth, 1977. ISBN 0 14 0561 15 3

Loyrette, Henri: 'Le concours pour l'Opéra de Paris: Viollet-le-Duc et Garnier', in exhibitioncatalogue *Viollet-le-Duc,* Galeries Nationales du Grand Palais, Paris, 1980.

Steinhauser, Monika: *Die Architektur der Pariser Oper. Studien zu ihrer Entstehungsgeschichte und ihrer architekturgeschichtlichen Stellung.* Prestel-Verlag, Munich, 1969.

Le Moniteur des Architectes, 1876, pp. 121 - 196 (Charles Laffitte: Le Nouvel Opéra).

The Architectural Review, 1949, pp. 303 - 304 (H.S. Goodhart-Rendel: Reassessment: Paris Opera House).

Documentation from the library of the Paris Opera House was also used.

THE REICHSTAG IN BERLIN

Cullen, Michael S.: *Der Reichstag. Die Geschichte eines Monumentes.* Frölich & Kaufmann, Berlin, 1983. ISBN 3 88725 036 2

Eggert, Hermann: *Die Konkurrenz für Entwürfe zum neuen Reichstagsgebaüde.* Berlin, 1882.

Graf, Otto Antonio: *Otto Wagner, Das Werk des Architekten 1860 - 1902.* Hermann Böhlaus, Vienna/Cologne/Graz, 1985.

Preisgekrönte Entwürfe zu den neuen Reichstagsgebaüde. Berlin, 1882.

Baumeister, Der, 1903, pp. 1 - 5 (M. Rabsilber: Paul Wallot).

Bauwelt, 1912, pp. 25 - 29.
— 1986, no. 6 (Reichstags-Operationen); no. 25, pp. 942 - 959 (Peter Rumpf: Königsplatz der Republik?).

Centralblatt der Bauverwaltung, 1883, pp. 227 - 229.
— 1894, pp. 411 - 500 (R. Streiter: Baugeschichte des Reichstagshauses).

Deutsche Bauzeitung, 1872, pp. 141 - 162.
— 1882, p. 313 ff.

THE EIFFEL TOWER

Eiffel, Gustave: *La tour de 300 mètres* (2 volumes). Paris, 1900.

Lemoine, Bertrand: *Gustave Eiffel*. F. Hazan, Paris, 1984. ISBN 2 85025 067 8

Design Trends, October 1939 (The Eiffel Tower: A Victory for progressive design).

Le Genie Civil, 1884/85, p. 107 ff. (Projet de tour colossale en maçonnerie de M. Bourdais).
— 1886, pp. 120 - 121 (M.N.: Tour de 300 mètres).
— 1887, pp. 267 - 268.
— 1888, pp. 29 ff. (Exposition universelle de 1889. Documents officiels et informations).

l'Illustration, 5 June 1886, p. 395 (Paul Eudel: Les projects du concours).

Journal of the society of Architectural Historians, XVI, 4, 1957 (Frank I. Jenkins: Harbingers of Eiffel's Tower).

Magazine de l'Histoire, October 1983, p. 96 ff. (Catherine Hodeir: l'Expo des Expos).

Le Moniteur des Architectes, February 1887 (Exposition Universelle; la tour Eiffel).

THE AUSTRIAN SAVINGS BANK IN VIENNA

Schorske, Carl E.: *Fin-de-siècle Vienna. Politics and culture.* Vintage Books, New York N.Y., 1981. ISBN 0 394 744778 0

Wagner, M. en Peter Tomanek: *Bankiers und Beamte. Hundert Jahre Österreichische Postsparkasse.* Verlag Anton Schroll & Co, Vienna, 1983.

Der Architekt, 1903, p. 76 ff. (Wettbewerb um den Bau des k.k. Postsparkassen-Amtes in Wien).
— 1916, pp. 1 - 14 (Dr. Karl Holey: Neubauten der Wiener Banken).

Österreichische Wochenschrift für den öffentlichen Baudienst, 1903, pp. 66 - 535 (Der Wettbewerb für den Neubau eines Amtsgebäudes der Postsparkasse in Wien).

Zeitschrift des Österr. Ingenieur- und Architekten-Vereines, 1904, pp. 57 - 62 (Mitteilungen des ständigen Wettbewerbungs-Ausschusses).
— 1904, p. 145 (Bericht über Fachgruppe für Architektur und Hochbau, Versammlung vom 12. Jänner 1904).
— 1907, p. 120 (Das k.k. Postsparkassen-Amtsgebäude).

We also referred to the 'Protokoll der Sitzungen des Preisgerichtes für den Wettbewerb um den Bau eines neuen Postsparkassengebäudes', as well as articles and comments found in the archives of the Vienna Savings Bank.

STOCKHOLM TOWN HALL

Cornell, Elias: *Ragnar Östberg, Svensk arkitekt.* Stockholm, 1965.

Architecture, 1924, pp. 49-50.

Arkitektur och Dekorativ Konst, 1904, pp. 65-66; p. 67 (by Torben Grut), pp. 68-82 (programme and jury's report of the first round).
— 1905, pp. 81-83 (by Torben Grut), pp. 84-102 (programme and jury's report of the second round).
— 1911, pp. 45-54 (Stockholms stadhus).
— 1917, pp. 131-132 (C. Westman: Stadhustornet).

Bouwkundig Weekblad, 1923, pp. 436-441 (Ir. G. Friedhof).
— 1924, pp. 221-226 (D.F. Slothouwer).

Byggmästaren, 1923, pp. 166-168 (C. Westman: Stockholms Stadhus).

Moderne Bauformen, 1927, pp. 65-79 (Willem Bäumer).

HELSINKI STATION

Abacus, Museum of Finnish Architecture, 3rd annual, Helsinki, 1983, pp. 49 - 77 (reprint of original text by Gustaf Strengell and Sigurd Frosterus, in English and Finnish: Architecture: a challenge to our opponents/Arkkitehtuuri; taistelukirjoitus jonka Gustaf Strengell ja Sigurd Frosterus omistavat vastustajilleen).

Hausen, Marika: 'The Helsinki Railway Station in Eliel Saarinen's first versions 1904', in: *Studies in Art History* 3/ *Taide Historiallisia* 3, pp. 59 - 113, Society for Art History, Finland/Taide-Historian Sevra, Suomi, Helsinki, 1977.

Arkitekten (ed. Bertel Jung), 1904, pp. 41 - 55.

Rautateiden Arkitehtuuri, Helsinki, 1984, pp. 48 - 59.

Wonen/TABK, 1985, no. 13, pp. 10 - 23 (Hans van Dijk: Eliel Saarinen's early work).

THE PEACE PALACE, THE HAGUE

Reinink, Dr. A.W.: *K.P.C. de Bazel architect.* Universitaire Pers Leiden, 1965.

Architectura, 1906, pp. 161-162, 173, 178, 211-214, 219-222 (W. Kromhout), 263, 269, 286, 370-371 (K.P.C. de Bazel).
— 1907, pp. 133-134 (W. Kromhout), 143 (H. Walenkamp), 157-161 (speech before the Dutch parliament, given by K.P.C. de Bazel, H.P. Berlage, W. Kromhout and others), 217-218, 277.

Bouwkundig Weekblad, 1905, pp. 499-500, 515-517, 542-543, 560, 570, 610-611, 696-698.
— 1906, pp. 325-328 (jury-report), 339-340, 369-370.
— 1907, pp. 193-194.

De Opmerker, 1906, pp. 153-154, 162, 185-187 (A.W. Weissman), 196-198.
— 1907, pp. 74-76, 89-91, 111, 129-130, 173-175, 234-236, 249-250, 263, 277-278.
— 1908, p. 46.

CHICAGO TRIBUNE TOWER

Goldberger, Paul: *The Skyscraper.* Alfred A. Knopf, New York N.Y., 1981. ISBN 0 394 74964 2

Jordy, William H.: *American buildings and their architects - the impact of European modernism in the mid-twentieth century.* Anchor Books, New Garden City, N.Y., 1976. ISBN 0 385 05704 0

Koeper, Frederick: *Illinois Architecture.* The university of Chicago Press, Chicago Ill., 1968. ISBN 0 226 44993 9

Roth, Leland M.: *A concise history of American Architecture.* Harper & Row, New York N.Y., 1979. ISBN 0 06 438490x

The Tribune Tower Competition - The international competition for a new administration building for the Chicago Tribune, 1922. The Chicago Tribune Co., Chicago, 1923.

The Architectural Record, 1923, pp. 151-157 (Louis Sullivan: The Chicago Tribune Competition).

Architecture, 1923, pp. 80-81 (Alfred Morton Githens: The Chicago 'Tribune' Competition - A retrospect).

Bouwkundig Weekblad, 1923, pp. 456-458 (J.J.P. Oud: Bij een Deensch ontwerp voor de 'Chicago Tribune').

Wasmuths Monatshefte für Baukunst und Städtebau, 1923/24, pp. 296-309 (Werner Hegemann: Das Hochhaus als Verkehrsstörer und der Wettbewerb der Chicago Tribune. Mittelalterliche Enge und neuzeitliche Gotik).

TERMINI STATION, ROME

Roma Termini, La nuova Stazione di Roma Termini, delle ferrovie Italiane delle Stato, raccolta di articoli pubblicati da 'ingegneria ferroviaria', C.I.F.I. Rome, 1951.

Roma Termini, La nuova Stazione di Roma Termini, delle ferrovie Italiane delle Stato, tavole fuori testo, C.I.F.I., Rome, 1951.

Architectural Review, 1951, pp. 209-215.

l'Architecture d'Aujourd'hui, 1951, pp. 51-54.

SYDNEY OPERA HOUSE

Giedion, S.: *Space, Time and Architecture.* 5th edition, Cambridge, Massachusetts, USA, 1964.

Hubble, Ava: *The Sydney Opera House, More Than Meets The Eye.* Lansdowne, Sydney, 1983. ISBN 0 7018 1722 4

Yeomans, John: *The other Taj Mahal.* Longmans, Green and Co, London/Harlow, 1968.

Architect and Building News, The, 1957, pp. 274-283 (jury report and award-winning designs).
— 1967, pp. 17-24 (Utzon and Arup on the construction of the roof).

Architects Journal, The, 1957, pp. 200-201 (award-winning designs); pp. 535-546 (designs by British participants).

Architectural Record, 1966, pp. 175-180 (Engineer's view).

Bauwelt, 1966, pp. 463-548 (Zum Theater-Streit in Sydney).

Canadian Architect, The, 1968, pp. 43-46 (Bring Utzon Back).

Progressive Architecture, 1957, pp. 95-97.

RIBA Journal, 1967, pp. 56-64 (What went wrong?).

CONGRESS BUILDING, KYOTO, JAPAN

Banham, Reyner: *Megastructure, urban futures of the recent past.* Thames and Hudson, London, 1976. ISBN 0 500 34068 4

Congress Building, Kyoto.
(containing jury's report, extensive documentation on award-winning designs, photographs and information on all designs; text Japanese only.) Publication of Ministry of Construction, Tokyo, 1967.

Japan Architect, The: *A Guide to Japanese Architecture.* Shinkenchiku-sha Co, Tokyo, 1984. ISBN 4 7869 0049 4 C1052

Riani, Paolo: *Kenzo Tange.* Hamlyn, London/New York/Sydney/Toronto, 1969. ISBN 0 600 35302 8

Riani, Paolo: *Contemporary Japanese Architecture.* Centro Di, Florence, 1969.

Japan Architect, 1963, no. 9, pp. 9-29.

Kenchikubunka, 1963, September; (number devoted to the competition, with discussions over many of the designs; text in Japanese).

Shikenchiku, 1963, September; (number devoted to the competition, with reviews of about 20 desings; text in Japanese).

Wonen/TABK, 1984, no. 16-17; (number dealing with Japan, see esp. pp. 11-20: Hans van Dijk: 'Tekens van Leegte' an overview of developments in Japanese architecture since 1960).

AMSTERDAM TOWN HALL

Brugmans, H. en A.W. Weissman: *Het stadhuis van Amsterdam.* Elsevier, Amsterdam, 1914.

Lutterveld, R. van: *Het raadhuis aan de Dam.* Heemkennis Amsterdam, vol. VIII. Amsterdam, z.j.

Roegholt, Richter: *Amsterdam in de 20e eeuw,* vols. 1 and 2. Het Spectrum, Utrecht, 1976 and 1979. ISBN 90 274 5842 1 and ISBN 90 274 6203 8

Bouwkundig Weekblad, 1937, pp. 24, 43, 67, 94, 118, 129, 133, 328, 368.
— 1938, pp. 1, 54.
— 1939, pp. 45, 53, 85, 101, 113, 125, 138, 248.
— 1940, pp. 34-35, 338.
— 1969, pp. 65 ff., 225, ff., 261 ff.

CENTRE POMPIDOU IN PARIS

Chaslin, François: *Les Paris de François Mitterand - Histoire des grands projects architecturaux.* Gallimard, Paris, 1985. ISBN 2 07 032335 8

Cook, Peter: *Archigram.* Studio Vista, London. ISBN 0 289 70302 6

Zaknić, Ivan: *Pompidou Center.* Flammarion. ISBN 2 08 012007 7

Déja Paris Demain Beaubourg Les Halles. Un dossier de Linhas-Paris réunie par Ned et Rival. Editions de la Table Ronde, 1974.

Architectural Design Profiles, no. 2: Centre Pompidou.

Domus, June 1972, p. 9 (A Parigi, per i parigini. l'Evoluzione del progretto Piano + Rogers per il 'Centre Beaubourg').

Techniques et Architecture, February 1972: Centre de Plateau Beaubourg Paris; concours international d'idées.

ARCHITECTURAL COMPETITIONS: A WATERSHED BETWEEN OLD AND NEW
Dennis Sharp

Adams, T.: *Recent Advances in Town Planning*. London, 1932.

Birrell, J.: *Walter Burley Griffin*. Queensland, 1964.

Cheney, S.: *New World Architecture*. New York, 1930.

Engel, G.H.: *American Architecture of Today*. New York, 1928.

Künstler, L. and G.: *Adolf Loos, Pioneer of Modern Architecture*. London, 1966.

Robinson, C.M.: *Modern Civic Art*. New York, 1903.

Sullivan, Louis: *Kindergarten Chats*. New York, 1947.

AA Quarterly; vol II, no. 2, pp. 36-48. (A. Cunliffe: The Competition for the Palace of Soviets in Moscow 1931-1933).

Sources of Illustrations

Per page, l. to r., top to bottom; names following a diagonal ('/') indicate the photographer.

Abbreviations used:

Arch.: archive; B&U: Beeldbank en Uitgeefprojecten; C.I.F.I.: Colleglio deglo Ingegneri Ferroviari Italiani; C.N.A.M.: Conservatoire National des Arts et Métiers; NDB: Nederlands Documentatiecentrum voor de Bouwkunst; PRO: Public Record Office; PSK: österreichische Postsparkasse; RIBA: Royal Institute of British Architects; TH: Technische Hochschule; TU: Technische Universiteit.

Dust jacket: TH Berlin-W/Archiphoto; 3: PSK Wien/Archiphoto; 5: Kisho Kurchawa Tokyo; ó: Sazakura Ass. Tokyo; 8: Foster Ass. London/Ian Lambot; 9: PSK Wien/Archiphoto; NDB Amsterdam; 11: NDB Amsterdam (3x); 12: Arch. Kenneth Frampton NYC; 13: W. Holzbauer Wien; 14: P&T Architects and Engineers Hongkong (2x); 15: Skidmore Owings & Merrill Chicago; YRM London (2x); Harry Seidler Sydney (2x); 16-17: Foster Ass. London; 18: Foster Ass. London/Richard Davies; 19 Foster Ass. London/Ian Lambot; 20: W. Holzbauer Vienna; 21: A. Alberts Amsterdam; 22: Cornell University Archives; 23: Associated Press Amsterdam (2x); 25-29: Maryland Historical Society, Baltimore Maryland; 30: RIBA London; Archiphoto; 31: B&U Amsterdam/Woodmansterne; RIBA London; 32: RIBA London; 33-37: PRO London; 39: Royal Commission on Ancient and Historical Monuments Scotland (copyright: Lawrence Blair Oliphant Blairgowrie Scotland); 40-41: B&U Amsterdam/Michael Hendrikse; 42-53: Bibliothèque de l'Opéra Paris/Archiphoto (19x); 52, 53: Archiphoto (4x); 54: Archiphoto; ABC Press Amsterdam (2x); 55: Archiphoto; TH Berlin-W/Archiphoto; B&U Amsterdam; 56-63: TH Berlin-W/Archiphoto; 64: B&U Amsterdam/Lauros Giraudon; C.N.A.M. Paris/Archiphoto; 65-71: C.N.A.M. Paris/Archiphoto; 67, 71: Archiphoto (2x); 73-75: Archiphoto (4x); 76-81: PSK Vienna/Archiphoto; 82: B&U Amsterdam/Hans Wretling; B&U Amsterdam/Jan Halaska; 83-92: Stockholm Stadsmuseum; 93: Stadhuset Stockholm; 94: Museokuva Helsinki (2x); 95, 97-98, 100: Rautatie Hallitus/Museokuva (5x); 96, 99, 102, 103: Suomen Rakennustaiteen Museo (6x); 104: B&U Amsterdam; 105-111: NDB Amsterdam/Frank den Oudsten; 112-113: NDB Amsterdam; 115: B&U Amsterdam; 116-123, 125: The Tribune Company; 124: BW 1923; 126: B&U Amsterdam; C.I.F.I. Roma; 127-132: C.I.F.I. Roma (15x); 130, 133-135: Francesco Montuori Roma (9x); 137: Arch. Architext Haarlem; The Architectural Press London (2x); 138: Archives Authority of New South Wales (5x); Sydney Opera House Trust; 139-140: The Architectural Press London (6x); 141: W. Holzbauer Vienna; 142: L. Prynn London; 143: H. Krall London; 144: TU Delft (2x); T. Bliss London (3x); 145: B&U Amsterdam; Sydney Opera House Trust; B&U Amsterdam; 146: Kyoto International Conference Hall (3x); 148: Junzo Yoshimura Architect Tokyo; 149: Samon Sano Tokyo; 150: M. Yendo Ass.; 151: Nikken Sekei Tokyo (2x); Sakakura Ass. Tokyo (2x); 152-155: Ministry of Construction Government of Japan Tokyo (12x); Kisho Kurokawa (2x); 157: Wilhelm Holzbauer Wien; Archiphoto; 158: BW 1937; 159: Arch. Duintjer Amsterdam (3x); NDB Amsterdam (1x); 160-161: NDB Amsterdam/Frank den Oudsten; 162-163: NDB Amsterdam; 164: HWT Rotterdam; Van den Broek and Bakema Rotterdam; NDB Amsterdam (2x); 165: E. Jelles Amsterdam/Paul Bessem; Hans Bosch Amsterdam; Herman Hertzberger Amsterdam; LRR Amsterdam; 166: L.J. Heijdenrijk Amersfoort; 166-167: W. Holzbauer Wien (4x); 168: Archiphoto; 170-171: William Alsop London; 172: Centre Pompidou/Archiphoto (3x); Robert Stones London; Centre Pompidou/Archiphoto; HWT Rotterdam; 173: Manfred Schiedhelm Berlin-W (2x); OD 205 Delft; 174-175: Kisho Kurchawa Tokyo; 176: Charles Vandenhove Liège; 177-178: Centre Pompidou; 179: B&U Amsterdam/Charles Rapho; Archiphoto; 180-183: Library National Capitol Development Commission Canberra; 185: The Tribune Company; 186: BW 192; The Tribune Company; 187-199: Arch. Kenneth Frampton NYC.

INDEX

Numbers followed bij an asterisk * refer to illustrations and captions.

Aalto, Alvar (1898-1976) 18, 141
Åberg, Hjalmar 94, 97*, 99
Abramovitz 203
Adams, Arthur Frederick 118*, 119
—, John (1735-1826) 28
—, Thomas (1871-1940) 182
Adler, Friedrich (1827-1908) 54
Agache, D.A. 182
Ahlberg, Axel 87*
—, Hakon 187*, 188
Alberts, Anton (1927) 21*
—, C.A. (1936) 165*
Alpar, I. 112
Alphand, J. 64, 67
Amsterdam, Frederiksplein 161
—, Exchange 11*, 13, 106*, 107, 110
—, Muziektheater 157*, 167
—, New Church 158
—, palace in Dam Square 156, 156*, 158, 159, 161, 166, 167
—, Palace of Industry 159
—, Pijp, the 161, 166
—, town hall 9*, 13*, 156*, 156-167
—, Waterlooplein 160, 166
Andersson, Erik 137*
Annapolis (Md.) 22
—, Church of Our Lady 65
Aran, Kemal 172*
Arretche, Louis 171
Arup, Ove (1895), see: Arup & Partners, Ove
Arup & Partners, Ove 141, 142, 168, 175
Ashihara, Yoshinuba (1918) 147, 150, 153, 153*
Ashworth, Henry Ingham 136, 138, 139
Asplund, Gunnar (1885-1940) 141
Atelier d'Urbanisme et d'Architecture 171
Athens, Acropolis 9, 16
Auer, H. 112

Babylon, New 176
Bach, Karl Theodor (1858-?) 72, 75, 79*
Bakema, Jacob Berend (1914-1981) 164*
Baldwinson, A.N. 141
Baltard, Victor (1805-1874) 170, 170*
Bamberger, Gustav 72
Barry, Charles (1795-1860) 30, 31*, 34, 35, 36*, 37, 38, 39*, 46
Basile. E. 112
Bauer, Leopold 72
Bazel, Karel Petrus Cornelis de (1869-1923) 107, 113*
Beck, Edward S. 115, 119

Behrens, Peter (1868-1940) 107, 193, 196, 201
Bélanger, François Joseph (1744-1818) 42
Belcher, J. (1841-1913) 112
Berghoef, Johannes Fake (1903) 158*, 160. 162*
Bergsten, Carl 82, 87, 88* 91*
Berindey, I.D. 112
Berlage, Hendrik Petrus (1856-1934) 11*, 13, 106*, 107, 107*, 113*, 187, 193, 201
Berlin, AEG-factory 196
—, Reichstag 54*, 54-63, 80
Bernini, Gianlorenzo (1598-1680) 10
Berthelin, Max 44*
Bianchi, Salvatore 127*, 128
Bijvoet, Bernard (1889-1979) 123*, 124, 156, 161, 166, 183, 185*, 186, 201
Bismarck, Otto Eduard Leopold von (1815-1898) 54, 58, 63
Bliss, Terence 144*
Bliss & Faville 116, 118*
Blom, Piet (1934) 165*
Blondel, Henri (1832-1897) 44, 49
Bloomfield Hills (Mich.), Cranbrook 184
Böckmann, Wilhelm (1832-1902) 54, 59*
Bohnstedt, Ludwig (1822-1885) 56*, 58
Boileau, Louis H. 187*, 201
Boissevain & Osmond 136, 139, 139*, 140
Bonatz, Paul (1877-1956) 188, 201
Booth, George 184
Borsi, Franco 202
Bosch, Hans (1939) 165*
Botrel 41, 46, 48
Boucher 67
Boullée, Etienne-Louis (1728-1799) 42
Bourdais, Jules Desire 65*, 66, 67
Bragdon, Claude 184
Brang, Peter Paul 75, 77, 80
Brecher, N. 136, 139, 139*
Breuer, Marcel (1902-1981) 153
Broek, Johannes Hendrik van den (1898-1978) 164*
Broggi, Carlo 190*, 196*, 202
Broggi, Vaccaro en Franzi 188, 189*, 196*
Brune, H. 64
Brunelleschi, Filippo (1377-1446) 9, 11*, 170
Buckler, John Chessell (1793-1894) 30, 33*, 34
Buffalo (N.Y.), Larkin Building 183
Bühlmann, Joseph (1844-1921) 58*
Bunning, Walter 138
Burnet, John (1857-1938) 187, 193, 199
Burnham, Daniel (1846-1912), see:

Burnham & Co.
Burnham & Co. 116, 117*
Burton, Decimus (1800-1881) 66
Busse, August (1839-1896) 60*

Cahill, J.J. 136, 139, 142
Calderini, Guglielmo 112
Calini, Leo 127, 129*, 131
Callet, F.E. (1791-1854) 170*
Campen, Jacob van (1595-1657) 156, 156*, 158, 160
Canberra 180*
—, competition 181*, 182*
Candidus 33
Canterbury, Cathedral 10
Capitant, René 172
Cardeillac 41, 46
Cardelli, Aldo 127
Caré, Enrico 127
Caristie, Augustin Nicolas (1783-1862) 41, 46
Carnegie, Andrew (1835-1919) 105*, 107
Carnegie-Foundation 105, 107, 110,
Carrére, John Merven (1858-1911) 112
Carrére & Hastings 112
Carshore, Andrew Mayfield 24, 25*
Cassien-Bernard 68*, 69*
Castellazzi, Massimo 127, 130*, 131
Cavos, A. 43
Cavour, Camille Benso (1810-1861) 128
Ceradini, Giulio 127
Charpentier, Claude 172
Cheney, Howard 119
—, Sheldon 184
Chicago (Ill.), Bayard Building 184
—, Chicago River 114*
—, Chicago Tribune-Building 114*, 115-126, 182, 186
—, Equitable Building 114*
—, Wrigley Building 114*
Chicago Tribune 14, 116
Choisy, J.L.C. 173*
CIAM 150.
Clarke en Reeves 65*, 66
Clason, Isak Gustav (1856-1930) 82, 84, 86, 112
Coch, Georg (1842-1890) 73*
Colbert, Jean Baptiste (1619-1683) 10
Collcutt, Thomas Edward (1840-1924) 105
Collignon, Ed. 64.
Collins Williamson, John 22
Cologne, Cathedral 65
Considerant, Victor Prosper (1808-1893) 199
Constant, see: Nieuwenhuys, C.
Constant-Dufeux, S.C. 41, 46
Contamin, V. (1840-1893) 64
Corbett, Harvey Wiley (1873-1954) 118*
Cordonnier, Louise Marie (1859-1938) 11*, 12, 105, 106*, 107*, 108, 110, 112
Cornell, Elias 85
Cosenza, Luigi 127
Cottingham, Lewis Nockalls (1787-1847) 32*
Couder, J.B.A. 43
Cremer, Robert 59*
—, Wilhelm 54, 63*
Crépinet, A. 41, 46, 48
Crompton, Dennis (1935) 170*
Cunningham, W. 136, 139, 139*
Cust, Edward 30, 34
Cuypers, Eduard (1859-1827, nephew of Petrus Josephus Hubertus C.) 112
—, Petrus Josephus Hubertus (1827-1921) 105

Dam, Cees (1932) 13*, 156, 167
Davidson, H.F.D. 165*
De Gisors, H.A. (1796-1866) 41, 46
Debat, Félix 109*
Debret, François (1777-1850) 42
Delouvrier, Paul (1914) 170, 171, 172, 176
Demiray, Matin 172*
The Hague, Peace Palace 104*, 105-114
Deneke, Albert 187*, 188
Deperthes, P.-J.-E. (1833-1898) 69*
Deudekom, M.C. van 164*
Diamond, James (?-1797) 26*, 27*
Dieltjen, E. 112
Dioscuren 193
Dratschevski, colonel 94
Duban, Félix Louis Jacques (1797-1870) 41, 46
DuBois, Macy (1929) 164*
Duc, Joseph Louis (1802-1879) 41, 48
Duchâtel, Ch. M.T. 42, 43
Dudok, Willem Marinus (1884-1974) 21, 18
Duiker, Johannes (1890-1935) 123*, 124, 183, 185*, 186, 201
Duintjer, Marinus (1908-1983), 159, 159*, .160
Dumas fils, Alexandre (1824-1895, French writer) 69
dumbbell houses 10
Dunster & Staughton 140*
Dutert, Charles-Louis-Ferdinand (1845-1906) 64, 68, 69*

Edgel, G.H. 184
Eggert, Hermann 61
Egle, Joseph von (1818-1899) 54
Egypt, Cheops pyramid 65
Eiffel, Gustave (1832-1923) 12, 64, 64*, 66*, 67, 67*, 68, 68*, 69, 69*, 71*
Eijkman, P.H. (?-1914) 113*
Eklund, Jarl 99*, 121*
Ellicott, Andrew 23, 24
Ena, Nello 127
Ende, Hermann (1829-1907) 54, 59*
Enfant, Pierre Charles l' (1754-1825) 22*, 24, 182
Engel, Carl Ludwig (1778-1840) 96, 97
Eriksson, Niels Einar 198*
Étex, Antoine (1808-1888) 43*
Eudel, Paul 68
Eugénie, empress (1826-1920) 10, 44, 52
Eyck, Aldo van (1918) 160, 165*, 167

Fadigati, Vasco 127, 130*, 131
Fagioli, Marco 127
Fahrenkamp, Emil (1885-1966) 187*, 188
Fairfield, Robert 164*
Faszbender, Eugen 72, 75
Faugeron, Jean 171
Favini, Leonato 127, 132*
Ferstel, Heinrich von (1828-1883) 60*
—, Max Freiherr von (1859-?, son of Heinrich von F.) 9*, 72, 75, 76, 81*
Fiorentino, Mario 127
Fischer-Essen, A. 188, 188*, 201, 202
Flegenheimer, Julien 190*, 200*, 202
Florence, Santa Maria del Fiore 9, 11*
Fontaine, Pierre François Leonard (1762-1853) 42
Forleo, Constantino 127
Formigé, Jean Cammille (1845-1926) 64, 68, 70*
Förster, Emil von 72
Foster, Norman (1935) 8*, 16*, 17*, 18*, 19*

Fourier, François Marie Charles (1772-1837) 197
Franchini, Gianfranco 168
Francis, Frank 168, 173
Franz Jozeph I (1830-1916) 72, 74*
Franzi, Luigi 189*, 196*
Frosterus, Sigurd (1876-1956) 98, 102, 103, 103*
Fun Palace 178

Gabriel, Ange-Jacques (1698-1782) 197
Gallen-Kallela, Akseli Valdemar (1865-1931) 95, 102
Galli, Adriano 127
Garden, Hugh M.G. (1873-1961), see: Schmidt, Garden & Martin
Garnaud, A.M. 41
Garnier, Jean Louis Charles (1825-1898) 12, 41, 45, 47*, 48*, 49, 50*, 52, 53*, 68, 182
—, Tony (1869-1948) 107
Gato, Carlo 187, 201
Gaudet, Julien 195
Gaulle, Charles de (1890-1970) 170, 171, 172, 173, 179
Gautier, Theophile 45*
Geddes, Robert (1923) 136, 139, 139*
Geneva, League of Nations Building 12*, 14, 181, 186, 190*, 192*, 194*, 201
Gerace, Claudio Longo 127, 130*, 131
Gerhardt, Paul 185*
Gerretsen, W.M. 165*
Gesellius, Herman (1874-1916) 102
—, Loja 102
Gesellius, Saarinen, Lindgren, office 102
Geste Architectural, Le 13
Ghiberti, Lorenzo (1378-1455) 9
Giannelli, A. 127
Giedion, Sigfried 140
Giese, Ernst (1832-1903) 54
Gilbert, Cass 184
—, Emile Jacques, (1793-1874) 41, 46
Ginain, P.R.L. (1825-1898) 41, 48, 49
Glasgow, Daily Express Building 183
Gleim, C.O. 97
Göbel, Marius (1939) 165*
Goki-Kai, 150
Goldberger, Paul 116*, 120*
Goodhue, Bertram Grosvenor (1869-1924) 116, 184, 184*
Gool, F.J. van (1922) 156, 161
Goossens, Eugene 136
Gouder, Amedée 46*
Gounod, Charles (1818-1893, French composer) 69
Graham, Gordon 17
—, James Gillespie (1777-1855) 31*, 37, 39*
Graham, Anderson, Probst & White, 114*
Granfelt, August 94
Granger, Alfred 115, 119
Granholm, Bruno 97
Granpré Molière, Marinus Jan (1883-1972) 159
Greco, Saul 127, 131
Greenley, H. 105, 108
Grenman, Bertell 122
Griffin, Walter Burley (1876-1937) 121*, 181, 181*, 182
Gripenberg, Sebastian 94, 98
Group GIA 156, 164
Groll, Jan F. 110*
Gropius, Martin (1824-1880) 57*
—, Walter (1883-1969) 123*, 124, 183, 191
Grossheim, Karl von (1841-1911) 54
Grut, Torben 90

Gugel, E. (1832-1905) 61
Guidetti, Louis 199*, 201
—, Pierre 199*, 201
Gulgonen, Ahmet 172*
Gunther, Walter 123*, 186*
Gyldén, Mathilde 102
Gyldén and Ullberg 99*

Hahmann, Friedrich 156
—, Hanna 156
Hall, Peter 136, 143
Haller, Martin (1835-1925) 46*, 54
Hallet, Stephen (?-1825) 26
Hamilton, Alexander (1755-1805) 23
—, David (1768-1843) 30, 34, 34*
Hare, H.T. 112
Harrison 203
Hastings, Thomas (1860-1929) 112
Haussmann, Georges-Eugène Baron (1809-1891) 10, 41, 43, 44*, 170
Heffron, Robert 142
Heijdenrijk, Leo J. 164, 166*
Hejda, Wilhelm 121*
Helmle, Frank J. 118*
Helsinki 96
—, Pohjola Office 102
—, National Theatre 96
—, railway station 94*, 94-104
Hennebique, François (1842-1921) 67
Henry 67
Herrmann, Heinrich L.A. (1821-1889) 56*
Hersent 64
Hertzberger, Herman (1932) 165*
Hitchcock, Henry-Russell (1903-1987) 186, 199
Hittorf, Jacob Ignaz (1792-1867) 40*, 41, 46
Hitzig, Friedrich (1811-1881) 60
Hoban, James (c. 1762-1831) 22, 23*, 26, 27, 28, 29, 29*
Hocheder, C. 112
Hoffmann, Josef (1870-1956) 107, 187, 193, 201
Holabird, William (1854-1923) 115, 116, 117*, 120
Holt, G.H.M. (1904) 159*, 161, 166
Holzbauer, Wilhelm (1930) 13, 13*, 20*, 141*, 156, 157*, 166, 166*, 167, 167*
Hongkong, Hongkong and Shanghai Bank 8*, 14*, 15*, 18, 19*
Hood, Raymond M. (1881-1934) 115, 116*, 120, 122, 124, 183, 184, 185*
Hoogstad, Jan (1930) 164*, 172*
Horeau, Hector (1801-1872) 43
Horrix, Paul (?-1929) 113*
Horta, Victor (1861-1947) 186, 193, 201
Howard, Ebenezer (1850-1928) 182
Howe, George (1886-1955) 124, 184
Howells, John Mead (1868-1959) 115, 116*, 120, 122, 183, 184, 185
Huet, J. Ch. 42
Hulshoff, Allard Remco (1880-1958) 159
Hume, Joseph (1777-1855) 30
Hunt, Jarvis 116, 119*
Hvittrask 102

Ihne, E. (1848-1917) 105
Immirzi, Vittorio 127, 130*, 131
Ito, Chubei 147
—, Shigero 147
IUA see Union Internationale des Architectes

Jacobsen, Arne (1902-1971) 18, 163*
Jeanneret, Charles-Edouard see: Le Corbusier

—, Pierre (1896-1971, nephew of Le Corbusier) 14, 16, 181, 188, 191, 191*, 193, 194*, 195*, 201
Jefferson, Thomas (1734-1826) 22, 23*, 24, 26, 28, 28*
Jelles, E.J. (1932) 165*
Johnson, Philip (1906) 168, 173
Jordan, V.L. 141
Jung, Bertel 95*
Jung and Bomanson 99*

Kahn, Louis (1901-1974) 18
Kalevala 95
Karczewska, Eva 164
—, Jan 164
Kayser, Heinrich Josef (1842-1917) 54, 63*
Kikutake, Kiyonori (1928) 147, 150, 153, 154, 154*
Klerk, Michel de (1884-1923) 107
Klijnen, J. 201
Klingenberg, L. 11*
Kloos, Jan Piet (1905) 159*
Kloot Meijburg, Herman van der (1875-1961) 159
Klophaus, Rudolf, see Putlitz, Klophaus and Schoch
Koch, Michael 72
Koechlin, Maurice 66*, 67
Komter, Auke (1904-1982) 159, 159*, 160
Kondo, S. 163*
König, Carl (1841-1915) 105
Kosel, Mansuet (1856-1919) 72
Kozielewski, Andrzej 164
Krall, H.D. 143*
Krausz, Franz von 72, 75, 78*, 79*
Kromhout, Willem (1864-1940) 107, 111*
Kruger, Alb. H.W. 125*
Künstler, Josef 72
Kurokawa, Kisho N. (1934) 5*, 147, 147*, 155*, 174*
Kyoto, City Hall 151
—, Congress Building 146*, 147-155
—, Takara-ga-ike 149

Labrouste, Henri (1801-1875) 195
Laclotte, Michel 168
Lange, Emil von 58*
Latrobe, Benjamin Henry (1764-1820) 22, 23*, 28, 29
Laurens, Henri (1885-1954) 141
League of Nations, see Geneva
Le Corbusier (1887-1965, pseud. of C.E. Jeanneret) 14, 16, 141, 150, 151, 151*, 173, 181, 188, 191, 191*, 193, 194*, 195, 195*, 196, 197, 199, 199*, 201, 202, 203
Le Pelley 144*
Le Vau, Louis (1612-1670) 10
Lebas, Louis Hippolyte (1782-1867) 41, 46
Lebrun, Charles (1619-1690) 10
Lefèvre, Camille 188, 189*, 190*, 200*, 202
Lefuel, Hector M. (1810-1880) 41, 46
Lejeune, August 42*
Lemaresquier, Charles 187, 193, 199
Leningrad 193
Lenormand, L. 41, 46
Lescaze, William (1896-1969) 124*
Lesueur, J.-B.-C. (1794-1883) 41, 46
Levallois-Perret 71*
Liddell, Thomas (1800-1856) 30, 34
Liebaers, Herman 168, 174
Liebknecht, Karl (1871-1919) 54*
Lindahl and Thomé 94, 98*, 99
Lindberg, Hugo 94, 98

Lindgren, Armas (1874-1929) 102
Lindhagen, Carolus 82
Lindholm, Charles 82, 85*, 88, 90*
Linge, M.E. van 200*, 201
Littlemore, David 136
Littlewood, Joan 176
Lo Cigno, E. 127
Lockroy, Etienne Auguste Edouard (1838-1913) 67, 67*
Lombardi, Pietro 127
London, Bank of England 10
—, Buckingham Palace 32
—, Crystal Palace 66
—, Daily Express Building 183
—, Houses of Parliament 10, 30*, 30-40
—, National Gallery 10, 34
—, Saint Stephen's Chapel 30, 32
—, Travellers Club 35
—, Wembley Park 70*
—, Westminster Palace 30, 32, 34
Lönnröt, Elias (1802-1884) 95
Lønberg-Holm, K. 124*, 124, 184, 186*
Loos, Adolf (1870-1933) 107, 185*, 186
Loschetter, L. 136, 139, 139*
Louis Napoleon, king (1778-1846) 156*, 158
Lubbe, Marinus van der (1909-1933) 63
Lugt, P.J. 160
Lund, N.O. 161
Luthmann, Julius Maria (1890-1973) 188, 198*, 201, 202
Lusson, L.A. 42
Luttwitz, Heribert Freiherr von 123*
Luxemburg, Rosa (1870-1919) 54*
Lyon, Gustave 195

Maaskant, Huig Aart (1907-1977) 156, 161
Maccari, A. 127
MacMahon, M.E.P.M. (1808-1893) 52
Madison, James (1750-1836) 29
Madrid, Escorial 9, 13, 17
Maillard, Henri-Pierre 168, 174
Maisonneuve, J.H. 166
Malmquist, S. 141
Malraux, André (1901-1976) 171, 173
Manchester, Daily Express Building 183
—, Saint Paul's Church 35
Mancini, G. 109*
Marcel, A. 105, 108, 109*, 112
Mardall, Cyril S. (1909), see: Yorke Rosenberg & Mardall
Marien, Hoym de 171
Marino, R. 127
Marion 68
Marot, Michel 171
Marseille, Unité d'Habitation 197
Martin, John Leslie (1908) 136, 139
Marzella, J. 136, 139, 139*, 140, 142*
Matsuda, Gumpei 147
Matthew, Robert (1906) 156, 161
Maupassant, Guy de (1850-1893, French writer) 69
Mayekawa, Kunio (1905) 147, 150, 151, 153, 154
Mazzoni, Angiolo 126*, 128, 128*, 130, 131, 131*, 131*
McCormick, Robert R. 115, 119
Meier, Richard (1934) 20*
Metabolism 147*, 153, 154
Meyer, Adolf (1881-1929) 123*, 124
—, Hannes (1889-1954) 183, 188, 189*, 191, 196, 197*, 199, 201, 202
Michelangelo, Buonarroti (1475-1564) 170
Milane, Giuseppe 135*

Milburn, S.W. 144*
Milles, Carl Vilhelm Emil (1875-1955) 186
Mitterand, François (1916) 18
Molinos 64
Moneo, José Rafael (1937) 163*
Monteiro, J.L. 112
Montuori, Eugenio (1907) 127, 129*, 131, 134*
—, Franscesco (son of Eugenio M.) 134*, 135*
Moore, Charles Willard (1925) 20
Moretti, Studio 134*
Morozzo della Rocca, Robaldo 127, 132*
Morris, Benjamin Wistar 116, 119*
Moscow, Centrosoyus 193
—, Palais des Soviets 191*, 193, 195
Moser, Karl (1860-1936) 187, 193, 201
Mouchez, admiral 64
Muggia, Attilo 187, 201
Mussolini, Benito (1883-1945) 128, 130
Mutinelli, Carlo 127, 131*

Nachon 68*, 69*
Napoleon, Louis (1808-1873) 41, 43, 49, 52, 168, 170, 170*
Napoleon III, see: Napoleon, Louis
Narducci, R. 127
Nénot, Henri Paul (1853-1934) 105, 190*, 200*, 202
Neumann, Franz von 72, 75
Neureuthen, Gottfried von (1811-1886) 54
Neutra, Richard 202
New Babylon 178*
New York (N.Y.) 10
—, Daily News Building 122, 184
—, dumbbell houses 10
—, Rockefeller Center 184
—, Woolworth Building 183
Nicolaas I, czar (1796-1855) 37
Nicolaas II, czar (1868-1918) 96, 105
Nicolosi, G. 127
Nielsen, Chr. (1910) 161, 162, 167*
Niemann, George 72
Niemeyer, Oscar (1907) 168, 174
Nieuwenhuys, Constant 178
Notti, Anna di 135*
Nouguier, Emile 66*, 67
Nyrop, Martin (1849-1921) 82, 112
Nyström, Gustav 94, 98
—, Usko 94, 100*

Ohara, Soichiro 147
Öhnell, Richard 82, 83*, 84, 86
Östberg, Ragnar (1866-1945) 82, 83, 83*, 84, 86, 87, 90, 91, 92, 92*, 93*
Okumura, Katsuzo 147
Olbrich, Josef Maria (1867-1908) 76, 107
Olin, H.S. 105, 108
Onderdonk, Holmes 115, 119
Onur, Selahattin 172*
Otaka, Masato (1923) 147, 150, 153, 155*
Otani, Sachio (1924) 146*, 147, 150, 152, 152*, 153, 154
Ott, Carlos 18, 20
Oud, Jacobus Johannes Pieter (1890-1963) 18. 124*

P&T Architects and Engineers 14*
Palladio, Andrea (1508-1580) 26, 28, 193
Pallotini, Mariano 127
Palmer and Turner, see: P&T Architects and Engineers
Paniconi, M. 127
Paris 18, 166
—, Beau Bourg 171

—, Bibliothèque Nationale 195
—, Centre Beaubourg, see: Centre G. Pompidou
—, Centre Georges Pompidou 5*, 14, 168*. 168-180
—, Champ-de-Mars 64*, 67*, 68*
—, Défense, la 173
—, Eiffeltower 64*, 71*, 178
—, Esplanade des Invalides 67*, 68*
—, Gare de l'Est 168
—, Halle de Blé 26
—, Hallen, de 168. 170*, 171, 172, 179
—, Louvre 10, 13, 178
—, Museum of the XXth C. 173
—, New Opera 12, 40*, 41-53
—, Palais de l'Industrie 67*, 68*
—, Palais de la Concorde 199*
—, Palais Royal 41
—, Parc de la Villette 18
—, Pavillon Suisse 196
—, Place de la Bastille 18, 20*
—, Plateau Beaubourg 13, 171, 173, 179*
—, Reseau Express Regional 171
—, Rungis 171
—, Salle Le Peletier 41, 42, 43, 49
—, St Eustachius church 170*
—, Tête Défense 18, 21*
—, Théâtre Champs Elysées 195
—, world exhibition 1889, 12
Parkes, Cobden 136, 139
Palmieri, G.C. 127
Pascoletti, Cesare 127, 132*
Patterson, Joseph Medill 115, 119
Peabody & Stearns 112
Pearlman, Wolfgang 172*
Percier, Charles (1764-1838) 42
Perrault, Claude (1613-1688) 10
Perret, Auguste (1874-1954), 107, 187*, 193, 195, 197, 199*, 201
Persius, Reinhold (1835-1912) 54
Petersburg, St, see: Leningrad
Petrignani, Achille 127, 131*
Peyre, Joseph (1730-1785) 42
Philadelphia (Penn.) 23, 24
—, Centenary exhibition 66
—, PSFS building 184
—, town hall 10
Philipps 64
Piacentini, Marcello 201, 203
Piano, Renzo (1937) 13, 168, 176, 177*, 178*
Picon, Gaetan 168, 173
Pintonello, Achille 127, 130*,131
Pius IX (1792-1878, G.M. Mastai-Ferretti) 128
Plumber and Sanitary Engineer 10
Pochet 67
Pomeranzeff, Alexander Nikanorowitsch (1848-?) 112
Pompidou, Georges Jean Raymond (1911-1974) 173, 178*, 179, 179*
Portzamparc, Christian de (1944) 20*
Poyet, Bernard (1742-1824) 42
Price, Cedric (1934) 178
Prouvé, Jean (1901) 168, 174
Provo 164
Prynn, Laurence 142*
Pugin, Augustus Welby (1812-1852) 30, 31*, 35, 37, 38, 39*
Putlitz, Erich zu, see: Putlitz, Klophaus and Schoch
Putlitz, Klophaus and Schoch 188, 198*, 201, 202

Qualls, G. 136, 139, 139*

Quaroni, Ludovici 127
Quentin, Robert 137*
Questel, Charles Auguste (1807-1888) 41, 46

Raczynski, Athanasius (1788-1874) 60, 61
Railton, William (1801-1877) 30, 34, 34*, 35*
Raimondo, G. di 127
Rasmussen, Steen Eiler 141
Raulin 69*
Ravesteyn, Sybold van (1889-1983) 159
Rebori, Andrew 116, 117*
Regard, Robert 168, 176
Regnoni, R. 127
Reichensperger, August (1808-1895) 62
Ricciardi, Guglielmo 127
Richardson 99*
Richelieu, Armand Jean Duplessis (1585-1642) 41
Rickman, Thomas (1776-1841) 32*
Ridolfi, Mario 127, 132*
Rietveld, Gerrit Thomas (1888-1964) 18
Rijnboutt, Kees (1934) 165*
Ritter, John 201, 202
Robert 68
Robinson, Charles Mulford 182
Roche, Martin (1855-1927) 115, 116, 117*, 120
Rochelle, la, town hall 13, 106
Rogers, James Gamble (1867-1947) 116, 117*
—, Richard (1933) 13, 168, 176, 177, 177*, 178, 178*
Rohault de Fleury, Charles (1801-1875) 12, 43, 44, 45, 48, 49
Rome, Aggere di Servio Tullio, 129*, 131, 132*, 133*
—, baths of Diocletian 127, 134*
—, Galleria di Testa 133*
—, Piazza dei Cinquecento 134*
—, Santa Maria Maggiore 127
—, station Termini 126*, 127-135
Ronca, Bruno 127, 131*, 132
Roosevelt, Theodore (1858-1919) 110
Rosenberg, Eugene (1907), see: Yorke Rosenberg & Mardall
Rossi, Carlo Domenico 127, 132*
—, Eugenio 127
Rouyer 68
Rowe, Colin 199

Saarinen, Eero (1910-1961, son of Eliel S.) 136, 139, 140, 141, 186
—, Eliel (1873-1950) 21, 94, 96*, 99, 102, 102*, 103*, 112, 112*, 113, 115, 120, 120*, 122, 124, 139, 182, 182*, 183, 183*, 184, 185*, 202
Sackerman, Fritz 125*
Sadenius, Yrjö 96
Safdie, Moshe (1938) 172*
Sakakura, Junzo (1901-1969) 7*, 150, 151*
Sakanaga, Kanashige 151*
Sala, Francesco della 127
Salvatori, Raffaello 127
Sandberg, Willem Jacob Henri Berend (1897-1894) 168, 173
Sanders, Th. 11*
Sano, Yukio 149*
Sato, Takeo 147
Sauvestre, S. 64, 66*, 67, 67*, 69*
Saverio de Merode, bishop 127
Scalpelli, Alfredo 127
Schader, J. 156
Schiedhelm, Manfred 173*

Schindler, Rudolf 202
Schinkel 188,
Schmidt, Friedrich von (1825-1891) 54
Schmidt, Garden & Martin 116, 118*
Schmieden, Heino (1835-1913) 57*
Schoch, August, see: Putlitz, Klophaus & Schoch
Schoder, Thilo 121*
Scholar, F.E. (1874-?) 188
Schröder, Gerhard 125*
Schulze, W. (1938) 164*
Schupmann, Ludwig 54
Schutz, Kurt 123*, 186*
Schwechten, Franz (1841-1924) 54, 60*, 105, 108, 112
Scott, George Gilbert (1811-1878) 4*, 58*
—, John Oldrid (1842-1913, son of George Gilbert S) 4*, 58*
Sébillot 65*, 66, 67
Seeling, Heinrich (1852-1932) 54
Seidler, Harry (1923) 15*, 20*
Sert, José Maria 203
Sevilla, Giralda 114*
Sibelius, Jean (1865-1957), Finnish composer) 102
Simonet, Jules Charles 44*
Sjöstrom, Einar 121*
Skagen, Christian 202
Skidmore Owings & Merill 15*, 115*
Skowron, Franz 3*, 80*
Slutzky, Robert 199
Small Jr, Jacob 24, 25*
Small Sr, Jacob (?-1791) 24, 25*
Smirke, Robert (1781-1867) 30, 31*, 32
Soane, John (1753-1837) 34
Soeten, H. de 165*
Sommer, Oskar (1840-1894) 63*
Speer, Albert (1905-1981) 193, 203
Speidel, R. 188, 188*, 201
Speyser 67
Sprecklesen, Johan Otto von (-1987) 18, 21*
Springer, Johannes Ludovicus (1850-1915) 112
Staal, Arthur (1907, son of Jan Frederik S.) 158*, 159, 160*
—, Jan Frederik (1879-1940) 158*, 159, 160*
Stalpaert, Daniël (1615-1684) 158
Statz, Vincenz (1819-1898) 54
Stern, Robert A.M. (1939) 184
Steur, Albert Johan van der (1895-1963, son of J.A.G. van der S.) 159
—, J.A.G. van der (1865-1945) 105, 110
Stier, Hubert (1838-1907) 54
Stockholm,
—, Steam Mill site (Eldkvarnen) 84, 91
—, town hall 82*, 82-93
Stones, Robert 172*
Strack, Johann Heinrich (1805-1880) 56*
Streit, Andreas 72
Strengell, Gustav 102, 103
Subiotto, George 140*
Sullivan, Louis H. (1856-1924) 122, 183, 184, 186
Sydney, Bennelong Point 137*, 138, 142*
—, Opera House 136*, 136-146

Takayama, Yoshizo 147
Tamm, G. 82
Tange, Kenzo (1913) 147, 147*, 150, 151, 152, 153, 154
Tarjanne, Onni, see: Törnqvist, Onni
Tauschenberg, E. 11*
Taut, Bruno (1880-1938) 123*, 124, 150, 183, 186*. 186

—, Max (1884-1967, brother of Bruno T.) 123*

Tavaststjerna, Alarik 100*

Tengbom, Ivar Justus (1878-1968) 82, 86*. 88, 91, 187, 193, 201

Tétaz, Jacques Martin 46*, 48

Thiersch, Friedrich von (1852-1921) 54, 60*

Tijen, Willem van (1894-1974) 160

Tilburg, A.S. van (1942) 164*

Todd, Lionel 136

Tohata, Kenzo 147

Tokyo, Metropolitan Festival Hall 151

Tölk, Josef 72, 75, 78*, 79*

Tonelli, Alberto 127

Törnqvist, Onni 94, 95*, 96, 96*, 99

Torulf, Ernst 82, 86*, 88, 91

Töry, Emil 109*

Tour Soleil 65*, 66

Tracy, Charles Hanbury (1777-1858) 30, 33*, 34, 36

Tremmel, Ludwig (1875-?) 72, 75

Treub, Marie Willem Frederik (1858-1931) 11*

Trevithick, Richard 65

Tropsch, Rudolf 121*

Tschumi, Bernard 18

Turin, Mole Antonelliana 65

Tvedt, Nils 121*

Uemura, Koshiro 147

UIA, see: Union Internationale des Architectes

Ulrich, Christian 72

Union Internationale des Architectes 161

Uotila, Paavo 94, 97*, 99

Urbinati, M. 127

Urioste y Velada, D.J. 112

Utzon, Jørn (1918) 136, 137*, 138*, 139, 140, 141, 142, 143, 145*, 173

Vaccaro, Giuseppe 189*, 196*

Vago, Giuseppe 189*, 190*, 200*, 202

Vandenhove, Charles 176*

Vegter, Joh. Jacobus Margarethus (1906-1982) 158*, 159, 160, 162*

Velde, Henry van de (1863-1957) 102, 107

Verlaine, Paul (1844-1896, French poet) 69

Vienna 72

, Franz Joseph-barracks 72

—, Georg Coch Platz 73*, 74

—, Lisztstrasse 73*, 74

—, Savings Bank 72-81, 73*

—, Ringstrasse 72, 74, 75

—, Stadtbahn 75

Vignola, Giacomo Barozzi da (1507-1573) 9

Viguet 44*

Villa Garches 197

Viollet-le-Duc, Eugène Emmanuel (1814-1879) 12, 44, 45*, 46, 48, 49, 49*, 52

Visentini, M. 127

Vitellozzi, Annibale 127, 130*, 131

Vivian, George (1800-1873) 30, 34

Vlugt, W. de (1872-1945) 159

Vorkink, Pieter (1878-1960) 159

Wagner, Otto (1841-1918) 61*, 72, 74, 74*. 75, 75*, 76, 76*, 77, 77*, 80, 99*, 105, 107, 108, 109*, 112

Walewski, A. de 41, 44, 46, 49

Wallace, Dwight G. 120

Wallot, Paul (1841-1912) 54, 55*, 57*, 60*. 61, 62*

Ware, James E. 10

—, William Robert (1832-1915) 105

Washington, George (1732-1799) 22, 23, 24, 27, 65

Washington (D.C.) 22, 28, 182

—, Capitol 24, 28, 29

—, obelisk 65

—, Washington Monument 10

—, White House 22*, 22-29, 23*

Weidner, Paul 54

Weisman, W. 136, 139

Weissman, Adriaan Willem (1858-1923) 107

Wendt, F. 105, 108

Werkstatt für Massenform 125*

Werner, Anton von (1843-1915) 54

Westman, Carl (1866-1936) 82, 84*, 86, 90, 91, 92

Wickman, Gustav 82

Wielemans, Alexander 72

Wiener, Karl von 72

Wijdeveld, Henricus Theodorus (1885-1987) 162*, 188, 189*, 201, 202

Wilhelm I (1797-1888) 54, 62

Wilhelm II (1859-1941) 62, 63

Wilkins, William (1778-1839) 34

Willem I, king (1772-1843) 158

Williams, Owen (1890-1969) 183

Winkler, Bernardo 156, 164

Winston, Denis 138

Wittwer, Hans (1894-1952) 188, 189*, 191, 197*, 201

Wolffenstein, Richard 54

Wouda, Hendrik (1885-1947) 198*, 201, 202

Wright, Frank Lloyd (1867-1959) 18, 141, 150, 182, 183, 184, 186

Wyatt, Benjamin Dean (1775-1850, son of James W.) 30

Wyatville, Jeffry (1766-1840) 30

Yanagi, Hideo 152*

Yendo, Masayoshi 150*

Yeomans, John 136

Yorke Rosenberg & Mardall 15*

Yoshimura, Junzo 148*

Zandstra, Piet (1905) 156, 162

Zess, Hermann 125*

Zimmermann, Heinrich (1845-1935) 62

—, Johannes 110*

Zwarts, Moshe E. (1937) 165*

Zwiers. H.T. 158*. 159

Idea for publication in book form by Jord den Hollander and Cees de Jong.
Designed by Vorm + Kleur, Naarden.
Research (text) by Maike Cannon, Ids Haagsma, Hilde de Haan and Harrie van der Meulen.
Research (illustrations) by Architext Haarlem, Loek Polders.
Dutch text edited by Hans Post.
English text edited by Lynn George and Wendie Shaffer.
Translations by Kerstin Bakker-Hesselblom (Swedish); Mariko Delvole (Japanese); Liisa Lindgren (Finnish); Harrie van der Meulen (Frans); H. Olsen (English and Italian); Adrienne Dixon, Lynn George and Wendie Shaffer (English); Dr Erwin Peters (German).
Advice and mediation by Marjan Beek (general); Han Tol (Rome Station); Mariko Delvole (Kyoto Congress Hall); Wouter Hubers (general); Harrie van der Meulen (Paris).
The following organizations and persons have also been of assistance in the preparation of this book:

AUSTRALIA
Harry Seidler, Sydney; Sydney Opera House Trust (Paul Bentley); Archives of New South Wales (Christine M. Shergold); National Capitol Development Commission of Canberra (A. Fitzgerald).

BELGIUM
Charles Vandenhove, Liège.

FINLAND
Museokuva, Helsinki (Ilari Järvinen); Rautatie Hallitus, (Finnish Railways), Helsinki (Olewi Lechtonen); Suomen Rakennustaiteen Museo (Finnish Architectural museum), Helsinki (Sirkka Valanto; A.P.B. Wolf).

FRANCE
Bibliothèque de l'Opéra, Paris; Centre Georges Pompidou, Paris; Conseil National de l'ordre des architectes (Jacques Tournier); Philippe Délis, Paris/Bordeaux; Paul Delouvrier, Fontainebleau; Bernard Dehertogh, Paris/Douaie; DLM, Paris, (Christian Larras); Musée National des Techniques, Conservatoire national des Arts en Métiers (Dominique Diguet); Renzo Piano, Paris; Société nouvelle d'exploitation de la Tour Eiffel.

GREAT BRITAIN
William Alsop, London; L. Blair Oliphant, Blairgowry, Scotland; Terence Bliss, London; John Forster Metcalfe, London; Foster Associates, London (Katy Harris); Hugh Krall, London; Laurence Prynn, London; Public Record Office, London; Richard Rogers Office, London; Robert Stones, London; The Architectural Press (Sheila Hind); The Royal Commission on the Ancient and Historical Monuments of Scotland (C.H. Cruft), Edinburgh, Scotland; The Royal Institute of British Architects, London; YRM International, Architects and Planners, London.

HONGKONG
Foster Associates, Hongkong; Naonori Matsuda, Hongkong; Palmer and Turner, Hongkong.

ITALY
Commune di Roma, repartitione Lavori Publici, Rome; Consiglio Nazionale degli Architetti, Rome; Francesco Montuori, Rome.

JAPAN
A + V publishing co, Tokyo (Toshio Nakamura); Sakakura Kenchiky Kaukyusho, Tokyo (Mr. Yamaki); Kisho Kurokawa Architects, Tokyo (Chihasu Senoo); Kyoto International Conference Hall (Nobuhiro Takuma); Kyoto; Fumihiko Maki, Tokyo; Ministry of Construction, Government of Japan (Shigeki Takahashi), Tokyo; Nikken Sekkei, Tokyo (Shoji Hayashi); Sachio Otani, Tokyo; Process Magazine, Tokyo (Bunji Murotani); Hideo Yanagi, Tokyo; Yendo Associates, Tokyo; Junzo Yoshimura, Tokyo.

NETHERLANDS
Architectengemeenschap Van den Broek en Bakema, Rotterdam; Architectengroep Loerakker, Rijnbout, Ruyssenaars, Amsterdam; Architectengroep Duintjer, Amsterdam (J.H. Kramer); J.H. Bosch, Amsterdam; Herman Hertzberger, Amsterdam; L.J. Heijdenrijk, Amersfoort; Hoogstad, Weeber, Van Tilburg, Rotterdam; E.J. Jelles, Amsterdam; Nederlands Documentatiecentrum voor de Bouwkunst, Amsterdam; Bibliotheek Technische Universiteit, Delft; Universiteits Bibliotheek, Amsterdam; Koninklijke Bibliotheek, The Hague; Maison Descartes, Amsterdam.

AUSTRIA
Otto Wagner Archiv, Vienna; Österreichische Postsparkasse, Vienna; (Doris Langeder); Wilhelm Holzbauer, Vienna.

UNITED STATES
AIA, American Institute of Architects, New York, N.Y.; Maryland Historical Society, Baltimore, Md. (Jef Goldman); Skidmore, Owings & Merrill, Chicago; The White House, Washington, Office of the Curator (William G. Allman); Tribune Company, Chicago, Ill.

WEST GERMANY
Manfred Schiedhelm, West Berlin; Technische Universität Berlin, Dept. of Plannsammlung, West Berlin (Dieter Radicke).

SWEDEN
Arkitekturmuseet, Stockholm (Ulla Eliasson); Stockholm Museum, Stockholm (Lars Johanneson).